Social Work
Constructivist Research

Mary K. Rodwell

Garland Publishing, Inc.
A member of the Taylor & Francis Group
New York & London
1998

Library of Congress Cataloging-in-Publication Data

Rodwell, Mary K.
    Social work constructivist research / Mary K. Rodwell.
            p.   cm.   —   (Garland reference library of social science ;
    v. 1134)
        Includes bibliographical references and index.
        ISBN 0-8153-2552-5 (alk. paper).   —   ISBN 0-8153-2567-3
    (pbk. : alk paper)
        1. Social service—Research—Methodology.   2. Constructivism
    (Philosophy)   I. Title.   II. Series.
    HV11.R53   1998
    361.3'072—dc21   98-19159
                                                                    CIP

Printed on acid-free, 250-year-life paper
Manufactured in the United States of America

To "Lilly,"
"Gina," and "Rose"

CONTENTS

SECTION II
Doing Constructivist Research

CHAPTER 3
Designing Constructivist Research

CHAPTER 4
Intervention in Constructivist Inquiry

PREFACE

From the early years of my career as a social worker, I have been struck by how difficult it is to make sense of the social work research literature. Further, it always seemed to me that what I found in the literature had little to do with my own reality in agency practice. I assumed that the reason the literature was not helpful to me was that I was not competent enough to understand what was being written. At least, that was my way of avoiding the consequences if I were to actually criticize what I was reading. If I criticized the lack of relevance, then I would have to find a way to make research relevant. Instead, I chose an explanation that I could control, and, based on my assumption that to see the relevance would take my developing further competence to understand research, I chose to pursue advanced training through a research doctorate. I wanted to be able to make sense of social work practice for myself and my colleagues by getting better at mainstream research methods, so I could understand research results. This is where my formal pursuit of research competence began.

But even before I was a social worker I had struggled with more fundamental questions about how one knows what is real. This may sound very abstract and metaphysical, but this concern is relevant and very real when you become immersed in a different language and culture, as I had during my time living and working in Latin America. None of what I knew to be "true" seemed to apply most of the time. And even though all my rules did not work, life did seem to go on quite nicely. I functioned even if I didn't understand what was going on much of the time. I began to realize that I was operating on a different level of data and a different set of assumptions than I did when I was in the United States. Could this possibly mean that rules can be relative? Could what works depend on a context? Could the point of view make all the difference in making judgments about what is right or wrong, what works and what doesn't?

This is a text that details an alternative model of social work research. It is about constructivist research for social work practice and brings together my two long-standing puzzles: how to get what is relevant and what is real into a rigorous alternative framework for knowledge building focused on effectiveness in social work practice. Much of what you will see may seem familiar if you have some experience with qualitative methods in social science research; but taken as a whole, this approach is altogether different. Set in a research paradigm that differs from the traditional empiricist/positivist perspective, it is built on different assumptions about the nature of reality and how systematic knowledge about that reality is derived. Constructivism, as conceptualized in this text, is greatly indebted to the works of Guba and Lincoln (1989; Lincoln and Guba, 1985), who first recognized the usefulness of constructivism as an alternative framework for evaluation research in education. This text transfers the constructivist research perspective and technology to the social work research environment.

Patience with the presentation of the material is important for the reader new to constructivism. The book is designed to allow you to experientially "get" this very different way of rigorous knowing. The text replicates the flow of the research process in how the material about constructivist research is presented and discussed. Constructivist research is not linear. The book is also not developed linearly. The information in the text circles back and forth through different levels of complexity and sophistication, just as the constructivist process weaves circularly and hermeneutically to greater degrees and levels of sophistication.

The structure of the text is intended to provide the reader with sufficient information to competently confront all the design, implementation, data analysis, and reporting elements of a constructivist inquiry process. At the completion of all sections, readers will know how the assumptions of constructivism differ from mainstream research primarily characterized by positivism or post-positivism. They will know how rigor expectations for research methods derived from different assumptions also differ. In addition, readers will know what types of questions can be appropriately researched using constructivist methods. They will know how to: determine the feasibility of undertaking a constructivist inquiry, when, and where it is possible; manage an emergent design; establish the trustworthiness and authenticity dimensions of a rigorous research effort. They will also know what is necessary to maintain a quality hermeneutic circle and a productive hermeneutic dialectic. For those interested in all aspects of constructivist research, there will be sufficient guidance to prepare them to act as a peer reviewer or auditor of a constructivist project.

The book is divided into four sections that, together, should give the reader the intellectual and practical background necessary to understand and undertake rigorous constructivist inquiry.

Section I: Thinking about Constructivism has a philosophical focus. It describes the intellectual history of constructivism and develops the logical linkage between constructivist philosophy and theory and social work practice. This section defines the perspective and its challenges and sets the stage for the methodological consequences that are derived from the assumptions of the constructivist perspective discussed in the first part of Section II.

Section II: Doing Constructivist Research is focused on the methodology of constructivism. It details the steps necessary to prepare the individual researcher to undertake a constructivist inquiry. It provides sufficient information for the design and implementation of a rigorous constructivist research project. In addition, this section includes the dimensions necessary to determine if a constructivist approach is appropriate and feasible.

Section III: The Results of Constructivist Inquiry details the final dimension of constructivism, the inquiry results. It provides the framework for creating a high-quality report of the research. The focus is on both the inquiry process and product and what is necessary to establish trustworthiness and authenticity. At the completion of this section, the reader will not only be prepared to develop a quality product, but will have sufficient information to act as a peer reviewer or auditor of other constructivist inquiries. This section ends with a realistic discussion of the major considerations when choosing to undertake an alternative, and potentially controversial, research process.

Section IV: A Research Example gives the reader a case study and rigor demonstration by way of a thick description, coding, and data documentation. Because an audit trail is included, the case report will allow the reader to analyze the strengths and weaknesses of the research. At this stage in the text, the reader, using case report quality criteria, and trustworthiness and authenticity standards, will be able to make a personal determination of the quality of the research process and product.

As an additional aid, at the conclusion of each chapter there are discussion questions and exercises that strengthen the reader's understanding of the material contained in the chapter. An annotated bibliography is

included that highlights additional philosophical or methodological resources compatible with the assumptions of constructivism. This should
encourage the reader to further develop his or her understanding of alternative paradigmatic thinking and methods based on these alternative assumptions. Also, because meaning is constructed in context, key terms
when introduced are boldface in the text and a glossary is included to reflect my meaning for these terms. Almost all the terms in the glossary
have been and are being used in diverse ways. So, in order to avoid confusion about my meaning, definitions have been provided that will allow
the use of concepts and terms in a way that is congruent with
constructivist principles as discussed in this text. This glossary will help
the reader to understand my approach to constructivist inquiry.

The reader who has some knowledge about the basic requirements of
traditional social research to serve as a comparative backdrop will probably benefit the most from this text. Knowledge about qualitative research
methods set in the positivist tradition or other perspectives, such as feminist, phenomenological, or ethnomethodological ones, would be a plus
for easy access to the material presented here. However, neither type of
educational or experiential background is required.

There is one caveat before beginning. Reading about constructivist
approaches will not be enough to create a full understanding of the fundamental differences of this research process. After studying the text, I
would encourage you to try to think and act constructively by undertaking a small constructivist inquiry. Only then will you understand the
power of the process, the power of the intervention—not only for you,
the inquirer, but for the participants, those who become your partners in
the knowledge-building process. In the end, you may not be comfortable
with this way of knowing. You may not want to be involved in such a tedious research process, but I guarantee that you will be forever changed
by a unique research experience.

ACKNOWLEDGMENTS

Writing a book such as this is certainly a solitary adventure. Clearly, all the errors and omissions must be borne by me alone. On the other hand, the shaping of my approach to the content was done in community. If there is a richness and clarity to what has been presented, it is due to the many important mentors and helpers in the years of developing the ideas that the book contains.

First, I am indebted to Drs. Yvonna Lincoln and Egon Guba for originating naturalistic/constructivist inquiry. I am particularly grateful to Yvonna for my introduction to the perspective and the methodology in her naturalistic inquiry seminar at the University of Kansas. She knew when I "got it" and has, over the years, encouraged me to develop "it" further. Thank you.

To Dr. Donald E. Chambers, the best mentor a person could have, thank you for teaching me to think and encouraging me to think even better. I know you were never quite convinced that alternative research was anything more than artful smoke and mirrors, but your supportive skepticism pushed me to a clarity and rigor that I might never have achieved on my own. You have an amazing mind and a wonderful way of presenting material. If I have done half as well in this scholarship as you have done in yours, I will be proud.

To the students in Virginia and Brazil who helped me work out the material presented here, thank you for never letting me off the hook. Your perceptive questions and struggle with the material, in combination with your enthusiasm about what you experienced and accomplished in constructivist inquiry, convinced me that a book was worth doing. I hope I have done your efforts justice.

At the risk of overlooking some, I am compelled to mention specific student collaborators whose influences are evident to me throughout every chapter. Thank you Susan Ainsley McCarter for allowing me to share your experiences and for reading and commenting on a final draft. Thanks to Wes Pullman, Sheila Crowley, Barbara Conklin, and Patrick Shannon for taking the risk to experiment with constructivist dissertations and to share your discoveries with me. William Beverly, Michael Crosby, Norma Geddes, Linda Hancock, Theresa Kraemer, and Janice Neil graciously shared their research experiences and ideas for the book. Thank you. To Jacques Jules Sonneville, thanks for helping me to work this out in Portuguese and for your enthusiasm for trying the method in the Brazilian context. Thanks, also, to two very special colleagues, Drs. Jaclyn Miller and Kia Bentley, for their criticism and encouragement.

Mary K. Rodwell
Richmond, Virginia
July 1997

Thinking about Constructivism

This section is designed to establish the philosophical tradition of constructivism and to clarify its congruence with social work values and goals, so that the basic methodological elements of both constructivism and social work practice are also seen to be congruent. In Chapter 1 a general overview of constructivism and its relationship to social work practice is provided. Constructivism is placed within the epistemological debate in social work. The major philosophical and theoretical underpinnings of constructivism are explicated through a discussion of positivist and alternative paradigm positions and constructivist and constructionist theories. The chapter ends with the challenges for social work when undertaking constructivist inquiry.

Chapter 2 presents the assumptions of constructivism with some of the areas of congruence between social work and constructivism highlighted. Also included is the decision-frame for planning a constructivist study. Because constructivist research is not always feasible or appropriate, ways of determining fit between constructivist assumptions and the research need are detailed.

At the conclusion of each chapter you will find exercises and discussion questions to strengthen your understanding. You are encouraged to spend some time with these portions of the text in order to develop the way of thinking and the vocabulary of constructivism.

CHAPTER 1

The Social Worker's Introduction to Constructivist Research

Chapter Contents in Brief

Similarities between constructivist inquiry and social work practice
Location of constructivist inquiry in the "ways of knowing" debate in social work
Philosophical and theoretical underpinnings of constructivism
Challenges for social workers engaged in constructivist inquiry

What does constructivism offer social work? Why should a student or a researcher/practitioner care about the material in this text? The answer to both questions is that people who are drawn to a helping profession out of respect for the human condition and a desire to effectively aid those in need will see a practical congruence between social work practice and constructivist research. In constructivist methods they will recognize familiar social work practice skills. They will also see in constructivism the promise for the creation of meaningful knowledge to guide useful practice. Basically, constructivist inquiry provides a mechanism for producing rigorous *and* relevant information for social work interventions. This text is designed to aid the skilled practitioner to extend those social work practice skills into knowledge-building skills for professional practice.

There exists a great deal of similarity between the techniques of social work practice and the methods of constructivist research. Both are exquisitely attentive to language and cognition. Both are attuned to communication and to interpretation of meaning. Constructivist research builds on the same elements of conscious practice and conscious use of self that social work has since its inception. In fact, the methods provided here will not only help extend knowledge needed for relevant practice, they will also assist those who perfect the methods to become even more skilled practitioners.

Constructivist inquiry will be useful in operationalizing many important value positions of the profession. Social work calls for flexible attention to individual client perceptions (starting where the client is), while also attending to the needs/desires of the context in which the client is found (person-in-situation). Built on alternative assumptions about what constitutes reality, constructivist inquiry provides practical guidelines for ways to understand and manage the context of multiple perspectives and diversity. By learning how to look at the "other" through the constructivist research lens, the reader will also learn alternative ways of reaching the client and the context in order to do the job of social work. Constructivist research provides a way to avoid racist, oppressive, or otherwise inaccurate information by assisting the inquirer to look at the world with more flexibility. By managing relativity, it provides a mechanism for the practitioner to understand data differently, and by doing so, allows for expanded uses of information to guide how to deal with problems and clients suffering with those problems.

Constructivist inquiry highlights perceptions. Its methods provide mechanisms for looking at another's world. These methods operationalize nonjudgmental interactions because they call for recognition of all possibilities. With constructivist inquiry guiding practice, fresh air enters the field. There is no need for the *right* answer because a variety of possible answers can be considered.

Social Work Practice and Constructivist Inquiry

There is a link between the epistemological perspective of constructivism and the social work frame of reference. Central to both is an interactive, context-bounded attention to dignity, individuality, empowerment, and mutual respect in the relationship between the individual and society. The social work profession values the individual in his or her uniqueness and holds that there is an interdependence between individuals and society in shaping the full potential of each person (Bartlett, 1958). Social work values hold that human knowledge is never final or absolute, as does constructivism. The social worker who conducts responsible, conscious, and disciplined interrelationships with clients must be prepared to deal with spontaneous and unpredictable human behavior, as should the constructivist researcher. Table 1–1 brings the assumptions of constructivism into alignment with the tenets of the social work framework by allowing a comparison along the dimensions of ideology, purpose, knowledge, and methods.

Ideology from both frameworks is very comparable. Both are pragmatic. Major elements of present-day social work show the influence of American pragmatist philosophers such as William James and John Dewey. Early social workers including Jane Addams, Mary Richmond, Jessie Taft, and Virginia Robinson drew from the American pragmatist tradition (Addams, 1910/1990; Richmond, 1922; Robinson, 1962; Taft,

TABLE 1–1

Comparison between the Social Work Framework and the Constructivist Perspective

	Social Work Framework	Constructivist Perspective
Ideology	Pragmatism	Pragmatism/functionalism
	Client self-determination	Human agency/autonomy
	Individualism	Multiple perspectives
	Interdependence	Contextualism/interdependence
	Self-realization	Human potential
	Personal/social responsibility	Social construction of societal standards
Purpose	Empowerment	Understanding/empowerment
	Choice	Informed choice
	Change	Effective change
	Problem-solving	
Knowledge	Nomothetic	Idiographic
	Idiographic	
Methods	Responsible, conscious use of self in relationship with an individual or group	Competent, reflexive use of human instrument
	Systematic observation and assessment	Persistent observation and inductive data analysis
	Continuing evaluation and professional judgment to determine direction of activities	Emergent, reflexivity, member checking to determine direction of activities

1937). Dewey, who never actually used the term *constructivism*, is instrumental in the development of constructivism in education (Lambert et al., 1995). His position about cognition and learning was that a person would not think unless he had a problem to solve (Dewey, 1933). Thinking was a goal-directed construction. It is also noteworthy that Dewey saw the individual as completely interdependent with the community and others "[A]part from the ties which bind him to others, he is nothing" (as cited in Campbell, 1995, p. 53). American **pragmatism** is based on the assumption that one uses what works in knowledge and action. Constructivist pragmatism focuses on what is done with the meaning we give to our lived experience (Fisher, 1991). Both social work and constructivist inquiry have functional aspects in the tradition of social workers Taft and Robinson (Robinson, 1934; Taft, 1937) because both look at useful meaning making and decision making in context.

This context-embedded pragmatism leads social work to focus on the client's own ways of responding to life's struggles via the social work relationship. Within the relationship, the client discovers what is most functional. This is self-determination, and is an important aspect of self-realization (Weick & Pope, 1988). Constructivism focuses more precisely on human capacity and autonomy. The constructivist assumes that every person determines his or her own meanings and constructions of events and that human potential is unlimited. Therefore, all meanings must be encountered as potentially possible and valid (Berger & Luckmann, 1976).

Individualism permeates American social work. This individualism not only recognizes individual capacity and responsibility, it also asserts that every person is unique, worthy of respect and affirmation (Hepworth & Larsen, 1993). Furthermore, there is a recognition that affirming someone's experience does not necessarily mean agreeing with or condoning the individual's views or feelings. For this reason, social work scholars such as Laird (1995) favor the contructivist influence in social work practice and education for its guidance in managing the **multiple meaning** context of most individually defined problems. Constructivist focus on **multiple perspectives** over a one "true" perspective overcomes some of the problems with overlooking important dimensions of problem solving when a unique, individualist view is maintained.

The person–environment construct in social work is an operationalization of the value of personal/social responsibility whereby both sides of the construct respond in appropriate ways to need. Constructivism sees potentially conflicting interests based on differing person/environment perspectives. Autonomy, for constructivism, comes not out of individualism, but is achieved and maintained through mutual negotiation and co-construction of mutually acceptable standards for performing societal responsibilities (Fisher, 1991).

Purpose for social work, since the 1890s, though varying language has been used to describe the "work" of social work, is a "shared power in partnership with others" (Cook, 1992, p. 16). Empowerment, or unleashing the client's own power through collaborative identification of both the problem and the solution, drives most activities called social work (Levy, 1983; Simon, 1994). Client choice is central to any social work change activity. Constructivism has a slightly different emphasis. The primary purpose of constructivism is understanding, but through understanding comes knowledge. Knowledge enhances the individual's power to make informed choices that can lead to effective change.

Knowledge in social work, according to Tyson (1992, 1993) and others (see for example Saleebey, 1990; Weick, 1987; Witkin, 1989), has been built both on a need to know the particulars of a case (idiographic knowledge) and nomothetic (or lawlike) knowledge, which is based on generalizable information that would apply to a class of individuals. Tyson (1995) makes a cogent argument that idiographic knowledge was the basis of practice until the profession embraced positivist methods and perspectives in the 1950s. It might be argued that, as a result of the recent epistemological debate in the social work profession (see Bloom, 1995), the nomothetic and idiographic are coming more into balance. Constructivism, on the other hand, due to its epistemological assumptions, is only idiographic in its approach to knowledge.

Methods comparison between social work practice and constructivism is a matter of semantic emphasis. In either framework, responsible, ethical, competent practitioners, using a reflective process, are conscious of their own feelings, intentions, and needs in relation to the others participating in a process with them. Both use systematic, persistent observation to provide data for analysis. Constructivist data are generally analyzed inductively (specific data to general categories), whereas social work practitioner data in a theory-guided practice are typically deductive in nature (from the general of the theory to the case specifics). Attention to needed adjustments throughout the process is a part of both methods. Professional judgment based on client and environmental feedback informs decisions about the direction in social work practice. Reflexivity and feedback from the environment, combined with other data sources, determine the emerging direction of constructivist activities.

The interactive nature of the education/change process, which is central to social work, is also paramount in constructivism. Just as in social work, constructivist strategy focuses on evidence of improvement in the participant's conscious experiencing of his or her world. This is based on a belief that through consciousness raising comes a more sophisticated understanding of the world. Social work does not entirely come to consciousness raising based on appreciation of alternative perspectives as constructivism does, but cognitive change via heightened awareness is a product of both methods.

Practice Principles

Demonstrating congruent practice principles makes the association between constructivism and social work even more explicit. The principles have been fashioned from the basic constructivist methods that are logically derived from the assumptions of constructivism (see Guba & Lincoln, 1989). The reader will also identify "best practice" of direct social work. The centrality of values, and the intersubjectivity and reflexivity of the social work profession, compare favorably to the basics of constructivist inquiry. The following principles operationalize some of the most salient commonalities between constructivism and social work.

- *Context-bounded nature of reality.* A social or individual problem under assessment or investigation is understood as a social world and explained primarily from the point of view of the actors directly involved in the social process. No useful understanding can be derived by the social worker or researcher without experiencing the **stakeholders** and the context of the social process under investigation. Assessment, investigation, or evaluation cannot be carried out except with field-based methods, taking full account of the local context. Note especially that a change in the social context of a problem changes judgments of the needs that should be addressed, the strengths, and the resources necessary or available to help.

- *Interactive nature of knowing and understanding.* The social worker or researcher, using good communication and empathic skills, is the main instrument to gather information. Only a social worker or researcher acting as the "person-in-situation" data collector can assure that the process leads to accurate understanding of the context, plus identification of the strengths and challenges of the various stakeholders in the social process under investigation.

- *Egalitarianism.* In the conduct of the assessment, investigation, intervention, or evaluation, the social worker or researcher is both a student of the stakeholders'particular constructions of social realities and a teacher, aiding others toward new insights about the constructions of other stakeholders. **Egalitarianism** involves respect and efforts toward equality.

- *Dialogic nature of knowing.* Information comes through conversation. Early in the process of coming to know, the dialogue serves to underscore differences in perspectives. Therefore, conflict, rather than consensus, is the expected condition surrounding an intervention in process. Multiple, sometimes conflicting, perspectives will appear when the goal is to uncover multiple meanings or perceptions of the participants. The role of the social worker or researcher is to utilize the learning/teaching process to manage the conflict and maximize the potential for consensus. The point is respectful negotiation among equal participants. In those cases where consensus is not possible, maximization of the contenders' understanding of their opponents' viewpoints should be the focus.

- *Viability of tacit knowing.* The social worker's or researcher's tacit/intuitive knowledge must be used full strength throughout the process to achieve the maximum value of the process. Conversely, **tacit knowledge** of all stakeholders in the process must be converted to propositional knowledge (that which has word form) so that the social worker or researcher can both think about it explicitly and communicate it to others.

- *Contextual nature of functional/pragmatic responses.* The intervention design and the theory within which to frame and understand the data collected must be allowed and encouraged to emerge from the helping or research process. It is in this way that multiple **constructed realities** can be encountered and folded into a practical or relevant practice or research intervention.

- *Consensus in reconstructions needed for lasting change.* Parties holding a variety of value postures must be involved in every part of the problem-setting or problem-identifying process and its product to assure that value pluralism (diversity) and stakeholder constructions are fairly preserved in the **reconstruction**. All participants should have a stake in the process and the product in order to commit to lasting change. Participation in all levels of the process is essential to ownership of the process. To that end, the social worker or researcher is taking a collaborative, rather than a controlling posture in the process.

- *Multiple perspectives for sense making and meaning making.* The social worker or researcher is duty bound to collect information relevant to all stakeholders; to collect information in ways that expose "facts" useful to all sides; and to release findings continuously and openly so their credibility can be examined by all.

- *Tentative nature of knowledge and goals.* **Generalizability** of findings or clinical results is not a matter of fundamental concern. Instead, negotiation between the stakeholders (including the worker or researcher) determines acceptable conclusions. The role of the worker or researcher is to mediate the process with equity and fairness, not as a judge, but as the moderator of a judgmental process.

These principles underscore the social justice/empowerment tradition of social work and constructivism, plus the importance of context and meaning in both (Lincoln, 1997; Popple, 1985; Rodwell, 1995; Simon, 1994). What is not as clear is the uncertainty, ambiguity, and ambivalence that is associated with each. The **relativism** versus **realism** controversy that plagues the philosophical dimension of the profession (Tyson, 1995, p. 345) also impacts the direct activities of the practitioner. How we know what we know and what we then do with it is central to the history of knowledge building for the profession and the debate that seems to have plagued us since our professional beginnings. This "ways of knowing" debate is crucial to finding a space for constructivist inquiry in social work.

Constructivism in Context: The Epistemological Debate in Social Work

The **epistemological** debate, or the debate on how we know what we know in social work, has gone in many directions. The complexity of the activities social workers are involved in, in combination with the range of client populations served, challenges the definition of social work as a profession and the development of empirically based social work theories. The debate is central to the history of what is necessary to professionalize social work.

In 1915 Abraham Flexner, an authority on professional education, declared that social work was not a profession because it did not have a body of its own knowledge to guide its practice. It was not scientific.

Embedded in the social science of the early 1900s, Mary Richmond, Jane Addams, Charlotte Towle, Virginia Robinson, and other foremothers, took up Flexner's challenge and produced much in the way of definitions and theoretical models (see for example, Abbott 1918; Addams, 1916, 1930; Dore, 1903; Richmond, 1917; Robinson, 1930; Towle, 1936). They helped to shape social workers' thinking about the scientific study of social work practice. Moving away from their roots in religion, philosophy, and humanism, the legacy that gave social work "its wisdom about the worth of individuals and fostered a commitment to the importance of values in the practice of social work" (Weick, 1987, p. 218), early social work leaders embraced logical positivism as a means of framing activities and garnering credibility and respect. The struggle continued at the 1929 Milford Conference (National Association of Case Workers, 1929/1974); was further explicated in the Hollis-Taylor Report of 1951; and is seen in the Working Definition of Social Work Practice, 1958 (Bartlett, 1958). This move toward positivism was finalized in the 1950s when the profession adopted the Social Work Research Group's commitment to "basic science" (Gordon, 1951; Maas & Varon, 1949). The emphasis on observation and measurement for knowledge meant forsaking intuition and other less rigorous and potentially "biased" ways of knowing. This ratified social work's movement in the direction, not only of Freud and the medical model of social work practice, but also of empirical practice including operationalization for measurement, control for generalizability, and the ongoing balancing act of embracing both knowledge and values in social work education and practice.

Mirroring the public professional dialogue in other disciplines and professions such as education, sociology, and psychology (see Adams, 1979; Blalock, 1979; Cronbach, 1975; Eisner, 1979), the debate reemerged in the late 1970s and early 1980s (Austin, 1978; Beckerman, 1978; Fischer, 1981; Gordon, 1983; Haworth, 1984; Heineman, 1981; Hudson, 1983; Imre, 1984; Karger, 1983). The limits of research findings, the inability of research to address complex social issues, and difficulties with effectiveness measures (among other problems) caused many to question the usefulness of a positivist perspective in guiding social work practice. Logical positivist and empiricist roots were, and continue to be, questioned.

Some, like Roberta Imre (1982), called for a return to our philosophical roots. Others call for more flexibility in pursuing ways of knowing (Berlin 1990; Fraser, Taylor, Jackson & O'Jack, 1991). Many suggest that quantitative evidence counts, but does not and should not stand alone (Dean, 1989, 1993; Heineman Pieper 1985; Scott, 1989; Tyson, 1992). Like its history, the social work profession continues to be challenged from the outside for lack of defined activities and effective measures and from the inside about what is good science for good practice (Gilbert, 1977; Grinnell et al., 1994; Thyer, 1986). Howard Goldstein (1992) even suggests that if our profession has not made progress as science, then might social work be art?[1]

Constructivist research fits in the realm of rigorous, systematic knowledge building possible from science, not the magical and visceral nature of knowing that comes through art. Therefore, the context for constructivist research in social work must be developed through paradigmatic, not aesthetic thinking. The controversy for social work, and most of social science, is not between art and science. Rather, it involves ontological and epistemological questions about what is human/social reality like: how we know and how this knowledge is being transmitted. The paradigmatic debate is about the assumptions that concern the essence of any phenomena under investigation. For example, is reality external to the individual or is it the product of the individual's consciousness? There are questions as to the ground on which knowledge can be obtained: Is knowledge hard, real, capable of being transmitted in tangible form? Or is it softer, subjective, spiritual, of a unique and personal nature that can only be acquired or personally experienced? What about human nature? Do humans relate to the environment in a mechanistic, deterministic way? Or are humans creative, creating their environments with free will?

Different answers to the above questions reflect different philosophical perspectives which incline the researcher/practitioner toward different methodological assumptions about what should constitute good research. These answers delineate different lenses (**paradigms**) for analysis of social theory, differing assumptions for analysis of social phenomena, and different concepts and analytic tools for social research.

Positivist and Interpretive Paradigms Compared

This section will detail two of the major perspectives in the paradigm dialogue in social work, the **positivist** and **interpretive paradigms**. We will not be discussing the more radical perspectives that have most recently been characterized by the postmodern and **critical theorists**.[2] The discussion reveals that the assumptions of the positivist position are fundamentally at odds with those of the interpretive perspective of which constructivism is a part. These perspectives do not differ so much as they compete.

As you will see, comparison is possible along some key dimensions such as the nature of reality, the relationship between the knower and the known, the possibility of generalizations, the possibility of causal linkages, and the role of values. It should also become clear that it is impossible to hold positivist assumptions along one dimension, while holding alternative, interpretive assumptions along another (Rodwell, 1990), even though it is possible to use either quantitative or qualitative methods or both in each paradigm. One might be able to combine both **quantitative** and **qualitative methods** while still attending to the **rigor** requirements built on the epistemological assumptions of each position. But how can one assume both single and multiple realities at the same time? How can one trust the separation between the researcher and the object of inquiry while supporting their interaction? How can one produce both a nomothetic and an idiographic body of knowledge in one research process?

In this text, we will not be arguing about the supremacy of one perspective over another. We will be describing both perspectives so that the reader can make a determination about how well the assumptions of each perspective fit the phenomena being investigated in social work research. It is not that one is better than the other. It is more a case that they are different, capable of producing different kinds of information for knowledge building. Earlier discussion of constructivism in relation to the social work frame of reference might suggest the interpretive paradigm's greater congruence with the values and goals of social work practice and research. In the final analysis, the true test is the relevance or the utility of each perspective as it applies to the practice of social work.[3]

The Positivist Position

In keeping with traditional positivist scientific thought, the mainstream in social work is in favor of an exclusively rational conduct of research and analysis of data, oriented to carefully defined structures including variables, sample frames, data collection, and data analysis strategies. Those supporting this perspective are oriented to **prediction**, control of events and variables, and are interested in the validity of research findings. Those operating from this perspective assume that study of human behavior should be modeled on the study of natural phenomena (Bloom, 1978; Fischer & Hudson, 1983; Grinnell et al., 1994; Rosen, 1978; Tripodi & Epstein, 1978). Research from this perspective is intent on the cumulative search for facts and **causes**, which can be assembled into laws, which, in turn, facilitate the explanation and prediction of human behavior. From this perspective, better operationalization, improved sampling, enhanced control of variation and testing, and use of statistical theory will result in the accumulation of powerful generalizations about human behavior and the practice of social work, comparable to those found in **natural science**.

Social work research and practice within the positivistic frame assumes that any social phenomenon has real existence, external to the individual; that knowledge is hard and factual; and that humans are shaped by their environment (Popper, 1968). From this frame, universal laws and the relationships between social phenomena are studied by the application of natural science research techniques (Diesing, 1991). The positivistic focus is on the objective nature of social reality and attending to what *is*.

THE NATURE OF REALITY   The social work researcher in the positivist tradition, assumes that there is a single, tangible reality "out there" that can be fragmented into independent variables and processes. There is also the assumption that these variables can be studied independently of the others. Through study of these variables and the accumulation of data, inquiry can converge on reality until it can finally be predicted and controlled. Social reality has real concrete existence above and beyond the individual. Hence, from the positivist perspective, human nature is **deterministic** in that it is shaped by circumstances and/or environments that constitute social reality. This reality, in turn, shapes action and perceptions. Finally, the positivist believes natural science methods can be applied to the study of social reality.

THE OBSERVER/OBSERVED RELATIONSHIP   In the positivist research relationship there is a subject–object **dualism**. The observer is able to maintain a discrete distance from the object of inquiry, neither disturbing it nor being disturbed by it. This **objectivity** is maintained through methodological controls.

THE PURPOSE OF INQUIRY   The purpose of all positivistic research is generalization. The aim of inquiry is to develop a nomothetic body of knowledge. This knowledge is best encapsulated in generalizations that are **truth** statements independent of both time and context. These truths will hold anywhere and at any time. Inquiry gets its purpose from the search for regularities and laws among social phenomena in order to predict and control those phenomena. Therefore, research is the search for the general and universal in reality.

THE NATURE OF EXPLANATION   Social workers using the positivist lens believe that identification of causality is not only possible, but central to the research enterprise. Every action can be explained as the result (effect) of a cause that precedes the effect temporally, or is simultaneous with it. In fact, the ultimate test of the success of a positivistic science is the ability to predict and control using knowledge of those causes.

THE ROLE OF VALUES IN INQUIRY   In positivism, the well-designed inquiry is value free. This is true in great part because of the subject–object dualism that objectivity can create and maintain. Objectivity and the bounding of values can be guaranteed through the methodology that is employed.

GOOD SCIENCE   In order to analyze relationships and regularities between various elements, positivist research must occur in a controlled setting using valid and reliable instruments to gather information through random sampling. The preferred method for data analysis is through quantitative/statistical methods. Experimental and quasi-experimental designs, formal measurement methods, and hypotheses-based deductive theory are also preferred.

Positivist research can be interventionist as in experiments or it can be naturalistic, evolving from the lived experience. **Interventionist research** is often preferred due to the control that is possible through its design and structure. Qualitative methods can be used, but are not generally preferred due to their potentially subjective nature. With either qualitative or quantitative methods, research issues revolve around definition of concepts, measurement, and identification of underlying themes because the researcher is looking for laws. The research must be systematic with the hypothesis, protocols, and techniques defined in advance and tested in the research process. This is considered acceptable scientific rigor.

The Interpretive Position

Those supportive of an alternative way of conducting social work science aim at understanding rather than description or generalization (Heineman Pieper, 1985; Imre, 1991; Tyson, 1995). For them, mainstream methodology is not suited to probing and understanding sociobehavioral phenomena. They reject a unilateral focus on an objective social reality in favor of an emphasis on empathic understanding of social phenomena from the actor or participants'point of view. This alternative, according to Reinharz (1979), represents a rehumanization of knowledge building to reflect that researchers are human beings dealing with human problems in human ways.

The interpretive perspective to research and practice in social work acknowledges that research and knowledge building are a mix of the rational, serendipitous, and intuitive. Though many modern positivist social workers would also recognize the serendipitous and intuitive in research and analysis, their goal is to control the nonrational in favor of the rational (Guba, 1990). From the interpretive perspective, the serendipitous and intuitive are not liabilities, but opportunities in the effort to understand human phenomena. This perspective assumes that, while producing accurate information, research processes and products can also be artistic. The research can be oriented to process, sensitively engaging participants in knowledge building, at the same time that it produces a product that aids understanding of a phenomenon. For interpretive researchers, research becomes personal and focused on the meaningfulness of findings for both the scholar and the user (consumer) communities. Science for social work, from this perspective, is a mix of objective and subjective orientations. It is capable of producing specific explanations, but not of identifying cause. Given the interest in the unique, although frequently occurring phenomena, and in generating concepts in vivo in the field, interpretive research recognizes the limits of its discoveries in favor of the relevance that develops.

Operating from this frame of reference, as a constructivist researcher does, means that there is an assumption that the world, as it is, can be understood and that understanding of the fundamental nature of the social world happens at the level of subjective experience. Hence, in the interpretive approach, individual consciousness and **subjectivity** are basic to understanding (Dilthey,1976; Polanyi, 1958) and people are active creators of reality (Gadamer, 1989; Merleau-Ponty, 1994.). From this perspective, universal laws are rejected in favor of the highly individual, unique, and emergent. Multiple constructed realities cannot be understood through the concept of law, universal or otherwise. Instead, these realities can only be studied holistically. As a result, research will naturally produce more questions than it answers, so prediction and control are unlikely and uninteresting (Burrell & Morgan, 1979).

THE NATURE OF REALITY   For those taking an intrepretivist perspective, there are multiple constructed realities that can be studied only in their totalities. Reality is the product of individual consciousness, so the "out there" has no reality other than what has been created and interpreted by each individual. Since free human beings participate actively in the creation and construction of their social reality, the existence of an external world is rejected in favor of the unique, the particular to the individual. Reality in the interpretive paradigm is relativistic. Therefore, inquiry into these multiple realities will inevitably diverge, so that prediction and control are unlikely outcomes. On the other hand, understanding of the ways individuals actively create, modify, and interpret the world in which they live is possible.

THE INQUIRER–PARTICIPANT RELATIONSHIP   The observer/observed is rejected in favor of the "inquirer" and "participant" to emphasize the interpretive research relationship. There is no subject–object dualism. The inquirer and the "object" of inquiry interact to influence one another. There can be no objective distance between knower and known. Since each is free and involved in a proactive role in the creation of reality, each is self-directing and self-correcting in the mutual interaction of the inquiry.

THE PURPOSE OF THE INQUIRY   The aim of interpretive inquiry is to develop a characteristic body of knowledge, particular to the participants in the inquiry. This knowledge is in the form of a series of tentative suppositions that describe the individual case. Here differences are as inherently interesting as similarities. The goal is to understand the fundamental, emergent nature of the social world at the subjective, experiential level. This is an idiographic, personalized, body of knowledge. The research showcases the meaning people give to their own situations.

THE NATURE OF EXPLANATION   Causal linkages are impossible to identify in the interpretive perspective. An action may be explainable in terms of multiple interacting factors, events, and processes that shape it and are part of it. From this view, all entities are in a state of mutual influence and shaping, so that it is impossible to distinguish causes from effects. This enmeshment suggests that cause is impossible to identify; the most that is possible is to establish plausible inferences about the pattern of the shaping that occurs in any given case.

THE ROLE OF VALUES IN THE INQUIRY   The inquiry is value bound by the inquirer's choice of problem to be researched; in the framing, bounding, and focusing of that problem; by the theory chosen to guide the investigation; by the inquiry paradigm chosen to inform the design and data collection; by the values that are inherent in the environment of the inquiry; and in the interpretation of findings. These values must be explicit and congruent if the inquiry is to produce meaningful results.

GOOD SCIENCE   Since in the interpretive position there is a belief in the relativistic nature of the world, the focus of good research is on the subjective experience of the individual in the creation of his or her social world. The methodological emphasis is on understanding what is unique and particular in the individual. In doing so, the process looks for firsthand knowledge of the subject under investigation and provides analysis of subjective accounts. It allows the subject to unfold its nature and characteristics during the process of investigation. Language-based or narrative-based data give voice to the unique, the individualistic. Aggregate data of the sort that are derived through quantitative methods are viewed as being insensitive to uniqueness and differences. Therefore, quantitative methods are not preferred; instead, qualitative methods with inductive data analysis are favored. Emerging theory grounded in the uniqueness of the context of the investigation becomes possible and desirable. Emergent theory, sensitive enough to differences to allow accurate reconstructions of the personal accounts, is the goal of interpretive inquiry.

There can be no question that constructivist inquiry is set in an interpretive paradigm, guided by interpretive philosophical principles. There is, however, question about its theoretical underpinnings.

The Theoretical Elements: Constructivism or Constructionism

Is constructivist research built on **constructionism** or **constructivism**? And does it matter? This section will describe and compare both theoretical perspectives with an eye to both theories' relevance to constructivist research. Cynthia Franklin (1995), in a recent article, does a reputable job of comparing and contrasting constructionism and constructivism, but the focus of her discussion is clarification for practice. Here, we are interested in the same sort of comparison, but as it informs a research model. Table 1–2 shows an analysis of the differences between constructivism and constructionism. These contrasts should be useful in determining theoretical congruence of both theories with constructivist research (see Table 1–2).[4]

Basically, both emphasize human agency and assert that reality is socially and psychologically constructed. Both hold an interactional view of human behavior and a connectedness between the individual and the social environment. Both assert a reflexivity in understanding and meaning making. Both reject the "received view" of reality in that for both there is no objective reality "out there" to be received/perceived and understood through sensory perceptions. Instead, there is no single reality, but many possible ways to understand behaviors, interactions, or events. Both assert that structures (cognitive or social) that exist beyond oneself cannot be completely objectively known due to the nature of language and social processes. Radical constructivists such as Keeney (1983), Maturana (1988), Varela (1989), and Watzlawick (1984) go even

TABLE 1–2

Contrasts between Constructivism and Constructionism

Constructivism	Constructionism
Nature of Knowledge	
Cognitive schemas	Linguistic negotiation (conversation)
A construction of the subject's experience and action	Generated between individuals who judge and correct
An invention of new interpretive frameworks or structures	Agreement regarding meaning
Evolutionary to more comprehensive interpretations	Product of claims-making, labeling and other constitutive definitional processes
Human Beings	
Proactive, goal-directed, and purposive organism	Personality and identity socially constructed and potentially changing from situation to situation
Human Interaction	
Structural coupling—fitting together structures and coordinating behaviors of self-organized systems	Linguistic coupling—negotiating meaning across cognitive, social, moral structures
Processes Relevant to Constructivist Research	
Schemas for analysis	Discourse analysis
Purposeful questioning	Stories
Managing paradox	Problems understood within the social network or context
Experiential data collection	
Restructuring of cognitive meaning	Circular questioning and emergent processes
Conceptual frameworks	Narrative reconstructions
Hearing the multiple voices	Opening spaces for conversation

further to suggest that it is impossible to know anything except what is in one's own mind.

However, the two theories diverge in conceptualizing how reality is shaped, formed, or constructed. Constructionists emphasize language, narrative, socio-historical, and cultural processes as primary factors in meaning making and in understanding our own constructions, our own knowledge base. Constructivists, on the other hand, emphasize cognitive structures, or **schemas**, such as organizing principles, deep structures, and **interactive** feedback from the environment. Internal consistency with existing knowledge structures and social consensus among observers validate knowledge within an interpretive framework for the constructivist. Even with this difference, for both there is a belief in the diversity of possible meanings and alternative interpretations that makes at least contextual relativity, if not true relativity, possible.

Linkage to Constructivist Research

For the purposes of creating a theoretical linkage to constructivist research, it would probably be best to view constructivism and constructionism as a fuzzy set of frameworks with mainly indistinct boundaries. Within each we will find diversity and contradictions. Within each we will find similar contributions to a very distinct way of being with clients that focuses on their own constructions of reality and their own strengths and possibilities.

What does this mean for constructivist research? Given the basic interpretive assumptions of the constructivist perspective to research, there do not seem to be contradictions with either constructivism or constructionism. Their commonalities are present in the research framework. Their differences, as will be clear later, are also part of the research process. From the constructivists will come schemas for analysis, purposeful questioning, managing paradox, experiential data collection, and restructuring of cognitive meaning (Franklin, 1995, p. 397). From constructionism **discourse** analysis, stories, problems understood within the social network or context, circular questioning and emergent processes, narrative reconstructions, and opening spaces for conversation will emerge (Franklin, 1995, p. 397). As the text unfolds, you will see that both theories give meaning to the research process. Both are congruent with the goals and procedures of constructivist research. In fact, both are necessary for the logic of the constructivist research methods.

The Challenges for Constructivist Research in Social Work

If the major skills in social work practice and constructivist inquiry are comparable, then the major challenges must also be comparable. It is reasonable, then, that the skilled practitioner and the trained constructivist researcher have been prepared to confront similar difficulties.

The relativity assumed in constructivism means that there can be no certainty in any state of affairs. Being conscious, introspective, and capable of engaging and targeting practice skills prepares the practitioner for the "never knowing for sure" aspect of the therapeutic intervention. The same is necessary for constructivist inquiry. Dealing with ambiguity and the ambivalence that result is part of the reflective training that mainly occurs in field experiences. These skills are demonstrated by such activities as process recordings for practitioners and in the reflexive journal for constructivists.

In constructivism the practitioner/researcher gives up even the illusion that he or she controls the process. The stakeholders have equally definitive input that shapes the process, rather than a single theoretical approach chosen by the researcher shaping the research design. The skilled practitioner appreciates diversity and respects the rights of the individual to hold different values and create different constructions. The ethnically competent practitioner, the one able to practice effectively among all types of differences, welcomes the opportunity to air and clarify these differences. He or she is not threatened by difference, but, in fact, embraces difference. The same preparation is also necessary for the constructivist, because everything about the quality constructivist process is related to respectfully managing all types of diversity.

The major challenge of the constructivist perspective for social work research comes from our experiences of being well-trained positivists. It is counter to our educational framework to reject one "true," "real" reality in favor of multiple perspectives that are held to be equally valid. As Bebe Speed (1991) said in her argument against constructivism and social constructionism, "Reality exists O.K.?" This is a philosophical argument which has no resolution because it is an assumptive argument based on a paradigmatic perspective. Constructivism is set in a subjectivist, interpretive framework in which reality is relative and perspectival. As well-trained positivists, our tendency is to drift toward research designs and language that suggest causality and generalizability of research results. To take constructivism into realism, objectivity, and generalizability would be to distort the assumptions upon which it is built. This distortion would then eliminate the results that are possible from the interpretive perspective.

Being comfortable with the "it depends" nature of a fluid and changing truth is also a major challenge to well-trained positivists. This is particularly difficult for rational, linear thinkers more comfortable in **dichotomous thinking**. The "either/or" of positivism is replaced by "both/and" fluidity of **nonrational** paradoxical thinking (Stone, 1988) in constructivism and the interpretive paradigm.

For a profession charged with the responsibility of assisting "individuals and groups [to] identify and resolve or minimize problems arising out of disequilibrium between themselves and their environment" (Working Definition of Social Work Practice, 1958, pp. 6–7), the many ways of expressing personal and social functioning supported by constructivism make attending competently to professional goals very difficult. We forgo the expectation that interventions will be found to be globally effective because, with constructivism, nothing is generalizable. In addition, determining who has a problem in need of remediation or prevention depends upon perspective. What warrants attention emerges over time. Constructivism means never knowing whether service targeting is accurate. It means never *really* knowing what you know. All knowledge is held tentatively and depends on context for its power and relevance.

What constructivism does mean is a shared exploration of issues in collaboration. This also means the shift in power that is at the core of empowerment (Simon, 1994). Constructivists don't "give" power to participants; they recognize that participants have power and attempt to facilitate its discovery among those participating in the inquiry. Constructivism, in sum, forces the abandonment of the role of the expert by the trained professional in favor of the role of a trained collaborator. In the final analysis, to find the space for constructivist research in social work, giving up the role of expert may be the hardest challenge of all!

Notes

1. Those wishing to know more about the "ways of knowing" debate in social work can read Bloom (1995), Brekke (1986), Chambon & Irving (1994), Cowger (1984), Dean, & Fenby (1989), Fischer (1981), Fraser et al. (1991), Grinnell et al. (1994), Hartman (1990), Heineman (1981), Hudson (1983), Imre (1984), Laird (1994), Peile (1988), Reid (1994), Rodwell (1990), Thyer (1986), and Tyson (1992).

2. We fail to do so with some hesitation because constructivist research, as it has evolved, has developed more **radical**, change dimensions that could comfortably fit within a **critical paradigm**. The more critical perspective calls for action or change as a direct result of knowledge building. In contrast, the positivist and interpretive positions are sanguine with the creation of knowledge for knowledge's sake. In the interest of clarity and with respect to the intellectual history of constructivist methods, the change dimensions of constructivism will be discussed as they relate to required rigor in an interpretive paradigmatic frame, instead of within any radical paradigmatic perspective or worldview, even though in personal conversation (April 11, 1997), Dr. Lincoln admits that constructivist methods implemented rigorously have radical change potential.

3. Those interested in philosophy of science and the paradigmatic discussion should read Burrell & Morgan (1979), Denzin & Lincoln (1994), Diesing (1991), Guba (1990), Guba & Lincoln (1988), Manecas (1981), and Rosenberg (1988).

4. Those needing more information about the differences and similarities between constructionism and constructivism should consult Berger & Luckmann (1976), Carpenter (1996), Doise (1989), Duffy & Jonassen (1991), Fostnot (1992), Franklin (1995), Gergen (1985), (1987a), (1987b), Gréco (1985), Harré (1984), Inhelder (1983), Inhelder & DeCaprona (1985), Mahoney (1988a), (1988b), (1989), Maturana (1988), Neimeyer (1985), (1992), (1993), Neimeyer & Harter (1988), Owen (1992), Piaget (1932), (1954), Sampson (1987), Spector & Kituse (1977), Viney (1993), von Glasersfeld (1984), Vygotsky (1962), and Woolgar (1989).

Discussion Questions

These questions will strengthen the reader's understanding of the linkage between constructivist research and social work practice as well as the overall philosophical and theoretical context of constructivist inquiry.

1. Using the dimensions of ideology or beliefs, purpose or goals, acceptable knowledge to guide action, and useful methods, discuss the similarities between constructivist inquiry and social work practice.

2. Where does constructivist inquiry fit within the "ways of knowing" debate in social work?

3. Give at least five reasons why it can be said that constructivist inquiry fits within the interpretive paradigm.

4. Identify two common elements of constructionism and constructivism found in constructivist inquiry. How do they differentially shape constructivist research?

5. Discuss three challenges for social workers engaged in constructivist inquiry. What might you do at this stage to overcome each
   challenge?

CHAPTER 2

Planning a Constructivist Study

Chapter Contents in Brief

Assumptions of constructivism
*Deciding to do or not to do constructivist research: Determining
the focus of an inquiry, the fit of the paradigm with the focus of
the inquiry, and the paradigm fit with the theory selected to guide
the inquiry*
Determining the feasibility of undertaking a constructivist inquiry

True constructivist studies must not only conform with the philosophical assumptions of an interpretive paradigm and the theoretical dimensions of constructivism, but must also be in keeping with the explicit assumptions and methods of the research model developed by Yvonna Lincoln and Egon Guba, who first labeled the perspective, "Naturalism" (Lincoln & Guba, 1985). In the early days of model development, confusion existed because positivistic research can also be **naturalistic research** when it occurs in natural, nonlaboratory environments (Denzin, 1971). Further, there was confusion, well articulated by Biklen and Bogdan (1986), between the tools and techniques of naturalistic (positivist) methods and the wholly different way of viewing the world involved in "thinking naturalistically." In order to make clear that this approach to inquiry was altogether "other," the title of the model was changed in 1989 (Guba & Lincoln) to "Constructivism." This change in label more accurately reflects its theoretical connections to social construction and its radical departure from conventional research designs and methods.

The first section of this chapter clarifies constructivist inquiry's departure from traditional research. The detailed analysis of the assumptions of constructivism will provide the ideological or value basis for the constructivist inquiry process and its methods. The remainder of the chapter covers the essential questions and the planning elements that must be addressed before deciding to undertake a full constructivist inquiry. In all the discussion that follows the reader should note the comfortable fit between constructivist inquiry and the interpretive paradigmatic perspective.

A Detailed Look at Constructivist Research Assumptions

It is essential to understand the specifics of constructivist assumptions because from them flow all the methodological dimensions of constructivist inquiry. To understand these assumptions will be to understand why only certain methods can be logically derived and used in constructivism. Understanding the assumptions is the first step to understanding the "otherness" of the research model. What distinguishes constructivism from traditional inquiry and what places it squarely within an interpretive perspective is the constructivist position regarding reality, the role of the inquirer and participants in the inquiry process, the desirability of generalization as a research product, the location of causality, and the role of values in research.

Constructed Realities

Constructivists assume that realities are multiple, constructed, and holistic. If this is so, then construction of reality must depend on some form of consensual language. Meaning is determined through the manipulation of words and symbols. Usually this is done in negotiation—negotiation with the environment and the individuals who people the environment. Constructivism recognizes perspective or standpoint. What gives meaning depends on one's perspective or position. There is no objective reality, only one that is created in relationship to perspective. Instead of being objective, then, reality is subjective. It is a personal reality that is self-created. Individuals create a reality that reflects their own view of the world and who they think they are in relation to it. For constructivists, there are multiple ways in which reality may be constructed and multiple rationales for doing so.

Central to constructivism is the understanding of the multiple reasons and multiple constructions through **Verstehen** (understanding), a concept introduced by Dilthey (1961) and elaborated by Weber (1949) into his methodological stance. Verstehen, for constructivists, involves coming to an understanding of the view of the world held by those people involved in the situation (an **emic** perspective) rather than adopting a "stranger" or outsider perspective (an **etic** perspective). Through the inquiry process, one attempts to enter the role of the individual under investigation in order to understand the individual's inner experience related to his or her outward actions. Instead of remaining at a distance and ascribing meaning to external processes that can be observed, the researcher comes to knowledge building through an interpretive understanding of the internal world of human affairs. The researcher attempts to reach understanding about the phenomena under investigation by understanding the internal and intangible processes of the minds of the inquiry participants. Constructivists are interested in the structure of the construct systems, the schemas or **cognitive maps**, that individuals evolve for themselves that allow them to impose meaning on their individual experiences. Through the cognitive structure, individuals construct their own truth. Constructivists participate in the creation of that truth.

"Truth" emerges in inquiry, not as one objective view, but rather as the composite picture of how people think. Truth is a constructed reality in the minds of the individuals involved in the inquiry process, including the inquirer. There are an infinite number of constructions and, hence, multiple realities. Definition of the truth, then, occurs through the use of common referent terms (consensual language), which will inevitably be understood (constructed) differently by different individuals (constructors) at different times.

For constructivists, there is no reality until reality is perceived. Constructivist inquiry, then, is the process of reality construction. Reality is constructed when that which is being investigated seems reasonable or makes sense (Weick, 1995). What first appears to be chaos is finally perceived (constructed) through sensemaking. Sensemaking is an inductive/deductive process in which one goes back and forth through information to give it form and meaning. Inherent in sensemaking is conflict that results from attempts to understand what could or should be, but does not feel like, complementary parts of a whole. All elements remain in play through a **dialectic** process involving dynamic tensions that focuses the sensemaking on wholeness. At different times this dialectic involves subconscious behaviors, tacit knowledge, and ex post facto reasoning to justify, explain, attribute, or make sense of behavior.

Reality construction imposes order on conflicting stimuli. It orders disorder and manages information overload. It is central to the methodological process of constructivism. A constructivist must recognize multiple realities, finding and presenting as many realities as possible for consideration in the sensemaking of the inquiry. For true sensemaking involving multiple realities, the constructivist researcher must manage and include all constructions that were involved in the dialectic process of the inquiry. It is in this way that movement to a greater level of sophistication about the phenomena under investigation is possible and can be demonstrated.

To honor and respect the multiple perspectives, the constructivist researcher must assure that legitimate stakeholders to the phenomena under investigation are identified. Those with a stake in the inquiry are encouraged to share, fairly and evenhandedly, what is assumed by constructivists to be their equally valid perceptions about the issues under investigation. True reality construction, one built on consensual language of an emerging shared perspective, then becomes possible in a hermeneutic process where all have equal voice about what is consented to and subsequently constructed. It is in this hermeneutic aspect of the constructivist process that there is researcher/participants shaping of a new, more sophisticated construction or understanding of the fullness of the reality under investigation. Multiple perspectives are articulated, understood, and moved to a more sophisticated whole in a sensemaking hermeneutic circle.

In constructivist inquiry, meaning and, therefore, reality, is constructed in a way that is reflective of all participants. Their views of their worlds, and what they think about the phenomena under investigation are the data for construction. What is constructed, what makes sense, is reflective of the minds of the individuals involved in the inquiry process only. At the conclusion of an inquiry, an infinite number of alternatives remain possible and, as yet, unconstructed.

Inquirer/Participant Relationship

Constructivism assumes that there is no objectivity, but that the knower and the known are interactive and inseparable. There is a rejection of the positivistic assumption derived from natural science that there is a discrete dualism between nature and the researcher. For constructivists, natural science principles do not apply when the object of inquiry is human. In constructivism, the inquirer and the object of inquiry interact to influence one another to such a degree that the knower and the known are inseparable. They are so inseparable that there is no way to select out this interactivity. This is accepted in constructivism because of the assumptions about important dimensions of the knowledge building process including:

- *Reactivity.* There is no reasonable design to eliminate the different, observable reactions to the research process. Participants, including the inquirer, are changed as a result of the research. In other research models, attempts to control **reactivity** through design control, unobtrusive measures, and other manipulation are seen here as deceptions or lies and are contrary to the empowerment values of constructivism.

- *Indeterminacy.* What we observe is not nature itself, but nature exposed to a method of questioning. This is known as the Heisenberg principle of mass/momentum in quantum physics (Heisenberg, 1972; Jeans, 1981). What we learn depends on what we ask; therefore, the observer not only disturbs nature, but shapes it.

- *Interaction.* The observation process and product are shaped by what is observed. The respondents are shaped by their perceptions and expectations about the research and the future use of their data. In constructivism there is an assumption that through interaction, the investigator and respondents create the data of the research.

There is the assumption that interaction cannot be removed from the research equation even if that is what the researcher wants. The impossibility of removal is clear because, from the constructivist perspective:

- *Theories and facts are not independent.* Any collection of facts is subject to meaningful interpretation within a variety of possible theories. Facts in and of themselves have no absolute meaning. Meaning is in the context of theory.

- *Purposeful or purposive sampling and emergent design, two cornerstones of constructivist research, are impossible without interaction.* Both require the presence of a continuously interacting and interpreting investigator.

- *Moving beyond objectivity* requires a level of mature judgment that can be achieved through continuous interaction. It is the moving back and forth among theory, research encounters, and subjects that allows maturity and sophistication to develop.
- *Research with humans is inherently dialectical.* It is fraught with contradictions and conflicts. Making sense of all this requires constant, sensitive, dialogical relationships with other humans.
- *Meaningful human research is impossible without full understanding and cooperation of participants.* This partnership is a reciprocal relationship. Constructivists must have participants thinking about the research. Thoughtful engagement is important in the emergent development of the "why" aspect of the inquiry and in determining what should be investigated. Constructivism requires full participation. This means that all stakeholders are totally informed about and fully participating in what is going on.
- *The quality of interaction provides the human instrument, the researcher, with the possibility of fully exploiting his or her own natural, flexible, responsive advantage.* All of human potential related to adaptability, insight, and use of knowledge can be realized through interactivity. Interactivity must be exploited to achieve the maximum possible from the human instrument. For constructivists, the research must be human-to-human to take advantage of interaction in order to get smarter about the subject under investigation.

From the constructivist perspective, this interaction provides another learning opportunity because of the mutuality involved. Here, in fact, any reduction of interactivity will reduce the wholeness of the inquiry process. For a positivist, this interaction is contamination. In positivism, investigator bias must be protected against by objectivity. However, in constructivism, objectivity is not expected. The assumption is that human instrument adaptability, insight, and knowledge will flow from interaction. They are balanced with fairness that is developed via the trustworthiness (rigor) criteria of the research product.

Constructivism takes full advantage of the richness of the interaction complexity in all its subjectivity, but this does not mean that rigor is sacrificed. Details about this will be provided in a later chapter, but for now it is important to see that implicit in the lack of objectivity in constructivist research is a need for balance and fairness. This is assured through the methodological requirements for rigor including **member checks, peer debriefing, triangulation, prolonged engagement, persistent observation,** a **reflexive journal,** and an independent **audit.**

Generalization

For a constructivist, the trouble with generalizations is that they do not apply to particulars. Generalizations are nomothetic or lawlike in nature. In order to use them for prediction and control, generalizations must be applied to particulars. This creates a kind of knowledge problem, called entrapment in the nomothetic/idiographic dilemma. What is interesting about generalizations is that they should apply to a specific instance, but they generally do not, so one is left wanting/needing the idiographic, when only the nomothetic is possible. A further challenge to constructivists is that generalizations, by their nature, tend to overlook the multiple perspectives that seem to be necessary to tell a full story. Generalizations depend on the norm or mean of aggregated information, overlooking what falls outside the norm. For constructivists, generalizations cannot provide the description of range or depth necessary to relate a holistic picture of a phenomenon under investigation. For them, even the data on the margins have merit.

As a further criticism of generalizations, constructivism assumes that only time and context-bound idiographic statements are possible for sensemaking and understanding. It makes no claims about human behavior being time- and context-free—necessary elements for generalization. There is no certitude through nomothetic statements. Instead, there are statements about "what we think we just proved about what we think we know, here and now." This is all that is relevant. Instead of generalizations, constructivist inquiry is based on "working hypotheses," statements about characteristics and presumed relationships in time-limited and context-limited frameworks.

There is a tentativeness about constructivist findings because all findings require understanding of context. What has meaning in one context may be meaningless in another time and place. The inquirer and other participants will not know what will be meaningful in another environment. Therefore, the desired product of a constructivist study is not one that generalizes to any other setting, but one that is an accurate, rich, reconstruction of the various perspectives within the context of the investigation. If the findings transfer, it is the responsibility of the reader of the inquiry report to make that determination, since it is only the reader, not the inquirer, who can be familiar with the time and context in which transfer of the findings might be possible. What is required of the inquirer is the preparation of a final report with sufficient richness that an informed reader can make the determination about relevance in another context. Instead of producing generalizations, the investigator is responsible for producing a detailed rich description of the working hypotheses in the context of the study. Subsequent testing and application of these tentative hypotheses in another setting remain the responsibility of the reader.

Causality

Constructivism assumes no cause. It assumes that all entities are in a state of mutual simultaneous shaping and that it is impossible to distinguish causes from effects. Instead of looking for causal relationships, it searches to identify functional relationships. Of interest are the recurrent regularities fundamental to shaping relationships. Here, at most, we are speaking of correlation, not cause and effect. We cannot assume cause and effect because to do so requires temporal precedence, simultaneity, determinism, and **reductionism**—all impossible elements from the constructivist viewpoint.

It is impossible to sort out cause in human inquiry, because humans are anticipatory beings with behavior that has a great deal of recurrent regularity that cannot be ascribed to causes. In addition, a multitude of factors impinge on and interact with humans. To reductively select one or a subset is to ignore the web of influences involved. Causes may be effects and effects may be causes.

This perspective means that **multiple causality** replaces linear causality. Multiple simultaneous shaping, multiple causality, is of interest because there is a need to understand and manage how elements relate. Constructivist inquiry will allow us to assert that factors are related, but in unknown ways. Patterns may not be regular and context may make the difference in the patterns, so it is important to understand the pattern in a given context. This approach to understanding allows for a description of interaction, but without directionality and with no particular outcome.

When the focus is on multiple simultaneous shaping there is an assumption that all elements are in mutual and continual interaction. It is also assumed that each element is activated by virtue of the configuration of all other elements in that place and at that time. This web or pattern of circumstance will never occur in that way again, giving the research participants a unique picture. These results cannot imply predictability or control, only tentativeness. What is produced is a here-and-now understanding of a pattern of relationship and a description of relatedness that seems to fit the current picture. It is limited, because no one pattern can be seen to take into account every aspect of the context. A time in the future may present very different aspects.

For a constructivist inquiry, the implication of this is that there is an inherent problem in determining when an interpretation of the relationship, which has been the focus of the inquiry, is sufficiently plausible to be persuasive. Most of the criteria for the **case study** and the thickness dimension are still evolving; but some methods, such as member checks, outside audit, persistent observation, long-term learning, and intensive interviews, that are part of case study rigor will help. These will be described more fully later. No matter what degree of rigor is developed in a constructivist inquiry, it will not be satisfactory to people looking for causes. Constructivism does not see cause as relevant.

Values in Research

Constructivism starts with the assumption that inquiry is value-bound and continues with further concern for morality and ethics in doing research. By taking a value-bound position, what constitutes an appropriate method depends on the situation, as does determining what constitutes admissible knowledge. The veil of objectivity is absent, so the risks involved in balancing perspectives and addressing the scope of moral, political, and personal challenges are more clearly delineated. When the research is value dependent, then every aspect of the rigor is dependent on the values being operationalized. A constructivist research problem is one where values are central.

True constructivist research can only be undertaken in an interpretive paradigm where values and intersubjective shaping are acceptable research issues. This allows for philosophical value congruence, but theoretical value congruence is also important. Theories guiding constructivist research must be open to mutual shaping or subjectivity such as constructivism, constructionism, or symbolic interactionism.[1]

Constructivism assumes that context is central to understanding and meaning making, so the questions that are asked and the participants who answer are entirely dependent upon the context of the inquiry. Assuming a value-bounded inquiry also assumes lack of certainty and stability, or coherence. This lack of stability may also have ethical consequences in the inquiry.

If we are to assume that researchers, regardless of perspective, believe that persons who participate in research should not be harmed or placed in harm's way; that they should give fully informed consent to the research endeavor; that there should be no deception; and that privacy and confidentiality should be respected, then it should be clear that ethical behavior in a value-bound, emergent, context-dependent process is more difficult to achieve than in the controlled processes of traditional science. The constructivist researcher has intentional personal involvement. He or she is living with the participant's reality in intense face-to-face contact. This makes maintenance of balance for good judgment difficult.

Constructivists assume that knowledge is power. Even though the researcher participates in an empowerment process that results from the learning and greater sophistication that comes from the hermeneutic process, the inquirer is still instilled with a great degree of power because the participants trust the investigator with their history and identity. Respecting that trust while protecting confidentiality is a challenge because of the intensity of the process. The reader will see that member checking and triangulation will naturally lead to statements like "I know who said . . . ," which will make protecting identity almost impossible.

In order for the dialectical process to have its best results, the inquirer needs the trust of participants and their rapport for negotiation. Somehow the participants must trust that the inquirer understands what they think and feel and that the inquirer will not hurt them. Unfortunately, when getting this close, the issue of framing the case study can create another ethical dilemma. How the case is framed can create a potentially less accurate reflection of the reality by what is chosen, what is emphasized, and what is overlooked. Some of those decisions are shaped by whose agenda the inquirer is implementing and whose reality is being recorded. It depends upon to whom the inquirer owes allegiance and where the inquirer fits within the personal and political frameworks of the environment. The potential for ethical dilemmas abound.

Whatever the context, values, morals, and ethics must be maintained at the forefront or the powerful process and product will be short-circuited. **Peer review** and honest member checking acts as a beacon to guide an ethical and value-congruent process. There should be no cheating in the research process. The demands of trustworthiness and authenticity, the mechanisms with which to demonstrate constructivist rigor for the research process and product, should guard against ethical lapses. More details of these and other methodological safeguards will be discussed in later sections of the text.

Constructivist Research Methods

All constructivist methods come from the basic assumptions of the model. To be constructivist, the research must, at a minimum, attend to all the following:

- *Natural setting.* The research is done in the usual context of the phenomenon because reality cannot be understood in isolation from the context that gives it meaning.

- *Human instrument.* Primary data gathering is performed by the human because an a priori nonhuman instrument cannot be devised with sufficient adaptability to adjust to the various realities encountered in the inquiry. Also, only the human instrument is capable of grasping meaning in interaction.

- *Tacit knowledge.* The tacit/intuitive/felt knowledge is legitimate to understand nuances. It should be used in addition to propositional knowledge for communication of meaning.

- *Qualitative methods.* Methods using words and observations are more adaptable and capable of dealing with multiple, less aggregatable realities because they expose more directly the nature of the transaction between the investigator and the participants.

- *Purposive sampling.* Sampling is done to increase the scope and range of data exposed in order to look for multiple realities.

- *Inductive data analysis.* Data are analyzed from specific raw units of information to subsuming categories in order to make sense in the context of the investigation.

- *Grounded theory.* Theory emerges from the inquiry based on inductive data analysis because no theory, developed a priori, could encompass the specifics of the multiple realities of a particular context.

- *Emergent design.* The research process emerges from the experience rather than being totally developed beforehand. This is because no inquirer can know about the many realities that will emerge to devise an adequate design before entering the process.

- *Negotiated outcomes.* The inquirer negotiates meanings, interpretations, and final products with the human sources of data because the participants own their data and because their constructions of reality are of interest.

- *Case study reporting mode.* The case study is preferred for being less reductionistic and more adaptable to multiple realities.
- *Idiographic interpretation.* Data are interpreted in terms of the particulars of the case rather than in terms of lawlike generalizations. Different interpretations will be meaningful for different realities.
- *Tentative application of findings.* Findings have no broad application because realities are multiple and different. They may not be duplicated elsewhere.
- *Focus-determined boundaries.* What is the real question and who knows the answer are based on an emergent focus that allows the multiple realities to shape and define the research.
- *Trustworthiness.* Research rigor is related to the quality of the research product and is analogous to positivist standards of validity and reliability.
- *Authenticity.* Research rigor is related to the quality of the research process and is attentive to the interactive dimension of the inquiry. It has a qualitative-change focus.

Constructivist inquiry, while attending to the above dimensions must be totally emergent. The inquirer will start based on prior experience, a review of the literature, or some other "intellectual itch," but this focus may change. The final form of the inquiry will be determined in interaction with participants and the context of the inquiry. What the "real" question is will be determined by all the stakeholders, including, but not limited to, the inquirer.

This emerging focus determines the procedures to be used in the inquiry. The appropriate methods to investigate any given question in any given context will depend on the context and the decisions made about focus. With this, then, theory emerges from the inquiry and is grounded in the context instead of being established beforehand. This does not mean that constructivist inquiry is atheoretical, but rather, that theory is never selected as the guiding framework for hypothesis testing because no hypotheses are tested in constructivist inquiry. Instead, traditional theories are used to shape only the foreshadowed questions and early, tentative, working hypotheses at the beginning of the enterprise. Instead of a theory that is tested, what is produced is **grounded theory**, a theory that is particularly grounded in the unique experience of the context of the inquiry.

The structure of the inquiry is emergent and so, too, are all the aspects within that structure, including rigor. Sampling cannot be determined in advance. For constructivism, sampling of data sources, known as stakeholders, serves to maximize the scope and the range of the information obtained in the inquiry. It must evolve with the process. Instrumentation for data collection is not external to the process, but becomes more refined as the inquirer becomes more knowledgeable in the process. Data analysis is open-ended and inductive. In short, all methods should change in response to the process of the emerging design and the theory definition. What constitutes appropriate rigor for a specific inquiry, then, emerges in and is influenced by the context and the process.

Just being aware of the constructivist assumptions and the methods that are logically derived for those assumptions does not mean that an inquirer is ready to undertake a constructivist inquiry. Not all research projects are appropriately addressed through a constructivist lens. The following section is designed to aid the reader in determining if the question about the phenomenon to be investigated and the context of the investigation fit within the assumptions of constructivism and if constructivist research is really feasible.

Constructivist Focus, Fit, and Feasibility

Determining constructivist focus, fit, and feasibility constitutes the first steps in undertaking a meaningful constructivist inquiry. It is essential that all elements of the following discussion are considered prior to designing and implementing a study. Failure to find congruence along all dimensions may mean, at best, the production of meaningless results or, at worst, involvement in untenable political controversy (see, for example Rodwell & Woody, 1994).

The importance of assessing all dimensions of feasibility and appropriateness cannot be overemphasized. When one engages in a constructivist project, one is participating in a research process that will be unfamiliar to even the most seasoned researchers. It will not look or feel the same to agency administrators, research funders, research teachers, or dissertation-committee members. The "otherness" might be seen as a threat or as an opportunity. A constructivist research proposal might be embraced enthusiastically or rejected in the most negative, visceral way. The researcher attempting to engage in this type of inquiry should know and should be prepared to argue that an emergent, essentially uncontrollable process like a constructivist inquiry is just what is needed to answer the questions at hand. You can know this by determining focus, fit, and feasibility.

Determining the Focus

The three main types of research: pure, evaluation, and policy are possible in constructivist inquiry. The difference from traditional research is that these three types can actually mix together in a constructivist process. An inquiry might begin as an effort to understand how to define neglect for the purposes of case-based decision making, but the context of the decision could become so important that "pure" research evolves into an evaluation of a particular child protective service system in a city. The actual evaluation would not be complete without a consideration of the intent of the federal and state policies in shaping case finding in child neglect. No matter where the inquirer enters a social work problem, chances are that dimensions of pure research, evaluative research, and policy analysis will evolve to importance in a constructivist inquiry.

Though the constructivist methodology was first developed for program evaluation, more specifically, educational evaluation (see Biklin & Bogdan, 1986; Bogdan & Biklen, 1992; Guba, 1987; Guba & Lincoln, 1981, 1982; Smith & Lincoln, 1984; Williams, 1986), it is amenable to most types of research questioning. Constructivist methods can be used to understand or describe a problem (Lincoln & Guba, 1985). This is what can be called "pure" research in that the focus is the defining of the depth and scope, the "ins" and "outs" of a phenomenon of interest. In social work, this could be anything from the meaning of neglect for all the stakeholders in a neglect decision to the role of race in the context of Alcoholics Anonymous meetings. Constructivist methods could investigate "justice" in social work practice or they could be useful in exploring "participant compliance" with research protocol in HIV/AIDS research. These questions explore values, meaning, and interrelationships within identifiable contexts.

Constructivist methods are useful in evaluation. They can be used to elaborate an evaluand—that which is being evaluated, a phenomenon, process, or context—to determine its merit (quality) or worth (value) (Guba & Lincoln, 1981). The evaluation, as in most models of evaluation, can be formative, "directed toward refinements or improvements in the evaluand" (Lincoln & Guba, 1985, p. 227) or summative, that is, "directed toward an assessment of its overall impact" (Lincoln & Guba, 1985, p.

227). I have suggested elsewhere (Rodwell, 1994) that constructivist evaluations can be undertaken when the goal is to understand the internal dynamics of program operations (process evaluation). It is appropriate when the goal is to understand how the program is perceived by important groups or when there is a sense that emergent or unmet needs are affecting the quality of the service process and outcomes. Constructivist approaches can also be very helpful when there is a sense that something is happening, missing, or needed, but the shape of the question is unknown. Finally, constructivism is useful when the goal is to understand or document individual client outcomes (case studies). Examples of appropriate constructivist evaluations could be assessing the quality of a family preservation program from the perspectives of the children and families receiving services, the therapists, the funders, the program administrators, and the court system; or evaluating the impact of self-esteem programs on inner-city, adolescent, African-American males.

Policy analysis or policy research can be undertaken using constructivist methods to determine the utility of current policy-in-intent, implementation, and/or experience (Guba, 1985; Skrtic, 1985b). Guba defines policy analysis as the "process by which policy decisions are illuminated and informed" (1985, p. 2). Constructivist inquiry into intent of policy would pursue the reality of policy makers and their constructions of what they want to have happen. This is a focus on the ideology of the policy. Policy is a statement of values (Guba, 1985) and, thus, policy analysis is an inquiry into choices and a process that is bounded by values.

Policy inquiry into implementation is how the policy-in-intent is translated into programs. Effects of programs serve as good proxies for policy effectiveness (Crowley & Rodwell, 1994). It is also with policy analysis at this level that constructivism can circle into program evaluation, because it is at the program level that most social policy is actually implemented. Evaluating the effectiveness of a program is also evaluation of policy-in-implementation.

Finally, policy-in-experience is how people with the social problem that the policy was designed to address experience what is generated as a result of the policy. A constructivist researcher is interested in assessing the worth of the policy as it is experienced programmatically. Values influence implementation; are reflected in programs; shape the experience of the beneficiaries; and are evident in their experience of the services, or their view of other benefits of the policy. Policy-in-experience is not just an assessment of the competence of service providers; it is an assessment of the co-construction about the values related to what the problem is, who has the problem, what should be done about the problem, and who should be responsible. All stakeholders in these values have a say in how public policy is shaped and their values will shape their view of the worth of the policy and the quality of the program. All stakeholders will have perspectives about the value or worth of current policy in intent, implementation, and experience, so all stakeholders must be tapped when inquiring into the experience of the policy.

Policy analysis, congruent with construcivist assumptions, requires values to be central to the analysis question. The inquiry could be focused principally on the subjective, or on attempting full understanding of multiple perspectives. An inquiry into the policy formulation or implementation process would be appropriate using constructivist methods. Examples of social work research appropriate for constructivist policy analysis include: inquiry into aspects of the implementation of federal housing policy, special education policy, welfare reform policy, "Learnfare," or interdisciplinary teams in early intervention.

Identifying the original focus, whether it be pure research, program evaluation, or policy analysis, is helpful to the inquirer because it indicates where he or she is beginning, even if this does not determine where the process will end. More importantly, determining a focus begins the development of an emergent structure for the research endeavor. At least at the initial stages, knowing what type of research is being undertaken will help determine the boundaries for the research process and the data inclusion/exclusion criteria. Knowing at the outset that a program evaluation will be undertaken clues the researcher in to the initial context of the evaluation (the agency setting) and the initial stakeholders in the process (clients, service providers, administrators, funders, etc.), but the final boundaries of the process will be problem-determined and emergent. It may develop that the real issue to be investigated is not program effectiveness in a children's mental health service, but the racial difference between service providers and service recipients. The final inclusion/exclusion decisions evolve with the evolution of the problem definition and the subsequent inquiry design.

Determining the Fit of the Paradigm with the Inquiry Question

Determining paradigm fit may require a quick review of the paradigmatic discussion regarding positivism and interpretivism in Chapter 1. The assumptions that undergird the research question and its focus must fit with the assumptions of the interpretive paradigm of which constructivism is a part. Specifically, *multiple realities* or constructions must be of interest. If the research is aimed at identifying the "cause" of child abuse instead of the multiple meanings of child abuse, then the research will be better conducted in a more traditional manner that would allow the control for generalizability necessary for identification of correlations and/or cause. For constructivist inquiry, the problem to be investigated must be one with many constructions.

Objectivity cannot be at issue. *Investigator/phenomena interaction* must not only be acceptable, but possible and of interest. The problem must require significant interaction between the inquirer and the research participants in order to achieve the level of understanding and sophistication sought. Mutuality must be possible in the context of the inquiry. If a study of teamwork in early intervention is, because of politics and other concerns, limited only to the perspective of the department director responsible for managing the team, or if the inquirer is only allowed to observe team activities and not interact with team members, then the interaction necessary to expand understanding is not possible. A constructivist inquiry would not be viable.

The problem under investigation must be *context dependent.* How the phenomenon manifests itself within a particular situation is assumed to be its unique meaning or reality for that time and place. The idiosyncrasies of the situation will shape the construction of meaning and understanding. For example, the specifics regarding the meaning of neglect in a rural community close to an Indian reservation will be different than those in a large multicultural environment where ethnic and cultural diversity predominates. If context separation is needed or expected, such as is obtained in controlled laboratory trials, then a constructivist approach would not be appropriate. The only acceptable laboratory-like constructivist question might be related to meaning making in a laboratory setting. Such an inquiry could investigate the meaning of the controls introduced in a laboratory experiment for all the stakeholders in that experiment.

A problem to be investigated by constructivist means should be a complex one. *No single cause* or combination of causes should be sufficient to explain the problem or phenomenon. Most social problems of interest to social work practitioners would be satisfactory from this standard.

In addition, *values* should be central to the problem. Returning to the neglect inquiry as an example, what constitutes good parenting is value or preference dependent when trying to determine when good parenting is absent and the child is neglected. The role of a child in a neglectful process depends on what value is placed on children and childhood. The role of the public servants charged with child protection also is value-sensitive in that labeling protective intervention as "overintrusive" or "underprotective" is a matter of ideological perspective or values.

If multiple perspectives or realities are of interest and if interaction between the inquirer, the phenomena to be investigated, and the context is important to understanding, then it is likely that the question to be investigated fits within an interpretive paradigm. If the question of interest is a value-embedded one, with complex dimensions suggesting no cause, and if understanding all of these aspects is of interest, then it is likely that a constructivist approach is appropriate.

Determining the Paradigm Fit with the Theory Selected to Guide the Inquiry

The type of **theory testing** that is central to positivistic research is not possible from a constructivist perspective. In constructivism, theory is grounded in the data (Glaser & Strauss, 1967) and will emerge from the inquiry process itself due to the context bounded nature of the constructivist assumptions about reality and knowledge building. The traditional research design step of determining theoretical fit with the paradigm is less important in constructivism than it might be in the traditional research process aimed at theory development or theory testing.

Since inquirers will generally be well-trained positivists with life experiences, they will not enter the research endeavor as tabulae rasae, or blank slates. Information gleaned through a process of lifelong learning will be informing the early stages of the inquiry. Therefore, knowledge of human behavior theories, sociological theories, or social work practice theories will influence how the foreshadowed questions or working hypotheses in the early stages of the research will be framed. In constructivist investigations the human instrument, the inquirer, is the sum total of an educational experience that will no doubt include exposure to theories of human behavior and social work practice. These are relevant in the early stages of the inquiry because they are the basis of the hunches that guide the inquirer's entry into the inquiry. But relevant theory for the context of the research must emerge from the data garnered in the research process. The theory that will be produced is the co-constructed meaning arrived at through the consensus-building process involving all participants, including the researcher.

Finally, if for some reason a theory must be stated in advance as a part of a research or funding proposal, it must be placed in the context of the constructivist assumptions. This means that a theory must be congruent with multiple realities, subjectivity, context dependence of meaning, and so forth. For example: critical theory, standpoint theory, empowerment theory, or symbolic interactionism could be acceptable on these grounds. In addition, if a theory must be put forward, it must be understood that it is a tentative means of constructing meaning. It can be introduced only to guide entry hypotheses or foreshadowed questions. If there is any research expectation regarding theory testing, then constructivism is an inappropriate research approach.

Determining the Feasibility of Undertaking a Constructivist Inquiry

Constructivist inquiry is a *political undertaking* (Rodwell, 1995). It is a process that, if successful, empowers participants and facilitates social change (Chambers, Wedel, & Rodwell, 1992; Guba & Lincoln, 1989). Effective social change must be based on honest declaration of the different perspectives so that they can be compared and contrasted in an attempt to reach the highest possible level of mutual understanding. If a sense of safety is absent as a result of high levels of anxiety due to conflict, then honest communication will not be possible because participants will be inclined to protect themselves from risk. The inquirer must know enough about the conflict potential and the context to manage the communication necessary to glean accurate constructions of the context. If an agency is in funding crisis and employees fear for their jobs, the chances of honest appraisal of the quality of services via constructivist means will be minimal. This would be particularly true if an outside funder was instrumental in the constructivist evaluation of the agency's service. This type of agency would not be appropriate for constructivist intervention because the level of conflict and overall risk would make honest communication unlikely even for the most capable constructivist inquirer (Rodwell & Woody, 1994).

Co-construction of meaning is fraught with potential for conflict. In fact, the dialectical process necessary to move to higher-order sophistication for the consensus in co-construction will have tension, if not conflict. In order to manage the level of discomfort that may be present, the *degree of conflict* in the context should not be so high as to bar honest communication. Participants must not be required to risk too much in order to be forthcoming about their position. They must feel safe and respected in order to be comfortable, disclose honestly, and openly consider alternative views on the subject under investigation. They must not fear for their jobs or their physical or psychological safety as a result of open discussion of their position.

The *external constraints* such as funding sources or report or dissertation time frames must be amenable to the unfolding nature of an emergent process. Since timing and budgets cannot be precisely predicted, outside interests to the constructivist process must be ready to accept the shifts that are inevitable as the process develops. It should not be surprising that the timing of a constructivist research project cannot be predicted. Budgets are also virtually unspecifiable, as are the end products. The specifics of the design cannot be given in advance. These must emerge, develop, or unfold as they are co-constructed in context. Failure to assure that undue pressure will not be placed on the process may mean that a full process, either in terms of inclusion of significant stakeholders or in the development of a quality of the hermeneutic circle (to be discussed in Chapter 4), will be prevented, thus short-circuiting the quality of the constructivist product as well as its process.

To determine if a constructivist inquiry is feasible, Guba and Lincoln (1989) have provided some guidelines. At a minimum, participants must be able to participate from a position of integrity. Honest presentation of personal perspectives must be possible without hidden agendas and other means of conscious obfuscation. Commitment of time and energy to the completion of an intense process must be possible so that the true consideration of alternative perspectives necessary to come to co-construction is possible. Contexts not congenial to the collaborative, teaching/learning nature of the process would not be appropriate. A highly hierarchical environment in which the leader is not open to input from "underlings" would not be appropriate, because the leader is most likely very invested in maintaining, not sharing power. The most amenable context will be one that can allow and support mutual respect among all stakeholding groups, no matter what their expertise or power. This will be the context in which the maximum benefit of the consciousness-raising experience of the co-construction will be possible because power sharing is or may be possible.

In addition to the fit between the focus of the inquiry, the paradigm, and theories guiding the research design, the technical requirements are central to the feasibility assessment. Information must be available; access to stakeholders must be possible; and the inquirer must have the capacity to draw out the important voices in the story.

Time and technical expertise must be available for data analysis. As in most qualitative research, data overload is a real possibility. The inquirer must have the personal or computer assistance necessary to manage, reduce, and reconstruct data according to constructivist guidelines, and the time to let this process emerge. Otherwise, the research will not result in a meaningful product. The time and real dollar costs must be in the realm of the possible, or it would be better not to start this essentially unpredictable and uncontrollable process.

The human and political feasibility must be of serious concern because of the power shifting potential of constructivism. Elsewhere we have discussed these in relationship to feasibility assessment in program evaluation (Chambers, Wedel, & Rodwell, 1992, pp.138–139), but human and political feasibility are particularly important to constructivist inquiry, no matter what the focus. The following questions should guide the inquirer's final decisions regarding the feasibility of undertaking a constructivist investigation:

- *Can the inquiry be undertaken with due regard to the maintenance of personal rights and integrity?* For example, could participants be harassed as a result of sharing their positions? Or would participants feel compelled to act or speak against their true position?

- *Could harm come to stakeholders as a result of the inquiry?* For example, could a participant risk losing his or her job or current status?

- *In what ways might the inquiry be detrimental to human functioning?* For example, could a child's recovery from the trauma of abuse be hampered by the inquiry?

- *Who are the potential gainers and losers for the inquiry product?* For example, if the findings are negative, who will be blamed and who will be pleased?

- *What kinds of political influences can be expected in the inquiry and from whom?* For example, who with power might be made uncomfortable by the process? Who might want to control, or be able to control, the process or the results?

- *What do the participants and the context have to gain or lose from the inquiry?* For example, what might participants learn that could be helpful or threatening, or what might positive or negative results mean for the agency?

As the result of this process, political imbalance will occur. For a final analysis of feasibility, according to Guba and Lincoln (1981), it is important to assess, as far as possible, whether the information likely to be derived from the constructivist process is sufficiently significant to warrant the resulting political upset. Only the participants can determine this. The researcher must help them by providing sufficient information to allow them to give fully informed consent to participate.

Doing constructivist inquiry is not easy, but constructivist research can be done. The next chapter will develop more fully this constructivist picture by providing you with all of the design elements and methods that must be utilized for an inquiry to be considered a constructivist inquiry. It will become evident that the skills developed by a competent social work practitioner can transfer nicely into making rigorous constructivist inquiry possible.

As the text unfolds, it will also become more clear how constructivist research can advance the empowerment agenda of the profession. Constructivist research is an empowerment intervention in which the sharing of power tools occurs. It represents empowerment practice because of the leadership development aspects of the hermeneutic process and because it shares information. It may be difficult, cumbersome, and tedious, but when it works, change occurs. People are stimulated to take risks, think creatively, take pride in themselves, and make commitments that require accepting responsibility (Guba & Lincoln, 1989; Lambert et al., 1995). Constructivist inquiry, when done well, can overcome its costs in time and energy by creating a "liberating education" (Freire, 1994, p. 17) of which our social work foremothers would be proud.

Notes

1. For those interested in symbolic interactionism, see Blumer (1969), Denzin (1989, 1993), Joas (1987), Meltzer, Petras, & Reynolds (1975), Plummer (1987, 1991), and Saxton (1993).

Discussion Questions

Discussion questions rest on the reader's ability to assess and determine if certain situations lend themselves to constructivist inquiry processes.

1. Imagine that you are interested in studying the experience of families with special needs children. Your particular questions relate to their treatment and participations in multidisciplinary teamwork. One of the service providers most involved in direct work with children with special needs is a local hospital. You want to look at the experience of families with the professionals in this hospital. A social worker on the team is a colleague and is very interested in your research, but her supervisor is concerned about "outsiders" engaging in research on their patients. What more would you need to know to determine if this context would be amenable to a constructivist inquiry? What information would indicate that this hospital would not be a feasible site for emergent inquiry? What assumptions of constructivism are relevant to your response?

2. You are interested in preparation for multicultural practice. You would like to learn about the perspectives of the clients being served, the professions involved in service, the students being prepared for practice, and these students' educators. What would be the original focus of the inquiry: pure research, evaluation research, or policy research? How might the research change focus? What additional assumptions of constructivism are relevant to your responses?

3. You have been investigating many aspects of child abuse and have yet to find a theory that usefully captures the cause of what you have come to see as a multilevel complex phenomenon. You know that stress theory, psychological theories, system theories, and cognitive behavioral theories have all been associated with the cause of child abuse. How might elements of these theories provide appropriate guides for foreshadowed questions in a constructivist investigation of child abuse? First, determine what aspect of child abuse would be appropriately investigated through constructivist means. Second, create at least four foreshadowed questions informed by the above theories. What assumptions of constructivism have been relevant to your response?

4. You have been asked to evaluate the Head Start program associated with a local school district. There have been a series of news articles about the need for quality child care at the same time that this particular program has come under scrutiny for potential licensing and code violations. What specific questions would you

have in order to determine the human and political feasibility to
undertake a constructivist evaluation of the child care services?

Doing Constructivist Research

Section II further develops the framework for constructivist inquiry by providing the design and development details necessary to create a rigorous constructivist process with the possibility of a meaningful constructivist product. Chapter 3 introduces the general form and flow of a constructivist research project. Details about constructivist research methods logically linked to constructivist assumptions can be found here. The elements of a constructivist inquiry, including the phases of a constructivist process, are introduced to clarify what constitutes constructivist methods. All dimensions discussed are necessary for implementation, if the research is to be called constructivist.

Chapter 4 explores the interventive aspects of constructivism. Praxis and research as an intervention are discussed to further clarify the affinity between social work practice and constructivist inquiry. The major messages in this chapter concern the hermeneutic circle and achieving a productive dialectic. Details are provided about how to maintain a quality hermeneutic circle, including the responsibilities of the inquirer.

The remainder of this section covers the constructivist methods or what is necessary to really "do" constructivism. Chapter 5 develops the various dimensions of constructivist research rigor including trustworthiness and authenticity. From this chapter, readers will have the basic information necessary to establish all aspects of a quality constructivist process and product with defensible constructivist rigor.

Chapters 6 and 7 lay out the data collection and data analysis aspects of constructivist inquiry. Though much information in these chapters will at first appear familiar to those schooled in traditional qualitative data collection and analysis, the required emergent nature and grounded theory development of constructivism will be emphasized in order to create the alternative, interpretive nature of this type of inquiry. This section ends with the most radical difference in constructivist inquiry, negotiating the results of data analysis with the participants in the inquiry, who are seen to both own the data and have a stake in the framing of the results. Continued linkage to the values and empowerment tradition in social work will be apparent.

Again, the reader is encouraged to participate actively in the learning process by completing the discussion questions and exercises at the end of each chapter. The exercises in this section are essential to understanding how to conduct constructivist data collection and data analysis. Completion of the exercises is guaranteed to save much time for the researcher who is interested in engaging in a full constructivist inquiry. Each activity has been tested by students who say that, because many of the usual mistakes in implementation will be made during the exercises, those mistakes can be avoided when the actual work of constructivism is undertaken.

CHAPTER 3

Designing
Constructivist Research

Chapter Contents in Brief

Form of constructivist inquiry
Methods of constructivist inquiry used in the entry condition, the
*   inquiry process, and the inquiry product*
Phases of constructivist inquiry
Planning data sources, data collection, and inquiry logistics

The central assumptions in constructivism regarding the context-dependent nature of reality, multiple perspectives, many ways of knowing, and the impossibility of generalizable knowledge suggest that research design in constructivist research involves giving the *most possible* structure to an emerging process and product that is actually without predictable structure. Though the exact details of any constructivist inquiry cannot be envisioned in advance, certain aspects can be foreshadowed. When engaging in constructivist research design, the researcher will be the architect of a process that Guba and Lincoln (1989, pp. 186–187) have described as the "flow" of a constructivist inquiry. This flow begins with what was discussed in the last chapter: determining the fit, focus, and feasibility. It also includes organizing the inquirer for undertaking this activity by being certain that the inquirer or the inquiry team is trained in constructivist principles and methodology. One cannot expect to conduct an effective constructivist inquiry without training or practice beforehand.

Next, the stakeholders, those with a stake in the phenomena under investigation in the context of the investigation, should be identified and the effort begun through a hermeneutic process to develop within-group joint constructions. This occurs when data are shared between and within the relevant stakeholding groups. Greater sophistication is then achieved by enlarging joint stakeholder constructions through acquisition of new information to expand the depth of meaning, to fill gaps, or to perform additional checks of credibility.

Consensus emerges as claims, concerns, and issues are identified and resolved. Those that remain unresolved are prioritized and opened to further information collection for added sophistication. Those claims, concerns, and issues that remain unresolved are then negotiated among the stakeholders, including the inquirer, in order to come to resolution. Those constructions where resolution has been achieved become part of the final **case report**. Those elements where resolution is not possible are part of a **minority report** and may also become a part of "recycling" (Guba & Lincoln, 1989, p. 226). Recycling occurs when the results of the inquiry are returned to the context for further consideration. Here the inquiry comes full circle for a final effort in co-construction.

Actually, constructivist processes are, by their nature, so emergent that the flow is never-ending. The inquiry will raise more questions than it answers. The unresolved claims, concerns, and interests remain a part of the context. This means that the results of the inquiry process and product will continue to reverberate in unexpected and uncontrollable ways even after the inquirer has left the process.

A variety of interactive qualitative methods must be utilized during the flow of the emerging constructivist inquiry. The implications of constructivist assumptions are seen in the research design, data collection and analysis, and reporting, and in the rigor expectations associated with a quality constructivist process and product. This chapter will discuss the range of what constitutes constructivist methods for use in planning and implementing a constructivist inquiry.

Though each research process is unique with respect to the time, place, and data sources, a constructivist inquiry can be discussed in terms of its form, process, and product. The major methods that constitute constructivist methodology are seen in the details of these three dimensions. Figure 3–1 depicts the form of the inquiry. Note that constructivist inquiry form is not as static as it is depicted on the written page. Instead, it is interactive, going back and forth in a constant process of data collection and verification, of theory construction and verification. The inquiry and the knowledge creation are on a course of continuous shaping involving discovery and validation. The process is always interwoven from the

FIGURE 3–1

The Form of a Constructivist Inquiry

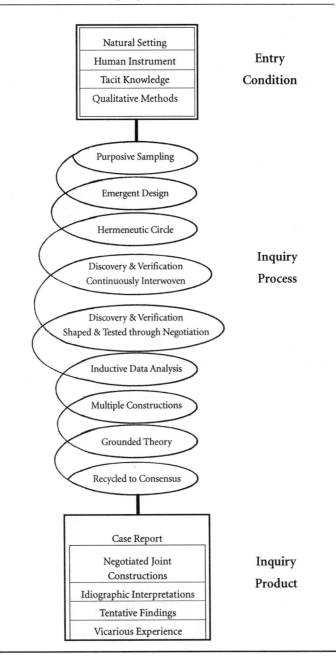

entry into the inquiry, through the co-construction of meaning, to the construction and negotiation of an inquiry product. Though the form appears linear, it is important to think of it in terms of multiple dimensions with many embedded circles spiraling toward a visceral conclusion. Note that in Figure 3–1 the only aspect that appears to have solid form is that of the entry condition. Therefore, if a natural setting cannot be investigated by a human instrument, combining tacit knowledge with qualitative methods of data collection, then a constructivist inquiry is not possible.

Constructivist Methods

In order to assure the constructivist form, certain methodological considerations are necessary. The following section will cover these methods. Note also that they constitute important methodological consequences of constructivist assumptions. Table 3–1 contains all methodological elements for both the constructivist process and the product.

TABLE 3–1

The Constructivist Research Design

Aspect of Inquiry	Methodological Element
Entry	Natural setting Prior knowledge
Research design	Emergent design Problem-determined boundaries Purposive sampling
Data collection	Qualitative methods
	Human instrument Tacit knowledge
Data analysis	Inductive data analysis Grounded theory
Rigor	Trustworthiness Authenticity
Inquiry product	Negotiated results Idiographic interpretations Tentative applications Case study reporting

Each is as important as the others. If all aspects cannot be undertaken, interesting research may result, but it will not be an inquiry process that can be called constructivist.

Entry

To enter a constructivist inquiry, the research must be mounted in the *natural setting* of the phenomenon or problem under investigation. Notice that the elements necessary at entry into the research process are related to the context embedded nature of constructed realities. The flexibility and adaptability necessary at the beginning stages of an inquiry will be ensured if they are present.

A natural setting is elemental to constructivism because reality cannot be understood in isolation of its context; reality cannot be separated into fragments or parts. The wholeness of what is real is only understood when attention is given to the factors that shape the environment, the patterns of influence that exist, the values that are accepted, and so forth. All of these elements shape the webs of relationships in which understanding is constructed. The researcher must be interacting with the setting and with its inhabitants in order to achieve the fullest possible understanding of them, their actions, and their constructions. Through these interactions, meaningful reconstructions will become the products of the process.

Some *prior knowledge* of the subject under investigation is necessary in order to determine what constitutes the natural setting for the foreshadowed questions (McMillan & Schumacher, 1993). Foreshadowed questions are those questions that guide beginning data collection. This knowledge comes from a thorough review of the literature, determining the focus of the inquiry (pure research, evaluation, or policy analysis), and performing what Spradley (1979) calls prior ethnography. Information about context, its "meets and bounds," human and political structure, values and culture comes from "hanging out" in the environment in a community site survey mode used in ethnographic community assessment (Lofland & Lofland, 1995). This same type of "hanging out" is used to identify the limits of a service unit, an agency, a neighborhood, or a community, all of which might be the natural setting of a social work research project.

Once prior knowledge can be combined with information about the natural setting of the phenomena under investigation, the other aspects of the inquiry can be elaborated. Constructivist design, data collection,

data analysis, rigor, and the inquiry product are also keenly imbedded in
and can be derived from constructivist assumptions.

Research Design

The research process develops according to an *emergent design*, that
comes from the experience rather than being totally developed a priori.
No researcher will know enough beforehand about the context and the
multiple realities that will emerge to adequately devise a design. Exposure
to the special circumstances and the unpredictable interactions will determine what is interesting and important to be understood, and who
should participate in the co-construction. All of the actors, values, and
peculiarities of the environment are allowed to shape the character of the
research design and process. Each inquiry process will be different because it will be created by the individuals involved (Burrell & Morgan,
1979).

Problem-determined boundaries are created by the participants to
limit and shape the focus of the inquiry. The realities and values of all
participants, including the inquirer, limit or expand the margins of what
the real question will be and who should participate in the construction
of the answer. The focus of the inquiry emerges with the design and is
shaped by the multiple realities encountered in the context. As the inquirer and participants become more sophisticated and knowledgeable
about the investigation, they determine when the formal investigation
should cease. This usually occurs when information redundancy is apparent. At this point, when no new perspective or information is useful, then
the problem under investigation has been bounded.

This evolving design requires a specific method for identifying potential data sources. *Purposive sampling*, not representative (random)
sampling, is needed to achieve the maximum variation of multiple perspectives in an emergent inquiry. This type of sampling for both *participants* and *research sites* is chosen when "one wants to learn something and
come to understand something about certain select cases without needing to generalize to all such cases" (Patton, 1980, p. 107). This strategy is
necessary to increase the scope and range of the data exposed in the
search for multiple realities. Purposive sampling is responsive to local
conditions in that the sampling frame can be identified based on the mutual shaping and values identified in the context. The typical, extreme,
political, and convenient cases (Patton, 1987) are generally selected for
inclusion in the sample. According to Skrtic (1985a), different types of

sampling may occur at different stages of the process to serve different emerging purposes as the inquiry evolves. In the beginning the "typical" cases might be selected to understand the depth and range of the issue under investigation. Later the "extreme" and "political" might be selected to bound the focus. Finally, "convenient" cases might be selected to push for data redundance while also assuring research feasibility.

Data Collection

Once potential data sources are identified, formal constructivist data collection can begin. *Qualitative methods* are preferred because of their intersubjective focus and adaptability in dealing with multiple, less aggregatable realities, which are of interest to constructivists. The qualitative skills of looking, listening, speaking, and reading found in normal, effective communication must be honed into specific data collection, recording, and analysis skills. The researcher entering into a constructivist inquiry should be prepared to undertake interviewing, observing, recording, and analysis of nonverbal communication and artifacts, depending upon what seems most appropriate as the inquiry emerges. The trained social worker will note that each of these qualitative methods has much in common with the purposeful interview and assessment practices utilized in most social work interventions in micro or macro practice.

These methods are capable of exposing more directly the nature of the transaction between the investigator and the participants because they accommodate multiple, conflicting realities, and are sensitive to interaction and mutual shaping influences essential for co-construction to occur.[1] The context for this occurrence is the ever more sophisticated teaching and learning of the hermeneutic circle (Guba & Lincoln, 1989). In addition, qualitative methods make it easier to access the biases of the investigator because, with most qualitative methods, all perspectives are more explicit.

The *human instrument* is the primary data gathering instrument in constructivist research. No nonhuman instrument can be devised beforehand to have sufficient adaptability to adjust to the various realities encountered in the natural setting. No questionnaire, standardized test, or other structured data collection tool would be capable of recognizing, sorting, or testing the multiple perspectives or the subtleties of meaning that shape attitudes and behavior in context.

In addition, only the human instrument is capable of grasping the meanings of an interaction; sensemaking when confronted by the irrational or the nonrational in human action and communication; intuiting meaning; or engaging in communication, the basis of co-constructed reality. A constructivist researcher can use measurement instruments such as questionnaires. However, their limits must be recognized and adaptations made in order to create a context boundedness reflective of the setting of the inquiry. Standardized instruments are not preferred because of the difficulty in accomplishing appropriate adaptations and the danger of collecting irrelevant or misleading information when the adaptation is not accomplished.

In data collection, as in most other aspects of the inquiry, constructivism exploits *tacit knowledge*. The intuitive/felt knowledge is as important as the knowledge that can be put into word form. A constructivist researcher believes some things must be experienced to be understood. In addition, following Polanyi (1966), constructivists recognize the difference between knowledge that is propositional (expressed in language form) and that which is tacit (unstated) by acknowledging that both are important for meaning making. The inquiry goal, for the purposes of co-construction, is to recast tacit knowledge into propositional form as soon as possible. Without this conversion, findings cannot be articulated to oneself or communicated to others for verification and modification. Confining acceptable data only to that which has language form limits the inquirer's viewpoint and the use of the human instrument at its highest potential (Guba & Lincoln, 1982). Readers will note that this tacit dimension of knowing is very much akin to the practice wisdom that often guides the decisions of competent, experienced practitioners.

Data Analysis

Though intuition is exploited in constructivism, formal data analysis of verbal and nonverbal data is also required. *Inductive data analysis* is preferred for constructivist research in order to assure that the findings are grounded in the context of the inquiry. Inductive data analysis goes from the specific to the general instead of from the general to the specific, which is characteristic of the deductive analysis method preferred by traditional researchers. With inductive analysis, the data are analyzed from specific raw units of information into subsuming categories. Each unit of data is compared with each other unit in a process of constant comparison for analysis (Glaser & Strauss, 1967; Rosengren, 1981). Inductive analysis assures an emergent design where no fixed parameters are set to guide analysis decisions.

Constant comparison of inductive analysis is utilized because from it *grounded theory* can be produced. No theory is identified a priori because no theory could be identified beforehand that could encompass the specifics of the multiple realities in the particular context. Just as the design unfolds in the context, so, too, do the results of data analysis. Grounded theory has the advantage of being able to expose the values, beliefs, attitudes, prejudices, and biases of all participants. When theory builds specifically in the context, there is difficulty in disguising these important dimensions of a **contextual reality**. In contrast, in deductive theory testing, value-rich data might be disregarded as not relevant to the research framework. In grounded theory all data are relevant because the theory is generated from all the collected data and unfolds as the inquiry proceeds (Glaser & Strauss, 1967; Lincoln & Guba, 1985; Strauss & Corbin, 1990).

Rigor

The standards for constructivist research quality are composed of *trustworthiness* and *authenticity*. Trustworthiness attends to the quality of the research product, while authenticity attends to quality in the inquiry process. Both must be demonstrated for a constructivist inquiry to be deemed rigorous.

Trustworthiness is analogous to the positivist standards of validity and reliability and demonstrates truth value, applicability, consistency, and neutrality via four elements (Lincoln & Guba, 1985): **credibility**, which involves activities to increase probability of credible findings; **transferability**, which is determined by how well the lessons learned can be understood so decisions can be made about their usefulness in other contexts; **dependability**, which accounts for the instability and design-induced changes that are inevitable in emergent research; and **confirmability**, which demonstrates that the results are linked to the data themselves.

Authenticity, including demonstrations of equal power, consciousness raising, appreciation of other's constructions, stimulus for change, and effective change, is the interactive result of the research process, not a product. This dimension of rigor was developed in constructivism to demonstrate its qualitative-change focus. It is through the level of achieved authenticity that the most radical and empowering aspects of the research perspective are evident.

Inquiry Product

The product in constructivism also merits attention on several levels. It must contain negotiated results, idiographic interpretations, a tentative application of findings, and a case study report to be reflective of constructivist assumptions.

In constructivist research, the results are constructed by the participants as they together co-construct the meaning of the phenomena under investigation. The process of meaning making occurs within the hermeneutic circle and is a process of negotiation. *Negotiated results* are part of the final product. The outcomes are the results, not just of negotiated meanings and interpretations from the hermeneutic circle, but also of a negotiated final product. The final product, the case report or case study, is shared with the human sources for their scrutiny and validation that it is an accurate reconstruction of their perspectives. This is done because the report reflects participants' construction of reality. They own their own data and have a right to ratify their use. This dimension of negotiation ensures that power shifts in the research enterprise. It is no longer the researcher who determines what is relevant and meaningful. Instead, those who own the data retain the power to determine if what has been produced is an acceptable reflection of their position. This is an important aspect of the empowerment focus of the entire process.

Idiographic interpretations are of interest in constructivist research to highlight participant perspectives. Emic (insiders') perceptions/constructions are more important than the etic (outsiders') perspectives. Data are interpreted in terms of the particulars of the case, rather than in terms of lawlike generalizations, because different interpretations are meaningful for different realities.

Further, no broad applications can be made of the findings, because participant realities are multiple and different and may not be duplicated elsewhere. Constructivism asserts *tentative application* of findings. The lessons learned in one inquiry are not expected to be generalizable, but may be found to be useful in other environments.

Finally, the *case study reporting mode* is preferred for a constructivist report because of its holistic potential. Since case studies tell stories, they are not as reductionistic as other means of scientific reporting. A case study is more adaptable to multiple realities and can show the concepts and grounded theories that emerged. The case study is developed with a thick description, a concept first used by Geertz (1973). The constructivist thick description provides enough information so that the naïve or informed reader can get a visceral experience that is both cognitive and affective. This holistic experience allows the development of an understanding of the phenomenon so that the reader can make his or her own judgments about the usefulness in other settings of the information provided in the case report.

Determining the Phases of the Inquiry

The research design emerges in constructivism depending on the uncovering of new insights and new experiences. This **emergence** is a planned process that has an identifiable structure. Though the contents of each stage will be unknown until the completion of the stage, three roughly successive phases occur. Each of these phases involve identifying the salient questions, determining the meaning, and checking the findings according to standards of rigor, so that final closure of the process can be gained (Lincoln & Guba, 1985, 1989). Those familiar with Kirk & Miller's (1986) phases of ethnographic field work will recognize their processes of invention, discovery, interpretation, and explanation. Explanation for Kirk and Miller (1986) and for constructivists is not intended to declare causation, but to communicate or package a message about the phenomena being investigated (p. 60). The following process, with more or less sequential phases, will unfold as stakeholder input regarding claims, concerns, and issues is used by the inquirer to organize the research.

Orientation and Overview—Phase I

The initial bounding of the problem and description of the context constitute the opening phase of orientation and overview during which the researcher has an idea about what needs to be known or understood. This idea comes from prior experience, exposure to the literature, or some other situation that has shaped an intellectual puzzle. The form of that puzzle is initially constructed by the researcher by way of foreshadowed questions (McMillan & Schumacher, 1993). These are the questions that the researcher thinks are important, given his or her personal experience and outsider's perspective. These questions are not the finely structured type seen in the traditional hypotheses testing research approach. Instead, these working hunches are a statement of what the researcher thinks is important in the bounding and shaping of the problem. These beginning questions are made more sophisticated as the researcher comes to know the context important to the shaping of the answer to the puzzle.

It is also at this stage that all dimensions of the inquiry rigor (to be discussed in detail in Chapter 5) should begin. The development of researcher consciousness about self, which is necessary to bound emotions, values, and reactions in what Lincoln & Guba (1985) call "progressive subjectivity," is begun in the reflexive journal (p. 345). Regular entries record events, decisions, thoughts, and feelings related to the emerging development of the problem and the process. This journal is continued throughout the research process to record the inquirer's personal journey of change, insight, and knowledge development.

The emergent methodology is also noted in a methodological log (Lincoln & Guba, 1985, p. 281) which is designed to record all the methodological decisions made as the design emerges. At this phase of the process, initial concerns, reactions, feelings, certainties, and uncertainties are recorded in the reflexive journal and beginning decisions about the form and process of the investigation are recorded in the methods journal.

Data first emerge through grand tour–type (Spradley, 1979) ethnographic activities, such as driving around an area, touring an agency, or chatting with neighbors or agency employees. These activities aid in the initial exploration of the environment that the researcher thinks is important to the puzzle or question (Atkinson & Hammersley, 1994). The foreshadowed questions shape what is initially noticed, but in this informal process, individuals in the context help the researcher become more informed about the problem or phenomenon to be investigated. This "hanging out" of noting, watching, and taking into account the physical and psychosocial dynamics of the environment also aids in determining the appropriateness of the context for the question of interest. It also provides information to determine the human and political feasibility of the project.

In short, the participants in the context tell the researcher what is important about the problem or phenomenon, what ought to be known, who has the competence to participate in the creation of that knowledge, and whether or not this is the right place to undertake such an adventure. At this stage of the research, questions are open-ended and tentative in order to protect and expand the emergent nature of the inquiry. The researcher's prior knowledge gives the questions substance, but initial questions should be open enough to allow individuals contacted in this stage the freedom to tell the researcher what he or she needs to know.

This is the phase where the researcher discovers what is salient, what might constitute the whole of the problem, and where the parts might be constructed. The details discovered here help to shape the more focused activities of the next phase. Important stakeholders or stakeholding groups are identified to be tapped at later stages. Salient aspects of the human and political environment are identified and incorporated into the emerging plan of action. This might include the identification of powerful **gatekeepers** to the issue as well as gatekeepers to the development of working hypotheses (Lincoln & Guba, 1985; McMillan & Schumacher, 1993) who incorporate the differing ideas about what should be included. This is the stage in which gaining entry and negotiating consent to participate are achieved, at least at the level of important gatekeepers. It will be the gatekeepers who will, for the most part, allow or facilitate access to stakeholders.

Focused Exploration—Phase II

Phases change when the researcher is able to move from general discovery activities and questions guided by the foreshadowed questions, which began the study, to more targeted probing, guided by the working hypotheses. The working hypotheses for Phase II emerge from the prior ethnography of Phase I. Analysis of information gathered from testing the foreshadowed questions in prior ethnography provides the bridge to the focused exploration via working hypotheses of the next phase. Phase I data analysis is informal because data are not formally deconstructed, as in unitizing, for later reconstructions through categorizing. Instead, themes emerge from the researcher's experiences in data collection and from rereading and reflecting on field notes. The themes become clearer through the researcher's thinking and journal notations that bring tacit information into propositonal form. Once themes are identified, they become the framework for the working hypotheses that will guide focused data collection and data analysis in Phase II. Having working hypotheses means the general dimensions of the inquiry have emerged enough for the researcher to know what requires further investigation and who should be tapped for co-construction.

The key activities of Phase II are data collection and data analysis. These are accomplished through the development and implementation of a plan involving persistent observation and in-depth information collection/construction from the sample. The membership of the participant group will continue to shift as the process emerges, but the analysis of the data collected in Phase I continues to guide the more formalized data collection and participant inclusion in Phase II. This means that sufficient time should be allowed from the initial overview and ethnographic efforts to the implementation of more targeted probing so that meaning can be constructed out of the data at hand. This is particularly important if more than one site will be included in the inquiry.

It is in this phase that the hermeneutic circle will be developed with its concomitant dialectic (to be discussed in Chapter 4); the preferred qualitative methods of interviewing and participant observation will be used to generate **meaning construction**; and formal data analysis will be undertaken. As in Phase I, analysis occurs first through informal data review, where general themes will be refined through further investigation for greater meaning. Follow-up questions about differing perspectives will be necessary. As the inquiry becomes more and more focused, so, too, do the questioning methods. More structured interviewing and observation techniques will be introduced to further focus the inquiry. It may be at this stage that a more structured interview protocol with established questions might evolve. Lastly, formal data analysis of the constant comparative type (Glaser & Strauss, 1967) is undertaken when data collection ceases, usually when data redundancy occurs.

All mechanisms for collecting, tracking, storing, and analyzing data must be in place at the initiation of this phase. The methodological structure must also be fully developed, in that all plans for methodological rigor are in place and implemented throughout this phase of the inquiry.

This phase closes when in-depth information with maximum variation in the participant viewpoints has been achieved. It is at the conclusion of this phase that some level of formal negotiation in the context of the hermeneutic circle may be necessary. If some disagreement about constructions remains, negotiation will be necessary to gain as high a degree of consensus as possible regarding the themes or constructions that emerge from the grounded **theory building** of data analysis.

Comprehensive Member Check—Phase III

The major activities of this final phase of the inquiry are the completion of the case report, conducting the final member check, and negotiation and implementation of an independent audit. At the completion of a successful audit, the final case report is written and returned to data owners for recycling for further understanding. If all dimensions of rigor are being tracked and documented, further activities may occur after the recycling of the final report in the form of an assessment of the effective change dimensions of authenticity rigor (to be discussed in Chapter 5).

Again, sufficient time should be allowed between the analysis in

Phase II and the case report writing in Phase III. The reconstruction in the case report is necessary after the deconstruction that occurs in grounded theory building. This requires sufficient time and distance to allow insights to develop. Creating a rich, thick description of the context, the problem, and the lessons learned takes time because it is not usually accomplished in the first or second draft of the report document.

A preliminary case report, in draft form, is returned to the participants and submitted to a comprehensive member check "to obtain confirmation that the report has captured the data as constructed by the informants, or to correct, amend, or extend, that is, to establish the credibility of the case" (Lincoln & Guba, 1985, p. 236.). Total approval or consensus regarding the report, though desirable, is not necessary. What is necessary is the opportunity for as many stakeholders as possible thoroughly and thoughtfully to consider the story. The stakeholders should experience sufficient negotiation between the researcher and the participants so the areas of disagreement become clear enough to be included in the final report. Comfort among stakeholders about the accurate reconstruction of participant perspectives is necessary before the report is submitted for outside, independent audit.

After the independent audit is performed, the final report is written, returned to the participants, and utilized in whatever ways were proposed at the origination of the project. It is at this point that closure is achieved. However, the hermeneutic process will continue in at least informal ways to construct and reconstruct the meaning of the inquiry. The process will evolve in unpredictable ways. Recycling will result in reexamination of information. The reverberation of a well-constructed inquiry will be associated with improved sophistication about the research subject and consequences of the process over time. In a successful constructivist inquiry, the participants will recognize change in themselves and the context as a result of the process.

A few of the elements in the phases will be discussed in the next section in more detail in order to assure that the initial planning of the research project is sufficiently well-developed to allow appropriate emergence rather than sloppy research.

Determining Data Sources for Maximum Information

Data in constructivist inquiry are selected for inclusion to assure maximum information or maximum variability in the perspectives and the sources of data. In order to accomplish this, sampling is purposive, directed at the purpose of the research. "Chatter" in the data is required because differences are as interesting as similarities when constructing reality.

Identifying Stakeholders and Selecting Participants

The first stage of inclusion/exclusion decision-making is related to the human data sources. The following should be considered in identifying the important stakeholders or stakeholding groups. The selection of participants should be based on the various considerations that follow.

Sampling should be purposeful. *Purposive sampling* of the type discussed by Patton (1980, 1990) is used to expand the scope and the range of the discussion and subsequent co-construction. Maximum variation is the goal in order to understand unique variations in adapting to conditions and constructing meaning about the subject under investigation. Sampling of the extreme or deviant case should be undertaken to search for the unusual, the troublesome, or the enlightening. In many cases, it is from the perspective of the outlier that new useful insights can be garnered. For example, in a study of the multiple meanings of neglect, parents who identify themselves as neglecting, but who have never been identified in the formal system, would be included for their unusual perspective. The family who fought the court and won when they rejected a label of neglect would also be helpful, as would a family who had an experience of child removal and damage as a result of neglect, whether they agree to the label or not.

Sampling of the "typical" case is important to avoid rejecting information that might be considered special or deviant. The typical will give you some sense of what is perceived to be "normal" in the context. The neglect investigation would need to include both the "standard, ordinary" parents doing the best they can in parenting and those of the type typically known to the agency involved in investigation and confirmation of neglect. Both typical perspectives, including the variations that come with age, race/ethnicity, socioeconomic status, and so forth, are important in the development of the important themes of the inquiry.

The "critical" case should be included to permit maximum application of information in the co-construction. An example of a critical case in neglect might be the family that was important to the judge in shaping his or her standards for the decision about whether or not neglect exists. The politically important or sensitive cases are also important, not only for the information that can be obtained, but also in creating attraction to and support for the research or deflecting objections to the process. An important case in the neglect investigation might be a family that is especially involved in the parents' rights aspects of child protective services and, as advocates, might have the power to encourage or deny access to other parents.

Convenience sampling is also an accepted and important element of the selection process to save time, money, or effort. Convenience is acceptable as long as the maximum variation goal is kept in mind. An inquiry composed of only a convenience sample would probably not provide sufficient variation to make the co-constructing of results meaningful.

Another important consideration, *serial nominations,* where individuals are included in the sample in the order that they have been nominated by other participants, assures that the sampling emerges with the process and that some structure is also maintained in the process. Since the sampling design emerges instead of being based on some a priori notions that must be satisfied, it makes sense to begin where a gatekeeper suggests that one begin. Recall that a gatekeeper is someone who has been identified as either particularly expert or powerful in relation to the concepts or context of the investigation. Gatekeepers will most likely be the individuals with whom negotiation must be undertaken to gain entry and to get permission to undertake the project, like a judge or an agency director. The gatekeeper nominates participants because of their position within the context, their particular viewpoint, or any other reason that makes sense, given the emerging focus of inquiry.

It is recognized that at the initial stage the researcher may not be sophisticated enough in the context or the problem to make inclusion/exclusion decisions to avoid manipulation in favor of unstated agendas held by gatekeepers. However, the sampling process allows for continuous adjustment of the sample as it is refined to focus on what might evolve to be the most relevant types of human data sources. This continuous refocusing occurs through serial selection of the participants.

New participants are included only after the previous list of nominations has been tapped and informally analyzed. Each participant is asked to nominate individuals or groups who might have the same or similar perspectives, those who might be entirely different, or those who might represent, from their perspective, a particularly salient view. Each new list is used for sampling only after a prior list has been exhausted. New participants are included according to the emerging need to extend information, to test constructions, or to fill in information on divergent perspectives. Selection of participants continues to the point of redundancy. This process is not as cumbersome as it might seem because redundancy in nominations will occur quite quickly in any well-defined investigation context. The same people will appear on various lists. The ideal is that selection for sample inclusion concludes when no new information is evident. However, it is more likely for selection to cease when time for the data collection phase of the project runs out.

The same general sampling guidelines apply for multiple site selection. Sites are serially determined when it is known which types of sites are most likely to yield research focus–related information. Initially, site identification is determined through the literature or through expert sources, like gatekeepers. For example, if there is interest in seeing how early-infant-intervention teams work with different levels of resources, then the researcher might identify an urban, suburban, and rural site for the inquiry. Openness to identifying other types of sites would be needed in order to allow the capture of all the important dimensions of differential resources. Which sites are finally selected for inclusion should be based on the same maximum variation goal. It is important to note that the definition of what constitutes a site will vary with each research project. For example, agencies, units within agencies, neighborhoods, communities, or, more recently, different web sites in cyberspace (Neil, 1996) could all constitute workable sites.

The initial site will most likely be selected for convenience. Whichever site is easier to access, either because of participant willingness or because of its location in relation to the researcher, is where the initial teaching/learning should be undertaken. Instituting the emergent design will be difficult enough without needing to overcome other personal, political, or logistical barriers. Subsequent sites should be selected for inclusion, serially, and should be chosen to represent contexts and perspectives as different as possible from the preceding one.

Fully *informed consent* must be obtained from all participants. When this type of research is conducted in connection with a university, this consent mechanism will be required by the group in charge of human subjects review, which assures that participants will not be exposed to undue risk as a result of the inquiry process and product. Because of the challenges in constructivism in determining ethical behavior in such an intense face-to-face undertaking and because of the power shifts that will naturally occur as a result of the design and process, participants must be clear about the risks and opportunities. Fully informed consent is an expectation in constructivism before undertaking the project, even if the human subjects review and approval is not a requirement.

In a constructivist inquiry, fully informed consent is negotiated. The population invited to participate is identified as much as possible and the nature of the study, at least as it is initially conceived, is described. Participants must be informed of all features of the research, including the potential confidentiality problems that may arise as a result of the co-constructive process. Freedom to decline or discontinue at any time should be emphasized. The consequences of leaving the project, including how their data will be returned, should be made clear. In addition, participants should be informed about how difficult it will be to forget or overlook their information if they choose to leave. They must understand the impact of the consciousness raising that comes from a successful hermeneutic process and how impossible it will be to return to a prior level of understanding absent the participant's data. For fully informed consent, clarity about expectations and responsibility among all participants should be evident, including the amount of time that might be necessary, and the manner in which data will be protected and analyzed.

There are several important steps in the process of obtaining fully informed consent, and it should be documented through a product, the consent form. This form should include the name of the person instituting the inquiry and how that person can be contacted regarding problems or questions. The purpose of the inquiry should be provided in detail. Specifics of consent and participation should be noted, including how confidentiality and anonymity will be protected as much as possible; what measures will be undertaken to protect the fidelity of the data; the measures that will be undertaken to limit access to the data; the risks that might accrue due to the nature of the initial questions or due to lack of perfect confidentiality and anonymity protections; the right to withdraw at any time, the steps of withdrawal, and what will occur with the participant's data upon withdrawal; and a statement of voluntary participation. The consent should be signed by both the inquirer and the participant. Both participant and inquirer should have copies for future reference.

Other Data Sources

Aside from human data sources, other information may be important to the construction of meaning. In some cases information will be provided serendipitously, as in pamphlets that are available in waiting rooms. Other information will be purposefully collected to add richness or to validate assertions collected in other ways. The principal nonhuman data sources are records, documents, and unobtrusive measures.[2]

Records, according to Lincoln and Guba (1985), are "any written or recorded statement prepared by or for an individual or organization for the purpose of attesting to an event or providing an accounting" (p. 277). Meeting minutes, excerpts from the *Congressional Record,* or case notes are examples of records. *Documents,* for Lincoln and Guba (1985, p. 277), include "any written or recorded material other than a record that was not prepared specifically in response to a request from the inquirer (such as a test or set of interview notes)." Annual financial reports, policies and procedures, pamphlets for recruitment of clients or to secure financial or other support would be considered documents under this definition. *Unobtrusive measures* are defined as "information that accumulates without intent on the part of either the investigator or the respondent(s) to whom the information applies" (Lincoln & Guba, 1985, p. 279). These are physical traces that can be observed or collected without the participant directly providing them. Examples of unobtrusive measures might be the number of people in the waiting room as a measure of service requests, the amount of material in an "in" basket as an indication of workload, or a worn path in the grass as an indication of students' preferred route between buildings.

Documents, records, and unobtrusive measures should only be included to expand, enrich, or test understandings as they are being constructed, because they are rarely created during the inquiry process. They really are not part of the context of the inquiry, at least from a current historical perspective. In most cases, this material will serve as background to the emerging design and questioning development. Only in rare cases will this material be pulled into the formal data analysis process, because it is only the rare record, document, or measure that will specifically grow from the process or context of the constructivist inquiry.

Planning Data Collection and Recording

Details regarding the "how" of data collection and recording will be provided in Chapter 6. For the planning stages of the inquiry, certain decisions will be necessary even before the first datum is constructed or collected.

Determining *instrumentation* is straightforward at the beginning. The human instrument will be the major source of data collection. However, training the inquirer in the various ways to collect data through structured or unstructured interview, observation, participant observation, and focus groups may be necessary. If a team is used, training to develop integration and agreed forms of data collection and behavior will need to occur before the inquiry proceeds. As the research unfolds, mechanisms must be designed to identify themes for persistent observations and to assure that information is appropriately tested from participant to participant. As activities become more focused, plans should be in place to allow for the development of more structured data collection tools.

Data recording tends to be somewhat controversial with new constructivists. There is a tendency to wish to tape record or videotape each data collection encounter in order to assure the fidelity or accuracy of the data collected. While neither manner of recording is unacceptable, field notes and expanded field notes (Spradley, 1980) are preferred because of their ability to use the human instrument at its highest potential for meaning making. The human instrument naturally screens for meaning. Audiotaping or videotaping will collect data that are irrelevant to the inquiry process. New constructivists fear missing important information. Once they become experienced, they see that the use of audio- or videotape sets the stage for tremendous data overload and a need for data reduction before analysis can proceed. Social workers, trained in process recording writing, have the skills necessary to undertake the interactive data collection method of field notes and their expansion without needing to acquire much in the way of additional skills or confidence in the collection/recording process. Whatever the decision for recording, mechanisms for transcription or data expansion and/or reduction must be in place prior to the first data collection effort. The same process must be continued throughout the inquiry to assure that the audit can be undertaken.

Planning *data analysis* should also occur before the first datum is collected. This is important because, depending upon what mechanism is selected, the format of collection and storage may change. Most new constructivists are attracted to the idea of computer-based data analysis, believing that it will be more "scientific" and rigorous. However, only a few computer packages are available that are capable of creating a grounded theory analytic process. *The Ethnograph* and *Nudist* are text management programs that can, with a good deal of effort, be adjusted to respond to the kind of emergence necessary for constructivist analysis. Most other computer programs on the market require the identification of the parameters of analysis prior to the analysis. In a grounded theory process, the parameters evolve as the analysis evolves. Failure to recognize the subtleties of these differences in requirements may mean that data entry time will be wasted.

Most researchers I know who have been involved in more than one experience of constructivist data analysis prefer a lower-tech approach to data analysis in which data units are identified and placed on cards to allow an "up close and personal" process of constant comparison and categorization. The details of this process will be provided in Chapter 7. At this stage of planning, the decision to be made is whether to go high tech or low tech.

Planning the Logistics

There is a "rule of thumb" that I learned long ago regarding qualitative research: whatever time you think it will take, double it and you may have the timeline approximately identified. Timing is even more of a challenge for constructivists. My experience suggests that this process can involve up to three times the originally intended amount. Often this protraction is due to a real inability to control the project's emergence, but most of the time it is due to a lack of good logistical planning. The point is that emergence cannot be predicted regarding time, and so forth, but attention to logistics in each of the phases of the inquiry can control some of the potential chaos.

Timing

All the dimensions of timing should be considered in order to get the full impact of the process of co-construction. Even when an inquirer is familiar with a context and even when participants are interested in the problem to be considered in the project, time is required to get the different permissions and approval. If research is being done as part of a research course, directed research, or dissertation, those involved in approving a proposal might need time to gain familiarity with constructivism prior to giving their approval. This approval, in combination with human subjects review, should be acquired before ever officially entering into the research context. A potential research context can be identified beforehand, but requirements established by review panels, instructors, or other stakeholders in the approval process must supersede any arrangements that have been made with gatekeepers in the **inquiry context** prior to gaining initial approval.

Gaining entrance into a site, even a site that is familiar to the inquirer, will require time and patience. No promises as to the shape or form of the process can be made prior to obtaining whatever formal approval is necessary. Failure to forestall discussions about entry until formal approval has been achieved through review bodies may result in the necessity of locating alternative sites for the inquiry. Sometimes original sites cannot or will not accept requirements mandated by those outside the context who are responsible for research oversight. This access difficulty, in turn, may result in the need to return to the original approving bodies for amended approval. Clearly, this takes time. Even without these unfortunate "bumps," gaining entrance requires fully informed consent. Those with the power to give permission must be identified and then they must be helped to thoroughly understand what they are saying yes to in a constructivist project. Their failure to knowingly embrace emergence in the process might mean that when the dialectically induced stress develops, in order to abate the stress, those with the power of permission-giving might withdraw permission before the process reaches its co-constructed conclusion.

Gaining support of participants also will take time. Serial nominations and serial sampling are time consuming, as is engaging in the negotiation process of obtaining consent and commitment to really participate in the process. The negotiation necessary to find meaning through the hermeneutic circle also takes time. Participants may not be available or willing to engage in co-construction when the inquirer is ready to test for meaning. The process develops as if on its own. The pace will be unique to the particulars of the environment. It must not be rushed or consensus and true rich meaning making will not occur. In addition, rushing usually means the standards of rigor required for authenticity will not be achieved.

Although the details of constant comparison data analysis will be considered later, it is important to note here that while data entry and data analysis in any type of rigorous research are time consuming, the degree to which they are necessary to get close to constructivist data will at times be overwhelming. Managing that overload, as well as coming to higher levels of abstraction and sophistication about the data, will take enormous amounts of time. In addition, failure to build in sufficient time for case writing will hamper the quality of the final product. In most cases, the inquirer will not know what he or she knows until the report has been written once. A second or third draft is usually necessary for it to reach the level of richness needed to assure transferability.

Proposals

Proposals for constructivist research, whether funded or unfunded, present logistical challenges. Clearly, when a researcher is intent on securing outside resources to support research, attention to proposal timelines, and so forth, is important. Extra work at clarifying the method may be required either in person, as in a proposal defense, or in writing. Clarity of details regarding the structure of an emergent design is essential to gain support for an effort such as this.

All essential details within a potentially changing process should be identified and planned for. Sites, participants, time frames (for gaining entry, collecting data, co-constructing results, and report writing), and costs should be predicted as much as possible. Since details of the content of the phases are not possible to describe, alternatives must be used to demonstrate that the inquiry is well structured and well thought out. Providing details of the plan for logistics while in the field, for following field-based data collection, and for closure and termination, as well as the logistics for maintaining the hermeneutic circle, trustworthiness, and authenticity will demonstrate for a proposal reviewer that, even though the plan is emergent, it has discipline.

Human Subjects Review

Depending upon the agency or institutional setting, the human subjects review process can be protracted or almost nonexistent. In some cases, this type of research will be exempted from the review process because of the perception that collecting word data (as opposed to number data) represents no risk to participants. Other cases will require much detail to prove the quality of the science involved with the inquiry. Because of the emergence and the qualitative methods used, some review panels will question whether or not this is scientific inquiry of the type that should be supported by the institution. In other cases, the proposed participants or the proposed context of inquiry may present a concern. Public institutions may not approve of direct contact with the clients they serve in such an uncontrollable way as would be proposed in a constructivist project.

The point here is that there is another context for the inquiry that must be taken into consideration and must be allowed to enter into the negotiation, or the research will never achieve approval. It is incumbent upon the researcher to know not only what types of permissions and reviews are necessary to gain entry and to implement the inquiry, but it is also essential to know the perspectives of the reviewers regarding what constitutes a quality design that has the possibility of producing good science. Failure to speak in the language of the reviewers may result in a project never getting off the ground for lack of approval by other relevant stakeholders to the process.

Notes

1. For more information on the transaction between the investigator and the participants see Josselson & Lieblich (1995); Lofland & Lofland (1995); Marshall & Rossman (1995); Reason (1994); Rubin & Rubin (1995); and Strauss & Corbin (1990).
2. The challenges and opportunities of records, documents, and unobtrusive measures for constructivist research have been discussed elsewhere. Those wishing to expand their understanding are encouraged to read Lincoln & Guba (1985), and Chambers, Wedel, & Rodwell, (1992).

Discussion Questions

The following questions cover essential issues in planning a constructivist inquiry. The focus is knowing what makes the inquiry a constructivist one and not another type of qualitative research.

1. Given the assumptions of constructivist inquiry, why is it that qualitative methods are preferred over quantitative methods? If quantitative methods are selected in a constructivist inquiry, what adjustments must be made to assure congruence with the assumptions of constructivism?

2. Why must a constructivist research project design emerge in the context of the investigation?

3. You wish to investigate underage drinking behavior on a college campus from a constructivist perspective. Who would have a stake in this question? Who might be important gatekeepers? In order to assure maximum variation, what types of students might you wish to engage in the project?

4. Define the three phases of any constructivist inquiry. What activities will be undertaken by the inquirer in each phase? What assumptions of constructivism are evident in each phase of the inquiry?

5. Describe why time is such an important element in constructivist
   inquiry? Why do proposal writing and the human subjects review
   process present particular challenges to constructivist researchers?

CHAPTER 4

Intervention in Constructivist Inquiry

Chapter Contents in Brief

Praxis and research as intervention
Interventive aspect of constructivist inquiry, the hermeneutic circle
   with its dialectic
How to maintain a quality hermeneutic circle
The responsibilities of the inquirer

Traditionally in social work, as well as with most other social sciences, dichotomous thinking has predominated approaches to knowledge building and action. What was being undertaken was understood as either research *or* practice. It was not, and could not be, both. This discussion was further complicated by questions about what constituted human knowing. Was it a process or a product? (Bernstein, 1985; Foucault, 1980; Weick, 1993).

Many, taking the position that human knowing is a process deeply rooted in and shaped by our culture, conditions, and psyches, saw knowledge as a creation or a construction. Bernstein (1985, p. 165) saw humans as dialogical beings, "always in conversation and always in the process of understanding." The logic of this position was and is that knowledge is really meaning- or sensemaking based on human interpretation. This opens knowledge building and the research process. This means that no knowledge maintains a privileged status (Gordon, 1980; Minnich, 1990) because both the expert researcher and the person on the street can establish knowledge. Further, all persons can be expected to see and evaluate knowledge within a larger sociopolitical context because all persons are capable of context-based interpretation. There is a recognition of a personal participation in knowing (Polanyi, 1966) and because of this, what constitutes knowledge is more provisional and exploratory.

In addition, professionals in many disciplines, including social work, were troubled by the apparent schism between knowing and doing. Schön (1983) helped to clarify the potential lack of dichotomy by calling what professionals engaged in as "knowing-in-practice" (p. 62). He suggested that professionals "reflect-in-action" (p. 62). This reflexivity allows the practitioner to reflect on his or her own thinking and feelings in order to judge, evaluate, and possibly change thinking. For Schön this is at the core of professional behavior. This knowing and acting in the moment, or the after-the-fact ruminating for future action, inextricably links knowing and doing. For those holding this more integrative perspective, the ability, power, and responsibility to negotiate meaning means that knowledge building is a process and a product and that research and action can also be inextricably linked. Knowledge, then, arises in and for action.

With the emergence of "emancipatory social sciences" (Lather, 1991), efforts to connect research methodology with consciousness raising and subsequent change on the part of the researcher and the researched helped to address another element of the dichotomy. Do researchers research or practice? When emancipatory social science declared that research was intervention, it became part of the postmodern discussion about the relationship between research and practice and theory and practice (Denzin & Lincoln, 1994). Constructivist inquiry is part of this discussion.

Constructivist inquiry is in accord with those segments of the social sciences that developed a position following the thinking of scholars such as Hesse (1980) and others against objectivist social sciences and in favor of an explicitly value-based social science with emancipatory social goals. "Praxis" oriented research became the goal. It was no longer enough to build new knowledge or to critique the status quo via empirical efforts. New knowledge needs to increase awareness and allow direct attention to the possibilities of social transformation inherent in the research process. From this perspective, theory illuminates lived experience in order to enhance the intellectual and political capacities of the participants, so they can come to understand and, perhaps, change their own reality.

Though the framers of constructivist methods never used the word "praxis" in early work on constructivism, they did design a change-enhancing, interactive, contextualized approach to knowledge building that includes the possibilities of transformative action. This is due to a model of investigation that builds on egalitarian participation, and guides consciousness raising through the hermeneutic circle (Guba & Lincoln, 1989). This chapter focuses on those aspects of constructivist inquiry that advance emancipatory knowledge, first, by further defining praxis and, then, by detailing the praxis dimension of constructivist inquiry seen most clearly in the hermeneutic circle and its dialectic.

Praxis and Research

Praxis-oriented research consists of "activities that combat dominance and move toward self-organization and that push toward thoroughgoing change in the practices of . . . the social formation" (Benson, 1983, p. 338). Praxis research is beyond action research as developed by Kurt Lewin (1946) or participatory action research (Cancian & Armstead, 1992) with their collaborative and participatory focus. Praxis is collaborative and participatory, but it also provides ways to connect research methodology to theoretical concerns and political commitments (Lather, 1986). Praxis focuses on the transformative possibilities of the research process and product through a cyclic process of action, reflection, and theorizing that is continuous, overlapping, and recycling (Lincoln, 1997). It embraces empowering approaches to generating knowledge. It leads to change as much as it generates knowledge.

Praxis mandates a type of self-reflection that leads to a deeper understanding of the particular situation being researched (Lather, 1991). There is a give and take between the researcher and the researched, between the data and the theory. There is mutual negotiation of meaning and power in the process and the product or inquiry, based on reciprocity, dialectical theory building, and a questioning of all elements of the research process. This negotiation involves recycling descriptions and emerging analyses and conclusions with the participants. As praxis, research is used to help participants (including the researcher) understand and change their situation.

The result is empowerment of the researched because they are involved in a collaborative theorizing (Kushner & Norris, 1980–81) in which negotiation is at the base of the process and the product of the investigation. They are changed simply by virtue of their association with the research project, but there is more. The dialectical practice of reflexivity and critique means that negotiation is desired and needed regarding the research design, the descriptions and interpretations derived, and even the final meaning of the research. This interactivity and reciprocity forces reflexivity and critique among all participants and guards against false consciousness. The possibility of imposition of meaning by the researcher is eliminated, as is any possibility of reification of the researcher. The researched are true participants in the knowledge building; they know it and begin to sense their own power because of it.

Praxis is dialogic. Meaning is constructed in conversation. Interpretations are negotiated because participants are involved in the research in more than just data provision. They participate in data interpretation as well as in theory building. There is reciprocity among all for construction and validation of knowledge. It is in this dialogue, only possible in an environment built on trust, openness, and support, that participants come to new self-conceptions (Fay, 1977). They become conscious of their own perceptions and feelings, which are also tested.

In this testing, dialogue can become a dialectic. The dialectic develops in discussion of potential false consciousness among participants. The dialectic is between participants' self-understanding and efforts to create a context to question the taken-for-granted beliefs and situations within the context (Bowers, 1984). It is dialectic when the forum is created to test the usefulness and the resonance of the conceptual and theoretical formulations that are emerging in the process. This dialectic has an energizing, catalytic role in the inquiry. However, the personal power generated by self-reflection and subsequent deeper understandings may conflict with other participants' constructions and meanings. The tension involved with clarifying different conceptualizations and recognizing paradoxes may be unsettling, but the dialectic allows participants to gain strength to accept and act on new insights. Critical self-awareness can give rise to active involvement in construction and validation of meaning. Change happens. Action cycles into further reflection and theorizing.

The reciprocity in the process allows dialogue to remain central. With dialogue central, reciprocal relationships and mutuality in the education that occurs in the process are also maintained. This reciprocity empowers participants. And through this, more useful theory is built to guide action. The whole process reorients, focuses, and energizes participants toward knowing reality in order to transform it. This is Freire's (1973) conscientization that can lead to the reality-altering impact of praxis-oriented research.

Constructivism allows for praxis. Constructivist research approaches research as an intervention. In this chapter, the reader will see that consciousness raising and empowerment are the natural results of constructivist inquiry. The inquirer is a researcher and intervener. There are expectations for both roles. In the following discussion we will focus on the interventionist expectations and challenges of constructivist inquiry.

Constructivist Research As Intervention: The Hermeneutic Circle

The intervention and change possibilities in constructivism are clearest when the **hermeneutic circle**, the central mechanism of co-construction, is considered. It is in the context of the dialectical discourse about perspectives that individual knowledge and attitudes change. With this power of knowledge also comes the power to affect useful larger scale change, if it is deemed necessary.

It is here that constructivism is most congruent with the empowerment tradition/agenda of social work. Longres's (1981) characterization of the progressive social work tradition is most apparent at the level of the hermeneutic circle. Opportunities for critical analysis, human liberation, or personal change can be seen in the **hermeneutic dialectic**. Within the dialectic can also be seen institutions' or agencies' struggles for liberation, with agents of social reform attempting to make private troubles public issues. The progressive social work tradition and constructivist research linkage is the hermeneutic dialectic at it most formidable and radical.

Not all constructivist experiences will be so radical. Not all hermeneutic processes become confrontationally dialectical or specifically radical-change oriented. But all hermeneutic processes will have an interventive aspect and all will create change at least at the level of individual consciousness. A quality hermeneutic circle can simply be the forum for serious consideration of alternatives. It can be a forum for dialogue aimed at co-constructed understanding, not radical change. Either way, radical or simply educational, the hermeneutic process will still be a strategic, interventive part of constructivist inquiry.

Definition

The hermeneutic circle of constructivism does not need to be a physical circle in which individual stakeholders are in constant interaction. What is required is that a circle of information sharing be created so that perspectives regarding claims, concerns, and issues are presented, considered, evaluated, understood, rejected, or incorporated into an emerging understanding of the phenomena under discussion or investigation. See Figure 4–1 for visual examples of the two types of hermeneutic circles. One is a true circle like those created in traditional focus groups. The other is the circle of information that is facilitated by the acts of the inquirer in sharing and testing information. Either way the hermeneutic circle is a methodological device "in which one considers the whole in relation to its parts and vice versa" (Schwandt, 1994, p. 121).

FIGURE 4–1

Possible Forms of Hermeneutic Circles

True hermeneutic circle with
participants in contact over time

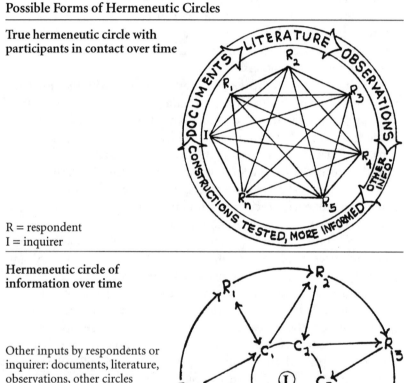

R = respondent
I = inquirer

Hermeneutic circle of
information over time

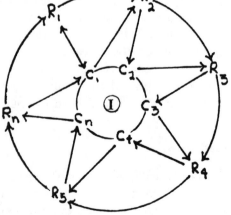

Other inputs by respondents or
inquirer: documents, literature,
observations, other circles

Each construction tested and
critiqued to become more
informed and sophisticated

R = respondent
I = inquirer
C = construction

The commonality in both is the "dialogic conversation" (Lambert et al., 1995, p. 86) that can occur either in a dyad or in a group wherein personal experiences, beliefs, and perceptions about an idea are accessed for assessment and reevaluation. The idea is to reflect on the information and the participants' personal relationship to it for a more sophisticated personal understanding and a more sophisticated co-construction in a reciprocity only possible when there is trust. Only in a trusting environment can old assumptions be broken and new constructions that have change possibilities be created. The creation of trust is primarily the inquirer's responsibility, but full, unencumbered participation is the responsibility of all participants. Trusting and being trustworthy are essential elements of a successful hermeneutic circle of dialogic conversations.

The reader is directed to Lambert's (Lambert et al., 1995, p. 89–99) clear discussion of several types of dialogic conversations, including inquiring conversations, sustaining conversations, and partnership conversations, each of which can be used in the development of the hermeneutic dialectic. In the same text, Zimmerman (1995, p. 109–115) provides specifics of the linguistic moves for the questioning that can be undertaken in dialogic conversations. In addition, a more detailed discussion of constructivist questioning for data collection and for co-construction in the hermeneutic dialectic can be found in Chapter 6.

The creation and maintenance of the hermeneutic circle is the responsibility of the investigator. It is the inquirer who facilitates, through dialogic conversation, the cycling and recycling of information for successively more sophisticated interpretation. This sophistication results from juxtaposing conflicting ideas. This happens when the inquirer initiates activities that support and extend a spirit of inquiry. Then participants are helped to live with the inevitable ambiguity and uncertainty that comes from this risk taking. Participants must be helped to trust that the initial chaos of juxtapositions will grow to a more complex understanding of what is being researched. They must trust that to force premature closure because of discomfort will short-circuit the communal connectedness and commitment to each other, to the topic, and to the kind of change that results from a successfully terminated intense mutual experience.

As in other dialectical processes, interpretive comparisons and contrasts are underscored for mutual exploration with the goal of synthesis, as in the Marxian tradition (Marx, 1988). Here the inquirer, in participation with the stakeholders, forms a connection between constructions for meaning making. Many of these connections are grounded in the inquirer's and participants' intuitive sense of things. To elicit and clarify this intuitive knowledge, the inquirer facilitates a reflection on actions to clarify and articulate what is known. By revisiting the familiar, we learn from our own stories. We make new individualized meaning. But this meaning making in hermeneutic discourse also results in consensus for education and empowerment on a larger scale, praxis.

All participants are affected in and by this process. The hermeneutic circle grows out of a belief, well articulated by Geertz (as cited in Lambert et al., 1995), that "it is possible for people inhabiting different worlds to have a genuine and reciprocal impact on one another" (p. ix). The hermeneutic circle is the context for this genuine and reciprocal impact. Via the hermeneutic circle, consciousness raising and empowerment are the natural results of constructivist inquiry.

Essential Elements

The constructivist hermeneutic process begins with purposive sampling and the protections necessary to assure the least amount of risk. To be productive, all participants must enter into the dialectical process from a position of integrity. Hidden agendas or other power needs can undermine the process. False fronts or deliberate deceptions should be exposed by subjecting the information to continuous and multiple challenges by the stakeholders.

All participants must be competent to participate (Lincoln & Guba, 1985). What constitutes competence depends on the foreshadowed questions and the context of the inquiry. Lincoln & Guba (1985) suggest that children need to have reached the age of reason, and other individuals should have the cognitive and verbal skills necessary for competent communication. But recent experiences with direct inquiry with young children (K through 5) (Rodwell & Wood, 1996), and experiences with data collection through the Internet (Neil, 1996) suggest that the definition of communication competence should be very broad, indeed. Competence to participate in this type of inquiry, which depends on a hermeneutic dialectic, should go beyond cognitive and verbal skills to include such interpersonal skills as trust and respect. Participants who are unwilling or unable to communicate forthrightly or to trust that other participants will as well, may not be competent to participate in a constructivist process. Trust and honesty are important aspects of competent participation that must be assessed by the inquirer, but also must be assured by those who agree to participate.

All participants must be willing to share power. The degree of this willingness is generally not known in the beginning of a process, so at a minimum, respect for human dignity and belief in human potential are elemental to hermeneutic discourse. The discourse process must have space for feedback, comments, elaboration, correction, revision, and expansions that are open to inspection. There should be no secrecy or information poverty. Leaving out important details or failing to give full disclosure for fear that participants might be unable to manage information diminishes the possibilities of the dialogic and dialectical process, and, therefore, the praxis dimension of the inquiry.

Participants, including the inquirer, must be willing to reconsider closely held value positions. Inquirer biases influencing outcomes are acceptable as long as the inquirer's construction is considered along with others and submitted to the same challenges, criticisms, and so forth. Both elements, openness to reconsider values and lack of inquirer control in the shaping, are important because only with these will the participants be willing to change if the results warrant it. They must recognize their true stake in knowledge creation or they will not be propelled by the inquiry results. Finally, participants must have the time and energy necessary to be open to consider the constructions and other inputs of others to come to a truly co-constructed result.

To assure that a real hermeneutic/dialectic process evolves, the investigator must manage the risk involved in honest reflection of beliefs and perspectives at least by creating emotional safety. The inquirer must also assure that there is a true range of perspectives for comparing, contrasting, and building to synthesis. This should come from sampling for maximum variation. The inquirer must also not shrink from the conflict that will naturally come from attempts at consensus building. Rushing to agreement or rejection in order to achieve a comfort zone does not enhance the possibilities of a more sophisticated synthesis. Throughout the dialectic, it is the inquirer's responsibility to model the appropriate, reflective, respectful, nondefensive behavior that is necessary for open discourse. In addition, the inquirer must model productive confrontational tactics to assure in-depth consideration of all perspectives in that discourse.

Methods

Most dimensions of the constructivist process also serve as methods in the creation of the hermeneutic circle capable of creating a hermeneutic dialectic. Sampling must be serial and contingent to assure range in perspectives and competence to participate in the process. There should be a continuous interplay of data collection and analysis. Respondents' constructions and the themes that emerge should be continuously compared with others' constructions with the goal of the creation of joint constructions. The inquirer must assure the grounding of the findings in the constructions of the respondents. They must "fit" and "work" so that the findings have relevance for the participants and the setting, or praxis with consciousness raising and resultant change will not be possible.

The emergent design attentive to multiple needs and perspectives supports the development of a hermeneutic circle. Ensuring an agenda for negotiation and the forum for negotiations when synthesis is difficult is also supportive of the circling of information. In addition, the process that results in a case report of joint constructions and an honoring of alternative divergent perspectives in minority reports contributes to a quality dialectic with change potential.

Role of the Researcher

The role of the researcher in the hermeneutic circle, not surprisingly, is similar to the researcher role in the overall inquiry. The researcher is not a describer as a photographer would be, but an illuminator, storyteller, historian, and judge. The researcher is not a controller, but a collaborator, learner/teacher. Finally, the researcher is not a discoverer, but is more an architect, a shaper of reality, and an agent of change.

To be certain that true discourse leads to dialectic and synthesis the researcher may also be required to serve as moderator of the conversation to ensure that all have voice. In addition, the researcher may be called on to serve as mediator of the conflicts and challenges that emerge when perspectives are compared, contrasted, and judged for relevance and meaning. Though the researcher positions himself or herself on the same plane of understanding as those who participate in the process, there must be another level of the researcher's conscious use of self (in the practice sense) that assures the use of the appropriate tool or role to carry out successfully the hermeneutic process as the process emerges.

Assuring Quality of the Hermeneutic Process

A conflictual process may be difficult to evaluate, but certain elements may be evident to indicate that the hermeneutic process is good enough to produce a quality co-constructed product. First, respondents must be selected for their variable perspectives and attitudes, not just because they are in support of the inquirer's original hunches that shaped the development of the foreshadowed questions. The respondents should be encouraged to nominate other participants for variation and range in perspectives.

Data inputs must be at least informally analyzed upon their receipt to identify salient themes that need to be introduced into the circle. Feedback should be elicited constantly. Participant constructions should be shared for comparison, analysis, reconstruction, and reconsideration. Participants should be asked for their comments on data produced at every stage of the inquiry for their elaboration, correction, revisions, or expansion. The shaping and testing, and the discovery and verification of the inquiry process should be ongoing and continuous. There should be immediate and continuous interplay of information, with continuous and multiple challenges to that information.

Generally, this will include going from unstructured to structured data collection as the circle achieves higher degrees of sophistication about the topic under consideration. Reconstructions should be collaborative between the inquirer performing the analysis and interpretation and the participants who provided the data. Comparisons of interpretations and reconstructions should be made for salience until redundancy is reached. The final case study should also be a collaborative, negotiated effort. Moreover, all dimensions of authenticity, the warrant for a quality constructivist inquiry process, should be documented and available for audit, if not public inspection, because these are indirect warrants that a quality hermeneutic circle was achieved.

Researcher's Responsibilities, Social Work Values, and the Research Intervention

Chapter 1 provided a discussion of the congruence between constructivism and social work practice. A review of that material might be useful before moving into a more complex value-based discussion of constructivist research as a potential social work intervention. This section will show how the specific responsibilities of a constructivist inquirer in the inquiry are a reflection of social work values embodied by the concepts of respect, dignity, and empowerment.

The first responsibility of the constructivist researcher is *identifying the full array of stakeholders* to the inquiry. The full array involves all individuals and groups who might have a perspective about the problem to be investigated. This responsibility illustrates a fundamental principle of constructivism, that of value pluralism (Guba & Lincoln, 1986), but it also illustrates the belief in an *equal opportunity,* without regard to power, position, or interest, to put voice to an individually or group-held perspective.

The constructivist must manage a design that will allow inclusion of new stakeholders whenever they become apparent. There is a belief that no useful understanding can be derived in an inquiry without the inquirer's thorough experience of the contexts and views of all the individuals and groups with an interest in the phenomenon. In this identification and inclusion of all participants with a substantial stake in the process and product, there is also recognition that any continuous and systematic effort of co-construction requires honest descriptions of perspectives. With honest revelation, for some, at least, comes risk.

Another dimension of equal opportunity is equal protection. For the purposes of constructivist inquiry, identification and inclusion of those with a stake must also include identifying those who might be at risk in the process. Beyond identification, the inquirer is responsible for arranging to *protect those at risk.* This protection may be as simple as assuring that the homeless person's voice is not drowned out by the politicians in the housing policy–making process by drawing out each perspective in individual conversations instead of in a group forum. But real risk may also be involved. Participants in a program evaluation may be at risk of loss of job or status if their real perspective can be identified. The constructivist evaluator must develop a way to release this construction without it being identifiably linked. This might be through "what would you think if . . ." suppositional probes to the administrator, or taking the role of learner with the administrator when literature reflecting the at risk individual's position is debated. The learning can then become teaching in which all perspectives are fairly considered.

This intrinsic fairness is central to another responsibility, *creating an atmosphere for eliciting the range of claims, concerns, and issues* relevant to the investigation. Recognizing that participants base their judgments on very different value patterns, there is a concern that no one be given unfair preference, but that each position is considered for its own merit and worth. All constructions must be honored by collecting information that is responsive to them for validation or lack of confirmation without regard to source. This *independence of thought* is necessary to create the insider's view of what is important. It also allows the framing and bounding of the research that prevents the inquirer from being the only one shaping the focus of the perspective.

The inquirer is also responsible for providing a *context for understanding and critiquing different perspectives*. This context must be the preferred environment for the participants. The individual must determine his or her own place and time for participation. This *self-determination* is enhanced through the use of various qualitative methods of data collection and data analysis that allow for an equal opportunity for various independent voices to be heard.

However, hearing the voices is not sufficient for constructivism. These different constructions and different claims, concerns, and issues must be understood, critiqued, and taken into account. Generally, in the context of valuing difference, material is circulated in a hermeneutic process so that merit or worth can be assessed in relation to the contexts and its particulars. *Generating as much consensus as possible* is the goal of this assessment process and must be facilitated by the inquirer. Though *valuing differences* will mean that uniformity in agreement will not always be possible, it is important in arriving at a co-constructed reality.

The concepts of negotiated processes and outcomes are central to constructivism. Value pluralism also invokes another criterion in the consensus of co-construction, that of *fairness*. Where true consensus exists, no challenge exists in moving toward a final product. Where there is no or incomplete consensus, the inquirer is responsible for *creating a forum for negotiation*.

Justice is central to this mediation of unresolved differences. All with a stake must have real engagement in the negotiation process to determine findings. The inquirer is responsible for preparing the agenda for negotiation, for collecting and providing the information called for in the agenda for negotiation, and for establishing and mediating a forum in which the negotiation can take place. The outcome should be at least reduction of differences, if not full agreement.

Justice is also central in *developing the final report*. When differences are reduced, those themes for which consensus exists become a part of the final report. The others serve to set the stage for additional efforts in negotiation or to become part of a minority report. All participants must feel part of the process by being able to see that their perspective is accurately represented in the final report. They must recognize their voice and agree that it has been fairly represented.

This recognition and warranting of voice is essential in executing the last major inquirer responsibility, *recycling*. This recycling is not only the return of the report to the participants, but engaging in and facilitating the management of unresolved issues that are apparent as a result of the process. *Fostering potential* is recognized as valuable here because management of unresolved disagreements is essential to continued growth in understanding. This makes subsequent ongoing meaning making and consensus-based co-construction a possibility. But more important, this facilitation of the recycling assures that all with a stake will have input into the courses of action that might evolve from the process.

Researcher As Research Instrument

Constructivist researchers, like social workers, are made, not born. Implementing a constructivist study, like implementing a clinical or macro intervention, requires the use of natural and acquired skills. Making initial contact, gaining entry, negotiating consent, building and maintaining trust, and identifying and using informants require the development of the human instrument. Designing a plan and allowing the phases of the inquiry to unfold, using the human instrument for information gathering, and collecting data from nonhuman sources in the context of trustworthiness and authenticity requires specific skills. Establishing a quality hermeneutic and preparing a negotiated case report, all require some educational preparation.

Natural Characteristics

The capable constructivist researcher must have intelligence, humor, flexibility, and creativity. Each is essential in handling uncertainty and in meaning making. Each is essential for communication. Each is essential for insight and understanding.

The constructivist must possess sufficient self-esteem to resist the need to maintain control or to be the recognized expert as a measure of self-worth. Giving up the expert role and giving up control can be taught, but the personal security to allow these important dimensions of constructivism to unfold is an integral building block for the other necessary skills. Additional qualities of honesty, respect, courtesy, and ethical behavior are important to engendering the trust that participants must develop in order to engage in the process.

Cognitive skills that include abstract thinking are also essential to the construction/reconstruction process of meaning making. Concrete thinkers will have much difficulty moving from the description of themes to reshaping them as needed for final negotiations of meaning and case study report writing. Genuine curiosity about the unknown is also a plus. With this curiosity will generally come an openness to risk that is essential to withstand the stresses involved in this all-encompassing, unpredictable, and unending process.

Acquired Skills

The preparation of a competent constructivist researcher involves skill development in the technical aspects of data collection and analysis. The human instrument as data collector and analyst, describer, and judge, requires skills that are combined in the collaborator, learner/teacher, reality shaper, mediator, and change agent roles that are essential to constructivist inquiry.

The human instrument as collector and analyst of information must first possess self-awareness. This is acquired through the skill of honest reflexivity. **Reflexivity** occurs when personal feelings and issues are identified, bounded, and controlled, so that the inquiry does not simply serve the conscious or unconscious needs of the inquirer, but the needs and preferences of all involved. This practice of introspection can be honed through the persistent use of a journaling process in which thoughts, feelings, fears, worries, reactions, values, philosophical positions, passionate responses, and preferences are recorded and observed in relation to how they shape the inquiry process. The insight acquired from this type of reflection leads to more insight and reflection in an ever better honing of the human capacity for adaptability, intelligence, and understanding. In most cases, this insight development cannot happen alone. For this and other reasons, the constructivist uses a peer reviewer who accompanies the inquiry to aid in monitoring through debriefing during the process.

Understanding is increased through frequent, continuing, and meaningful interaction between the inquirer and the participants. This interaction, which will result in the mutual shaping of co-construction, is possible only when the inquirer has a sensitivity and appreciation of diversity. The inquirer's understanding of and appreciation for cultural, social, and spiritual diversity will be enhanced by studying the elements of a multicultural society and discrimination resulting from persistent social, educational, political, religious, economic, and legal inequalities. This appreciation of diversity is the basis for a recognition of the strengths and possibilities found in difference. The approach to others that is desired is one in which the individual right to hold individualized perspectives is valued and encouraged. It is achieved through appreciation of diversity in combination with the critical self-awareness that comes through analysis of personal values and a resultant bounding of passions and biases.

Honest reflexivity, as described above, demonstrates a dimension of critical analytic thinking necessary in all dimensions of constructivist investigations. Critical thinking allows the constructivist to identify the value-embeddedness of beliefs and knowledge. It allows the constructivist to assess dispassionately the costs and benefits of positions and to ferret out the most salient and relevant matters in the context of the study. This critical stance allows distancing from personal feelings and thoughts, while maintaining genuine involvement in the communications and actions of the inquiry. Critical thinking uncovers leaps of logic and other mechanisms that can flaw reasoned descriptions and judgments. The skills in critical thinking develop through practice when the inquirer releases himself or herself from the requirement of being or doing "right." The result is a change in expectations from perfection or truth to maximum feasibility or maximum viability.

In addition to critical self-awareness and the ability to be reflexive, the constructivist must also be articulate in both written and spoken communication. This articulateness, in connection with reflexivity, facilitates the effective use of intuition in the investigation. Sensing salient factors, devising ways to follow up on them, and articulating those hunches in propositional statements so that they can be tested in the hermeneutic circle for meaning, comes with practice. Trusting the hunches and acting on them comes when the inquirer trusts his or her own competence, but is humble enough to recognize the tentative nature of the hunch.

Confidence in competence comes from several directions. First, the inquirer needs the clinical skills necessary to engender trust, establish honest communication, and question participants appropriately. Second, the inquirer must have the basic qualitative data collection skills of interviewing and observing. Third, constructivist investigators must have skills in data management including data recording and analysis. The data collection, management, and analysis skills can be acquired through the use of this text. The information and learning experiences provided in the text, in combination with thorough grounding in social work practice skills, will enable the reader to develop the confidence and freedom to undertake constructivist research.

Distinctive Features of a Constructivist Inquirer

There is congruence between constructivist research and social work practice. Due to this congruence, constructivism links research and practice in ways different from traditional research. This means that the constructivist researcher is different from the researcher engaged in a traditional research project. The following discussion highlights those distinctive features to dramatize the changes in the research process and the role of the researcher.

Constructivist research is a social/political process mediated and enhanced by the inquirer. Data are being created and judged in a hermeneutic process of meaning making. The inquirer understands the need to make judgments about the merit or worth of the various constructions, but instead of judging, the inquirer mediates the judgment process because all stakeholders have equal rights and equal responsibilities in making these essential judgments.

The inquiry process is a teaching/learning process that is continuous, recursive, divergent and never ending. The inquirer is just one stakeholder in the process and participates from a collaborative rather than a controlling stance. All those involved in a quality hermeneutic circle learn about the different value positions and perspectives held by the participants. All participants also teach each other about each others' constructions. The inquirer facilitates this process by assuring fairness and equal opportunity. Control is given up in the name of consciousness raising and empowerment.

Constructivist inquiry is a process that constructs a new reality based on a more sophisticated understanding of the various perspectives of the stakeholders. The inquirer is the *reality shaper* because when constructions emerge, he or she facilitates the dissemination and testing of perspectives. In this facilitation, personal values and preferences are reshaped to include the consequences of exposure to alternative perspectives. Inevitably the perspective of the inquirer also finds its way into the reconstruction or co-construction. In fact, all participants, together, create the data that result by their continuous mutual shaping in the hermeneutic circle.

Inquiry designs can never be specified in advance. Every element in the process emerges as a result of or in relationship to the other emerging elements. No one, including the inquirer, can determine in advance what will result from a collaborative process that is open to choice. All aspects are open to negotiation, including the future consequences of the negotiated results. The inquirer role inevitably emerges as one of mediator and change agent. Constructivist research is, then, a practice intervention with micro and macro consequences. It is praxis. The following sections of the text will show the reader the specific details of managing the constructivist investigation to assure that praxis will result.

Discussion Questions

These questions will augment the reader's knowledge of the basic skills and elements in the implementation of constructivist research, including instituting a quality hermeneutic circle.

1. What makes constructivist intervention praxis?
2. Why is constructivist research seen as an intervention?
3. Describe the dialogic and dialectic nature of the hermeneutic process.
4. Identify at least five responsibilities of the researcher in assuring the quality of the hermeneutic circle.
5. How does the hermeneutic circle and the circling of information therein relate to the other aspects of the constructivist process, specifically entry into the process and the case study report?

CHAPTER 5

Rigor in Constructivist Research

Chapter Contents in Brief

Trustworthiness including credibility, dependability, confirmability, and transferability
Maintaining field journals and an audit trail
Authenticity including fairness, and ontological, educative, catalytic, and tactical authenticity
Establishing mechanisms for achieving authenticity

It is at the rigor level that most criticism is lodged against alternative ways of knowing (see for example Berkenkotter, 1993; Grinnell et al., 1994; Thyer, 1986, 1989). Most of the argument is in response to the positivistic assumptions about what is real and knowable. The rigor criticisms, then, are extensions of the paradigmatic/philosophical discussions where there can be no conclusion because there probably can be no consensus. If Kuhn (1970) is correct, the criticisms and cross-criticisms, the battle and backlash, will continue until a new paradigm reigns as "good science."

In the meantime, alternative forms of rigor regarding what constitutes "real" knowledge or "good" science are built on alternative paradigmatic assumptions. Even these are not without regard to the "gold standard" (the standard against which all are measured) of positivism. Any discussion of rigor of any systematic effort of knowledge building must acknowledge positivist and post-positivist expectations in the conduct of inquiry. Therefore, constructivist rigor must be considered on two dimensions, one that is in response to the general expectations of traditional research, trustworthiness, and another that is congruent with the alternative expectations of constructivism, authenticity.

Two Dimensions of Constructivist Rigor

Trustworthiness, or accounting for the truth value, applicability, consistency, and neutrality (Green et al., 1988; Guba & Lincoln, 1982, 1986; Lincoln & Guba, 1985, 1986; Schwandt & Halpern, 1988) of the research, was developed in response and reaction to the standard expectations associated with traditional positivistic research including validity, reliability, objectivity, amd so forth (Lincoln & Guba, 1985, 1986). The aspects of trustworthiness were developed to replace the old conventions used to assess the credibility of knowledge. However, it cannot be overlooked that these decisions were also based on a need to warrant the legitimacy of the alternative research methods (Guba & Lincoln, 1986; Lincoln, 1989). In much the same way that social work sought professional legitimacy through the language of positivism, the initial iteration of constructivist rigor sought legitimacy through processes and language that could cross paradigms from interpretive to positivistic.

The language of trustworthiness, though attempting to show the real difference in the perspective, was developed to be understood by those actively researching in the traditional positivistic framework. Clearly, this decision had political undertones, because these traditional researchers also tended to sit in review of constructivist research proposals needing funding and manuscripts needing publication (see Hammersley, 1995, and Diesing, 1991, for excellent discussions of the politics of science). In the early days, it was clear that those reviewers and their constituencies, not constructivists and their followers, were going to assess and warrant constructivist inquiry's legitimacy, if legitimacy were to occur. In the early days of development, it was within traditional scientific language, and with traditional scientific standards, that there was any hope of establishing the alternative perspective as "at least as reasonable and useful as those of either positivism or postpositivism" (Guba, 1990, p. 9).

As a result of this attention to legitimating constructivism, the initial efforts were not truly congruent with the relativist, interactive, value-bounded assumption and goals of the constructivist inquiry *process*. Instead, they were a reflection of the positivist concern for a valid research *product*. Therefore, trustworthiness demonstrates elements necessary to ensure that there can be confidence in the research *findings*.

On the other hand, authenticity grows from the constructivist alternative assumptions. This second dimension of constructivist rigor attests to a rigor unique to the approach. **Authenticity** captures the value pluralism, multiple perspectives, and qualitative change focus of constructivist inquiry. It attests to the interactive results of the research *process,* not the product (Lincoln & Guba, 1985, 1986). Though still evolving, aspects of authenticity are an effort to depart from parallel trustworthiness criteria that are reflective of positivist standards. The authenticity standards are developed both as a symbol of the uniqueness of constructivism in an interpretive paradigmatic perspective and in an effort to establish quality standards for the inductive, grounded, creative processes involved in reality co-construction. They are reflective of the methods' value base and respond to the ethical challenges, largely ignored in standard investigations (Newman & Brown, 1996) of human subjects research. Authenticity is also reflective of an interest in the quality of a process that seeks to educate and empower, and, through that empowerment, to elicit action toward change. Authenticity speaks to praxis via a quality hermeneutic circle.

An outside assessment of the level of trustworthiness, authenticity and the quality of the hermeneutic circle occurs through an audit of the process and product of the constructivist inquiry. Much like a financial auditor, an outside auditor of constructivist inquiry reviews all elements developed to document rigor and attests to the degree of trustworthiness and authenticity in the inquiry process and product. Details of the auditing process can be found in Chapter 9.

Aspects of Trustworthiness

Trustworthiness standards are used to judge what was produced and how it is reported. Trustworthiness is attentive to the preferred techniques of constructivism and the appropriateness of researcher decisions regarding data collection, analysis, and display. These standards are credibility, dependability, confirmability, and transferability. Credibility parallels internal validity in traditional positivist research. Dependability is analogous to reliability. Confirmability relates to objectivity. Transferability is related to external validity to the degree that it allows decisions regarding the applicability of results and interpretations to other audiences in other contexts. Together, these elements are intended to aid in the assessment of quality and the defensibility of the methods, results, and conclusions of a constructivist inquiry (Green et al., 1988).

Credibility

Credibility attests to the process and product accuracy in understanding the depth and scope of the issues under study. This dimension of rigor attends to the "truth" value of the findings. Credibility also speaks to the accuracy of the results and interpretations as viewed by important stakeholders in the context. The intent is to prevent obfuscation on the part of the stakeholders and misinterpretation on the part of the inquirer. It is of the utmost importance that the inquirer's analysis, formulations, and interpretations are believable to those who participated in the construction of the reality represented in the final report. The outside audit will attest to this. The concern in the audit is with emic rather than with etic confirmation. Confirmation through the audit of the accuracy of the insiders' perspectives speaks to the reflective, responsive, and ethical goals of constructivism.

A variety of activities are recommended (Lincoln & Guba, 1985) to increase the probability of credible findings including prolonged engagement, participant observation, triangulation, peer debriefing, and member checks.

Prolonged engagement involves lengthy, purposive, intensive contact with the context and the stakeholders connected to the phenomenon or problem of interest for the investigation. This is intended to assess possible sources of distortion and to discover information salient to the investigation. Prolonged engagement tends to dilute the distortions introduced by the presence of an outsider. It also serves to build the trust in the outsider necessary for honest communication. Prolonged engagement is documented in the chronology of research activities.

Persistent observation is an in-depth, focused pursuit of the information found to be salient from prolonged engagement. It is through **persistent observation** that emerging themes become familiar enough to be understood and appreciated, or rejected as irrelevant for the purposes of the particular inquiry (Atkinson & Hammersley, 1994). Persistence allows the inquirer to achieve depth and exact specifics related to the major characteristics of the focus of the study. These will normally be reflected on and reported in either the reflexive journal or the methodological log.

Triangulation occurs when one data source is compared to another. Denzin (1978) describes the process as pitting a variety of data sources, different perspectives, theories, or methods against each other to cross-check information and interpretations. Guba and Lincoln (1989) have moved from triangulation as a credibility check, feeling that its overtones are too positivist, because triangulation results in a determination of "truth." However, the general idea of cross-checking, assessing, and otherwise considering perspectives or constructions is central to the hermeneutic process. It is also central enough to current understanding of the triangulation method to warrant continued recommendation of the process. Triangulation should be used for comparison, distillation, or convergent validation, or to see if the information holds up under comparison to something else. From our perspective, triangulation aids in attaining a full understanding of the reality in construction. The results of triangulation will be recorded in either the reflexive journal or the methodological log, depending upon the direction of the relevance of the findings.

Peer debriefing involves working with a peer who is uninvolved with the inquiry process, but knowledgeable enough about the methodology, if not the substance of the inquiry, to assist in bounding the subjectivity of the inquirer. The peer reviewer's role is to ask the difficult questions, explore next steps, support, and listen. The peer reviewer gives advice, adds perspective, offers technical assistance, and helps to process the strong feelings, anxieties, and stresses that naturally result from such a complicated, intense process so that these do not negatively affect the inquiry. The peer reviewer, in many ways, functions as a clinical supervisor does for a social work practitioner. The debriefing that occurs aids in monitoring the inquirer's progressive subjectivity and the developing constructions to assure that what is developing is truly a joint construction. Results of these debriefings should be recorded in the inquirer's reflexive journal. A debriefing journal should be maintained by the peer reviewer.

Member checks consist of formal and informal testing of the information with the participants for convergent validation. Participant reactions are solicited both in the process of construction as a part of the data collection and of the hermeneutic dialectic. Reactions to the final report are also elicited to confirm the accuracy of the reconstruction provided in the case report. Results of the member-checking process will find their way into either the reflexive journal or the methodological log of the inquiry.

Dependability

Dependability speaks to the point that all procedures employed to collect, analyze, and interpret data fall within the expectations of constructivist research practices. Methodological instability and emergent design–induced changes are accounted for and tracked through dependability. The central mechanism for dependability is the methodological log. In it are recorded all methodological decisions and their justifications as they emerge. Other elements include the following:

Triangulation which is used to establish credibility, also helps to establish dependability. The justification of changes in data collection or analysis are supported through the feedback provided in triangulation.

Records of data collected are all field notes and other "raw" information. This includes all records, documents, unobtrusive measures, and other sources of information that can be deconstructed into data units.

Records of data analyzed involve not only data deconstruction evidence seen in data units and subsuming categories, but also all data reduction and analysis products, all data reconstruction, and synthesis products. Process notes during the analysis are included, as is material related to inquirer intentions and dispositions regarding meaning making. Also included are all stages of the coding efforts. Keeping a record of coding will help in connecting and tracking each stage of the analysis process.

Decision rules are a subset of the data analysis record, which documents the logic of placing a unit of data in one category instead of another.

Analytic categories are the labels assigned to the decision rules that have been developed to describe the category properties.

Dependability audit is performed by an independent external auditor using all the above material in a planned, systematic review to determine the degree to which procedures used coincided with commonly accepted constructivist practices.

Confirmability

The point of confirmability is to assert the reasonableness of the inferences and the logic of the theory that evolved from the data. The goal of confirmability is not to assert that "truth" was achieved because the findings are demonstrated to be replicable, but that the results as reported are linked to the data. Another researcher using his or her own cognitive processes might construct something different with the same data. What is important here is that an outside auditor can discover and follow the logic that took the inquirer from the initial raw data to the final product. Auditor agreement with the construction is not the purpose, nor is it relevant.

However, it is important that the results are related to the context and the participants and not just a reflection of the inquirer's cognitive processes of meaning making. As with credibility, what is relevant is that all voices or perspectives are present in the data and the analysis, thus ensuring that all those with a stake have had the opportunity to have a voice in the final reconstruction. The participants' warranting of the accuracy of the final product is most salient, though a confirmability audit warrants confirmability for the outside consumers of the product.

To ensure that the results are linked to the data and to establish confirmability, the researcher is responsible for the successful completion of several activities. Primary is a respect for the rights and perspectives of all participants. In addition, the following means are useful either to guard against loss of credibility or to test for it.

Triangulation and *member checking* used in other dimensions of trustworthiness also support confirmability. *Records of data collected* and *records of data analyzed,* along with *decision rules* and *analytic categories* used for dependability are also useful in confirmability. These, along with the *interpretations and conclusions* found in the final report are the material sources for a *confirmability audit.* This aspect of the auditing process includes the close examination of the data and the inquirer's reconstructions to see that they are linked to the raw data collected in the context of the inquiry. This usually involves the auditor reconstructing the analysis process by following a sampling of assertions in the final report back to the raw data upon which the assertions were based.

Transferability

Care must be taken in order not to confound transferability with generalizability. Transferability allows for the possibility that information created and lessons learned in one context can have meaning and usefulness in another. The question is how the working hypotheses of one inquiry can be useful in another. Transferability is another aspect of the pragmatics of constructivism. Though there is a belief that every context and every inquiry experience is unique and that there is no immutable truth, there is also the recognition that through deconstruction and reconstruction, the tentative findings in one context might have applicability or functionality in another. This, then, is not generalizability, but a consideration of how useful a tentative application of findings might be in other environments.

The decision about usefulness in other environments remains with the consumer of the case report. The inquirer is responsible for providing sufficient description to allow the reader to determine if transfer of all or part of the findings is possible. The description provided is known to be a "thick description" (Geertz, 1973; Ryle, 1968), the details of which will be discussed in Chapter 8. In short, the narrative must be richly descriptive enough to impart a vicarious experience of the setting, the problem, and the findings. The outside audit of transferability is to establish that enough "thickness" has been provided regarding the setting, the participants, and the problem for an outsider to decide on his or her own if the findings are useful and applicable elsewhere.

Establishing Trustworthiness

Acceptance of the logic of the trustworthiness dimensions is not enough to guarantee a quality product. What is required is a system that assures the development of trustworthiness, tracks its development, and safeguards the products of the inquiry. The following discussion outlines some basic elements of a good system, but each researcher will develop his or her own documentation style and preferences that are matches for personality, time, and resource availability. What is essential for trustworthiness and auditability is that a system is developed and consistently maintained. The system is documented in the form of the audit trail, which includes relevant documentary evidence for trustworthiness. It should have sufficient internal logic to be explainable to an outside party, the auditor.

Trustworthiness is entirely dependent upon quality data collection and data analysis, which are the subjects of the next two chapters, so the discussion here is built on the assumptions that the collection and analysis is or can be done competently. The discussion that follows is more focused on the conceptual aspects of systems development and maintenance. By paying attention to the step-by-step discussions in the next several chapters, the "doing" of trustworthiness will be taken care of.

Maintaining Confidentiality and Rigor Protections

Given the intense, value-embedded nature of the constructivist process, and due to the centrality of the notions of respect for human dignity, fairness, honesty, and justice, confidentiality and rigor protections are central to the ethics and, therefore, the trustworthiness of constructivist investigations.

Confidentiality in most social science research means that no real names or other identifying information about the persons and places of the inquiry will be reported (Lofland & Lofland, 1995). These types of protections to ensure anonymity go without saying in social work practice. But in constructivism, protections that truly protect participants from being identified in the process of co-construction can be instituted only in a matter of degrees. When stable communities or ongoing groups are involved in the process, or when the hermeneutic circle is developed in a face-to-face fashion, strict confidentiality protections are virtually impossible. Even if the structure of data construction makes true identification impossible, in these contexts, participants can many times make relatively accurate guesses about who said or did what.

As in protective service investigations, the inquirer is obligated never to willingly identify a data source, nor confirm the identity of the source, even if another participant accurately guesses, or if outside interests (like reporters or agency administrators) press for information. The inquirer must also ensure that all participants know and are willing to comply with, as much as possible, the standards of identity protection. Participants in focus groups, hermeneutic circles, or any other type of joint construction must agree that what is discussed within the context of the process remains with the process at least to the degree that the "he-said-she-said" aspects of the conversations, dialogues, or dialectics remain a secret.

The inquirer should plan how this confidentiality standard should be presented in the consent form and in any group data collection processes. Having the dimensions of confidentiality developed beforehand will do much to facilitate the process of gaining entry into a site. Formalized statements of information protection, including who will gain access to raw data and how that data will be stored, all support positive aspects of trust building necessary for true understanding and meaning making. As another element in honoring the rights of the participants, the risks involved in the inability to guarantee complete confidentiality must also be made clear, especially in negotiating fully informed consent. Finally, identity must be disguised in the case report, but this effort must be carefully orchestrated so that in protecting identity, meaning does not also become obscured. For example, in research about relevant dimensions of justice for social work practice, changing the identity of an African-American male respondent to a female obscures important dimensions of meaning that pertain to being an African-American male in American society. The idea that just by being a black male fear is engendered, and that this fear of male power is sometimes sensed by a male is replaced by the idea of fear of males that is sometimes experienced by women. These important distinctions can change meaning for the participants and the reader of the final report.

Distortion is guarded against by rigor protections. Distortion due to an outsider's presence in the site or with the participants is managed through prolonged engagement and peer review. The inquirer must engage the site and the respondents in the inquiry long enough to create relationship. Depending upon the persons and contexts, this may require 15 minutes, days, or years. Consciousness of this aspect of rigor must be evidenced in the projected timelines for data collection. It should also be reflected in appropriate journals used to document the process.

Distortions that are due to the close, direct, and personal involvement with participants must also be managed. It will be natural to "side" with the respondents with whom the inquirer has much in common; but, just as with clinical practice, the inquirer must maintain sufficient distance to assure evenhandedness in all aspects of the process. Serious, persistent involvement with the peer reviewer in debriefing and planning sessions should aid in this "boundary management" challenge. Further reflectivity, as demonstrated in the reflexive journal, will also aid in the management of the intimacy, but will also document achievement of standards for the purposes of trustworthiness.

Distortions from personal biases must also be managed. Peer debriefing and personal reflexivity are important here. Just as important is continual checking with the context and the data sources through member checks and triangulations. Some distortions are possible just from the process of data gathering. Distortions are real possibilities in a process of mutual shaping, so all parts of the process must be monitored for evenhandedness. Assessment of respondent credibility, member checks, triangulation of data, themes, and coding mechanisms will assure maximum consistency and evenhanded co-construction.

Maintaining Field Journals

Journals should begin even before the initial research design is developed. Both the methodological and the reflexive journals should begin as the idea for the inquiry develops in order to document the early stages of human instrument development. All journals should be continuously maintained as essential elements of the audit trail. Without the journals, no evidence of the project's emergence will be available; the researcher loses documentation of individual growth and development; and the elemental work of bringing tacit knowledge to propositional form will be lost.

The first journal to begin and the last to finish is the *personal log* or *reflexive journal*. The reflexive journal should be the diary of the inquirer's journey through the project. What should occur is a reflective conversation with oneself that investigates possible meanings from what is happening in relation to one's own values and interests. This journal, then, explores the essential relationship of the human instrument with the method and the results. It does not document methodological decisions or findings, but rather the growing awareness that inevitably leads to shifting design decisions and meaning making.

In most cases the *methodological log* grows from this kind of reflexivity. It documents methodological decisions and the rationale for each. It is not sufficient to simply log the history of methods decisions; the reasons for making them must also be included. This log should accompany all phases of the inquiry and record the reasons for the instability in the research design. It is important to remember that this journal is the primary mechanism for documenting the dependability of the research process and product. Therefore, it must be assiduously maintained throughout the process including during the writing of the final report.

Data collection is recorded in a series of *field journals*. Field notes are a concept borrowed from anthropology and other disciplines using ethnomethodological methods (Marshall & Rossman, 1995). These notes are an "in the moment" accounting of the events, interactions, thoughts, and feelings of those participating in the interviews or observations as they occur in context (Punch, 1986).

One of the best detailed accountings of how to move from the scribbling of note taking in the field to a more organized and clear accounting that can serve for further analysis can be found in Spradley (1980). He suggests that a "condensed" journal be used during the actual interview or observation. Direct quotes (as close as possible), key words, specific behaviors, inquirer questions, or themes for persistent observation are jotted down simply to jog the inquirer's memory when the expanded account is developed.

Data should be expanded and recorded in an *expanded field journal* as soon as possible after the data collection activity. Lofland (1971b) recommends real expansion into full sentences and including material that might not have been noted, but is remembered in the act of expansion. To avoid confusing one data collection activity with another and to refrain from making inferences, data should be expanded within 24 hours of the data gathering.

A *log of day-to-day activities* need not be anything more elaborate than a calendar wherein appointments and other activities are recorded on the day and time they occur. This log should be maintained throughout the process as a measure of persistence.

Developing and Maintaining the Audit Trail

Details of what constitutes acceptable content of all the expected aspects of the audit trail and how to create them will be developed over the next several chapters. For now it is important to understand the minimal elements of the trail, because knowledge of this plays into the choices and plans that are made early in the inquiry process. Decisions made early on will have ramifications for the duration of the process, because the audit trail is cumulative and the logic must be developed before it is built. The trail must delineate all methodological steps and decision points and give access to all data in all their forms.

The audit trail should include all raw data. This data must be linked to its expanded form in the field journals and to its reduced form by way of the data reduction and analysis products. All the iterations of the data reconstruction and synthesis are documented and their products become part of the audit trail as well. Instrument development information, either related to structured formats for data collection or to the developing human instrument, must be archived as part of the trail. The case report is the final aspect of the audit trail, but all steps that precede its construction, including inquirer and participant intentions and dispositions, are also audit trail material.

Dimensions of Authenticity

Authenticity is the most potentially radical dimension of constructivism. It is also the element of research rigor that will be of utmost familiarity to the social work practitioner. Any practitioner who operates from a change-agent perspective will appreciate the attention given to the qualitative change focus contained in constructivist inquiry. It is at the level of authenticity that we see the most pragmatic aspect of the research perspective. It is not sufficient to have an exquisite research product; something must occur as a result of the process. This is an excellent demonstration of the difference between knowledge for knowledge's sake (as in producing a good case study) and knowledge for action (as in effective action based on the mutual education resulting from the process). Authenticity speaks to the integrity and quality of the interactive process in constructivism that is attentive to multiple constructions shaped by the context. It also calls on the inquirer to attend to contextual betterment which should also result from the action orientation of the teaching/learning that goes on.

Authenticity is composed of five aspects, some of which are more developed than others: fairness, ontological authenticity, educative authenticity, catalytic authenticity, and tactical authenticity. Fairness is the criterion that is probably the most well developed both by Lincoln & Guba (1985, 1986, 1989) and by other research scholars with an interest in operationalizing social justice in the research context (see for example: Fetterman, Kaftarian, & Wandersman, 1996; House, 1976; Lehne, 1978; Miles & Huberman, 1994; Newman & Brown, 1996; Strike, 1982). The other aspects only have good conceptual or philosophical development. There are few guidelines for assuring the standards of the other aspects of authenticity (Manning, 1997). For the more adventuresome constructivist researcher, this means that the practical implications of establishing authenticity still require the inquirer's investment in testing out personal ideas.

Fairness

Fairness involves evenhanded representation of all viewpoints. As another aspect of honoring value pluralism, the fairness criterion ensures that different constructions, perspectives, and positions are not only allowed to emerge, but are also seriously considered for merit and worth.

As this attempt at evenhanded consideration is undertaken, there is the potential that conflict will result as a by-product of the dialectical conversations. The inquirer is responsible for managing this conflict or discomfort so that all persons have true voice, by ensuring that their perspectives are aired, clarified, and considered in an honorable and balanced way. The inquirer establishes fairness when all stakeholders have the power to have voice.

Having voice does not just mean having the capacity to overcome fear so that an individual narrative is considered in the construction process, nor is it just providing data. It also includes participation in the analysis and interpretation stages of the inquiry. Fairness requires that participants competently participate in the negotiation process of consensus building. If participants are not capable of doing this, then the inquirer is responsible either for aiding in the skill development necessary or in developing a negotiation process in which less powerful perspectives are protected. Participation from equal positions of power and with equally complete information are also important for fairness.

Finally, fairness calls for serious attention to minority reporting mechanisms. Constructivist consensus building is not a democratic process in which the most popular or most promoted viewpoint is used to represent the whole. Instead, it is a process of mutuality, in which all those with a stake involve themselves in educating themselves and each other about alternatives in order to determine the most viable construction of the phenomenon under investigation. Even when a particular effort in negotiation attempts to shape diversity to mutuality, sometimes incomplete or total lack of consensus will ensue. Material disagreement remains an important part of the process and product of the hermeneutic circle and the constructivist process. Fairness dictates that perspectives that depart from consensus remain evident, as in a minority report of the results.

Ontological Authenticity

Increased awareness of the complexity of the constructions of the phenomenon under investigation is the goal of **ontological authenticity**. This aspect of rigor attends to the construction and reconstruction of a person's perspective as it becomes more sophisticated. The interaction with other perspectives due to the hermeneutic circle is intended to improve the participants' conscious experience of the subject of the investigation and of the context in which the investigation is being undertaken. The aim of this form of disciplined inquiry is consciousness raising that leads to greater sophistication. It may mean "getting smart" about the sociopolitical, economic, or cultural contexts that aid in the framing and bounding of the reality under investigation. It should mean greater appreciation by all stakeholders and stakeholding groups as to the complexities involved in the problem. This should also include a more complete or complex understanding of self and others.

Educative Authenticity

Becoming smarter about the issue at hand is not enough for constructivist research. In addition, there should be increased understanding of and respect for the values of others as well as how these values frame their perspectives. This is **educative authenticity**. The issue here is increased appreciation of the complexity as it is shaped into others' perspectives. An agreement with the alternative perspective may never develop, but sympathy for it should be developed. There should be enough appreciation and respect for others' constructions to allow participants to agree to disagree. It should be possible to conceive of honorable people holding markedly different positions without one position or the other being termed "bad" or "evil."

Not only should participants understand and appreciate the positions of the other stakeholders, but there should also be some increased understanding about what seems to evoke these alternatives. The sources of different opinions, preferences, judgments, behaviors, or preferred actions should be known, understood, and appreciated. In many ways, educative authenticity is another cut at multiculturalism, in that the process of co-construction is a process of crossing individuals' cultures with care and respect in order to come to sensitivity and real understanding of what has merit in even the most opposite of positions.

Catalytic Authenticity

Shared understanding, creating new knowledge, is not enough for constructivist inquiry. The process, in order to demonstrate **catalytic authenticity**, must also facilitate, stimulate, or otherwise evoke action. This is knowledge for action, praxis. Catalytic authenticity documents relevant knowledge that actively affects the lives of the participants and their shared contextual experience. Some degree of rethinking or reshaping, as a result of the teaching/learning process, should occur. If knowledge is power, then powerful participants should be enabled to use their voices in collaboration for change.

In many cases this empowerment process has not come full circle, or the consequences have not unfolded sufficiently when the inquiry is terminated to be able to warrant this aspect of authenticity. Generally, at the conclusion of the inquiry it will be impossible, either due to paradigmatic assumptions or because of contextual complexity, to assert or claim that a change is the result of the inquiry process in a cause/effect sense. But in follow up, the inquirer may hear from participants about their sense of enhanced possibilities for change. Without follow up, evidence of collaboration created by the hermeneutic circle can be said to support the change possibilities envisioned by this dimension of constructivist rigor.

Tactical Authenticity

Tactical authenticity holds the inquirer and the constructivist process not just to a change standard, but the change must be effective from the points of view of the stakeholders. There must be desired change due to the empowerment or redistribution of power among the stakeholders. Here, again, subsequent contact in the context will be necessary to assess the degree to which this standard was met.

Establishing Authenticity

Very little of specific guidance is found in the literature regarding strategies and techniques for meeting each of the above criteria. Most are yet to be devised. Constructivists have been experimenting with ways in which these criteria and their warrants (for the purpose of auditing) might be developed (see Green et al., 1988; Manning, 1997; Rodwell & Byers, 1997). The following is based on ideas gleaned from students and researchers currently involved in this aspect of the methodology's evolution.

Elements Redundant with Trustworthiness

Due to the relationship between the quality of a research product and the quality of a research process, at least to some degree, demonstration of elements of trustworthiness will also serve the purposes of authenticity. The following are examples of how warrants in trustworthiness also can act as warrants in authenticity.

Credibility in understanding the depth and scope of the issues involved will ensure that a balance of the various views, *fairness,* has also been established. Credibility also suggests that increased awareness about the complexity of the issues is achieved. With this, *ontological authenticity* can be asserted. If a quality hermeneutic circle has been constructed to achieve credibility, an increased understanding of the constructions of others also should have developed, thus assuring that *educative authenticity* has occurred.

Dependability will demonstrate the appropriateness of methodological shifts that occurred during the emergent process. Appropriateness can be asserted if all perspectives were allowed to have voice and if the data analysis and report represent the multiplicity of perspectives, regardless of assigned or inferred power. If this is demonstrated via participant and data inclusion, then *fairness* is also demonstrated.

Confirmability demonstrates that the findings are grounded in the data. Credibility also establishes that the results are related to the participants and are not just a reflection of the inquirer's point of view. A recognition of the salience of the participants' warranting of the accuracy of the final product is also a measure of *fairness.*

Newly Emerging Mechanisms

Clearly, all dimensions of authenticity cannot be demonstrated through trustworthiness, the rigor that attests to the quality of the research product. Authenticity is still in development, so what follows are examples and ideas that have been utilized to operationalize the intent of each aspect of authenticity. The reader is encouraged to experiment with these or other strategies to both ensure and demonstrate authenticity. Certainly, in this aspect of the methodology, there is a need to work together to make this empowerment dimension real and realizable in an emergent, context dependent inquiry.

Fairness strategies attend to sampling and data collection methods to ensure that all stakeholders have an equal voice and that the case study presents a balanced view. This begins with fully informed consent to participate and continues with real and persistent member checking and negotiation throughout the process. Negotiation to achieve a balanced view is necessary. It should be an open process, carried out with skilled bargainers from equal positions of power, in which all participants have complete information. The negotiation should follow rules established and approved through prenegotiation (Lincoln & Guba, 1986). There should be a grievance mechanism for both the process and the product that is known and accessible to all for use by participants when they feel that they or their perspectives have been unfairly treated.

Though most inquirers ensure that member checking occurs continuously among those who participate in the investigation, most constructivists do not have the time and resources to have all participants involved in the final grand member check of the final product. This is unfortunate, because completing a full, final, member checking process is an excellent support to fairness. If a less than total final member check is undertaken, then representative stakeholders, agreed upon by the stakeholding group they represent, must be included to ensure fairness in the final negotiation of the case study product.

To ensure that equal capabilities exist in all the negotiation processes, including the hermeneutic circle, attention must be given to race, class, gender, and special needs issues. This attention might take the form of preferring individual interviews over group forums, or, if a group process is necessary, ensuring that groups are not composed of individuals with varying degrees of power. Attention to power inequalities might also include managing how the data unfold by moving from the least to the most formally powerful participant. For example, a study of welfare reform might start data collection at the level of the recipients and move only to the level of state welfare authorities at the later stages of data construction. This allows the voice of the least empowered to be heard first, without the power filter of others.

Another strategy might be to allow a participant's story to unfold in other ways than verbally. Enactments, music, or drawings can help participants articulate what they want to say. These products of the construction process must also be shared for inclusion in the group construction.

Two major warrants of fairness include the product of the process and the voices of the participants regarding the process. If evenhanded representation of all viewpoints is clear in the case study, and if the testimonials of the participants indicate that they felt included, respected, and heard, then there is a good chance that the process was fair.

Strategies to demonstrate *ontological authenticity* go beyond those that demonstrate fairness. Ontological authenticity must show that participants have learned more about themselves and others in the context of the inquiry. Continuous dialectical conversation creates this education and can demonstrate this aspect of authenticity. Ensuring that conversations are dialectical is important, because education for empowerment through consciousness raising is not didactic. No one is more in charge and more capable to teach than another, so an adult education model, andragogy (see Darkewald, 1982; Knowles, 1962, 1980, 1984, 1990), is a more appropriate model to create mutual teaching and learning as described by Freire (1994). Absence of a didactic style can be traced in the expanded field notes. In addition, evidence of the use of andragogy should appear in the methodological journal.

Dialogic strategies should be introduced in each interview so that participants investigate each others' thinking. Inquiring conversations, sustaining conversations, and partnership conversations (Lambert et al., 1995) of the Socratic method should be modeled in data collection. That way the participants learn to participate in the circular questioning that includes shared intentions, search for sensemaking and understanding, respectful listening, and reflection. With the feedback of these investigatory forays, rethinking to overcome biases, superstitions, and naiveté move participants to new assumptions and potential change.

Short of observing the hermeneutic dialectic in action, warrants of dialogic strategies to enhance ontological authentication could include data from member checks and testimony of participants. Participant responses, including those of the researcher, should show an appreciation of how complex the issue under investigation is. Statements about possession of a better understanding of self and others are adequate warrants that consciousness raising has occurred.

A third aspect of process rigor, *educative authenticity*, involves appreciation and respect for others' constructions. It begins with being attuned to the language of the concrete situation in which the participants operate. All participants must be helped to understand the structural conditions in which the thoughts and language of the participants are dialectically framed (Freire, 1994). Coming to an understanding of alternative perspectives means gaining an appreciation of the participants' perceived limits and freedoms.

The inquirer aids in developing all participants' appreciation of individual cognitive and emotional bounding of lived experience by helping to share the stories and by acting as an interpretive bridge between stories (Rodwell & Blankenbaker, 1992). This may mean translating the words from one framework to another, such as helping city children to understand the words of the children who live in the mountain "hollers." At times, the researcher does not have sufficient ethnic or cultural competence to perform this role competently. In those cases, the use of a cultural interpreter, in addition to the inquiry's peer reviewer, is warranted for advice giving and skill development.

Understanding how perceptions curb or limit and how they enhance or empower is important with educative authenticity. At issue is the understanding of the rootedness of different perspectives in values and experience. There is no real intention to force a change in beliefs, attitudes, or behaviors, nor should participants feel guilty about them, or feel compelled to adopt the values or experiences of others. The intention is to simply (or not so simply) appreciate them and understand their sources.

The continual circling of communication in the dialectic hermeneutic can achieve individual consciousness about personal values and experiences as well as appreciation and understanding of the values and experiences of others. Respectful rendering of perspectives must be apparent in the case report. Evidence that the inquirer has incorporated ideas from one perspective into the conversation with individuals from another perspective, as demonstrated in the field notes, is a beginning measure of educative authentication, at least on the part of the inquirer. When these field notes also demonstrate that other participants are forging accommodations to other viewpoints, then full educative authenticity is apparent. If evidence of these accommodations is not apparent in the data collection phase, it may be present as testimonials as the inquiry process is terminating in the final member check.

Catalytic authenticity results when people in concert produce and act on new ideas. Catalytic authenticity captures the praxis dimension of knowledge. According to Freire (1994), "there is no true word that is not at the same time a praxis. Thus, to speak a true word is to transform the world" (p. 68). Reflection on meaning is an action, but understanding meaning should also generate at least the consideration that improvement in the status quo is possible. Change in this process is inevitable, because participation in knowing is participation in change. It is praxis. When knowledge is created, a qualitative change occurs. It is felt, even if it cannot, as yet, be measured.

The inquirer facilitates praxis by continuing the circular questioning of the hermeneutic circle for all to consider not just what has been constructed, but also what might "be" constructed. Praxis continues with the dissemination of the case report. Reading and discussion of the case report might be sufficient to stimulate a rethinking among the inquiry participants and other consumers of the report that can lead to personal and contextual change.

Testimonials which suggest that respondents have never approached the issue in this way, or that they now have new insights as to the need to make some changes in the organization, the context, their communication style, what they expect, and so forth, would be a demonstration of catalytic authenticity. Openness to collaboration and to making change should be part of the testimonials. Evidence of changing attitudes, ideas about reform, or change in policies or in their implementation all serve as warrants for catalytic authentication.

Finally, *tactical authenticity,* or effective change, represents the greatest challenge for a time-bounded inquiry. For example, at the point of termination, the inquirer will not know if the system changes contemplated in the investigation of child abuse will result in a more effective treatment of at risk children and their families. There may not be real indications that the achievement of federal goals related to homelessness, special education, or welfare independence have been achieved.

What is possible is to determine for whom the research has been empowering or impoverishing. If all of the participants are better off because of having participated in the process and are able to provide evidence to demonstrate this, then there is hope that the real emancipatory elements of the inquiry have been implemented. There is the possibility that effective change will develop as the consequence of the redistribution of power and information and that it will continue to reverberate among the participants and throughout the context of the inquiry. Whether these possibilities will actually emerge is impossible to determine at the time that the inquiry is terminated. Unfortunately (or fortunately, depending upon your perspective), return to the context at a later date is probably the only viable way to directly document tactical authentication.

The challenge of creating a framework for managing rigor while attending to the uniqueness of each inquiry experience is great, since a specific set of standards themselves would work against the results that constructivist research hopes to achieve—unique, evenhanded understanding within a specific environment. Fixed standards will not allow for uniqueness to emerge, but a range of elements to consider will ensure that the investigator at least asks the right questions to ensure that, to the degree possible, all dimensions of trustworthiness and authenticity have been addressed. The reader is encouraged to participate in the development of these questions to guide the research practice.

Discussion Questions

What follows are real problem situations in constructivist research that involved establishing, maintaining, or documenting trustworthiness and authenticity. Test your knowledge and understanding of the criteria by developing a strategic response to each situation posed.

1. You have decided to undertake an inquiry into the meaning of child neglect and want to see how it might differ in different contexts. You decide to ask the major stakeholders: families, judges, law enforcement officers, lawyers, and social workers about this in urban, suburban, and rural environments. When you begin the inquiry, you discover that there are many types of parents who should be included, like neglecting, nonneglecting, those who have had formal charges, and those who see themselves as neglecting, but have never been charged. You fear the number

of participants will double, making the research financially
unfeasible. What issues must you consider in order to justify
changing the sampling from three sites to two while still maintaining constructivist rigor? How would you make and justify the
decision? Where would you record your thinking and your
decision?

2. You are in the midst of data collection regarding the role of
   parents in early intervention services and you realize that you
   have been prevented from accessing stakeholders who might have
   perspectives that are different from those of the program
   director's. You need to access participants differently. What
   should you do? What information would you record about this in
   your reflexive journal and what would be appropriate for the
   methodological journal?

3. You have taken five pages of notes in an interview with a parent
   whose son is in a detention facility. You have recorded key words
   about the mother's perspective about how she sees her child's
   treatment. What will you do to move from the rough notes to
   expanded field notes to allow auditor tracking backward to the
   raw data?

4. You have completed the analysis of the meaning of welfare reform. You have written a draft case report and have begun the
   process of negotiating the final product. After several participants
   had a chance to read your report you begin getting feedback like
   "I never thought about this before"; "Now I understand why my
   client took offense to what I was saying"; "I can't believe that I
   said this at the beginning of this process. I certainly don't think
   that way now"; "Based on the questions you asked I have re-
   thought the way I approach my clients"; "Because of the information you shared with me from others in the project, I have decided to change . . ." Which of these responses can be used to
   document ontological, educative, or catalytic authenticity?

CHAPTER 6

Constructivist Data Collection

Chapter Contents in Brief

Elements in determining instrumentation
Data collection mechanisms including: the interview, nonverbal data,
  focus groups, nonhuman data sources, and methods of data
  enhancement
The role and use of tacit knowledge
Recording and data storage
Data collection links to social work practice

Constructivist research has as an important goal the creation or construction of meaning. Meaning involves statements about characteristics and presumed relationships in a particular time and context. These statements are constructed principally through words. Even though behaviors and their observation feature in qualitative data, words are the basis of meaning shaping and construction. It is through words that the meaning of behaviors and of other words are negotiated. Words are also the basis of the data deconstruction for analysis and reconstruction in the case study. It is with words that the melange of descriptors about the subject and its context are created for the final case report. Therefore, words are the primary data sources for most aspects of constructivist research. Data collection and management, words for meaning making, are important in all phases of the inquiry, from orientation and overview, through more focused data collection, to the preparation and testing of the final product.

This chapter will focus on the major considerations of word management, data access, and recording processes for meaning construction. For most constructivists, this stage of the inquiry is the most exciting and invigorating. But sometimes, the fun of creating relationships through words creates challenges in collecting or assembling data, and asking the questions of the data that allow meaning to emerge. Many times the interpersonal relationships that develop in the process take precedence over the disciplined approach to maintaining the structured system that must also develop to protect the rigor of the process. This chapter will address the safeguards and skills necessary to ensure that the individual researcher can enjoy the fun of human connectedness, while also implementing rigorously the data collection/construction aspects of a constructivist process.

Determining the Instrumentation

Clearly, the human instrument will be the major data collection tool in constructivist inquiry, but this data collection process involves more than people just talking. It is a structured, thoughtful process that must have form in order to produce meaningful results. This section discusses the issues that must be taken into account as the questioning process evolves to its most sophisticated format.

Foreshadowed Questions and Context Imbeddedness

Foreshadowed questions begin the data gathering, but how are they constructed and how do they change shape in the context and as the process develops? Concepts and their meaning in relationship are the cornerstones of a socially constructed reality and of constructivist inquiry. Concepts are always part of the specific language of the context within which they are constructed. Therefore, foreshadowed questions about the concepts to be investigated grow out of the inquirer's context and experience.

Foreshadowed questions are the inquirer's questions. They emerge from the researcher's knowledge of the technical vocabulary in the field; from review of documents, academic literature, books, articles; from personal experience, including preliminary interviews and participant observations; and from tacit knowledge. They are a product of the inquirer's personal/autobiographical history, and conceptual work, and they are the tentative assumptions that guide the initial steps into the inquiry context.

The researcher has used an inductive stance to explore all that he or she knows, including what seems to be missing or "wrong." These questions will inevitably suggest the "hunches" about what the researcher expects to be important in the sensemaking of the inquiry. This is not a theory to be tested, simply a framework from which to start.

The work in shaping the research question moves from the real world of the researcher's personal observations, dilemmas, and questions to the real world of the lived experience of the stakeholders, and finally to the initial inquiry questions. This information in the specifics of the stakeholders' language will result in the working hypotheses that will serve to shape the meaning making. Working hypotheses (Lincoln & Guba, 1985) are questions developed in the context of the inquiry. They take shape based on what is important to all those who are participating in the inquiry. This means, then, that working hypotheses remain "working." They must remain fluid in order to allow the process to emerge. They, like conversational guides that will be developed in a later section, remain in flux, never becoming rigid, just more focused.

Accessing Data

The most skilled data collector armed with well constructed foreshadowed questions will go nowhere without access to individuals and groups who have an interest in the subject or problem that the inquirer wishes to investigate. The beginning constructivist may choose to evolve the study in the context in which the foreshadowed questions were developed. The agency or community where the constructivist lives or works might be a place to begin, because access appears easy. But this ease of access may mean that the researcher's potential as a competent inquirer is initially bounded by the view that others have from previous associations with the researcher. In this case, access will require demonstration of competence to undertake the inquiry and persistence in overcoming resistance and gaining acceptance in a new role, that of constructivist researcher.

Whether you are known to the environment or an outsider, entry will depend on the cooperation of people inside. To achieve access to data and data sources, the inquirer must count on friends, colleagues, direct and indirect connections, and personal and professional networks for help. The researcher must always remain cognizant about why people are helping. It may be because friends just want to help you out, or it may be in service of someone's political agenda. In many cases, help must be taken in order to access environments in which the inquirer is a stranger, but care should be taken to avoid the situation where the politics of the access come with so many strings attached that honest communication becomes impossible. For example, it is okay to accept the help of the local juvenile judge in identifying who might be interested in investigating neglect, but understanding those connections, relationships, debts, and obligations will help to put what is said by those accessed in context. Persistence here is important to get at real, honest conversation.

Access is most difficult when the researcher proposes crossing class, cultural, or racial boundaries. A connection must be established to allow access across boundaries. This connection may occur as a result of inquirer participant observation with the goal of becoming familiar with the setting and the vocabulary across the boundary. The bridge or connection may be made by a "cultural interpreter" who knows and trusts you and is known and trusted in the context. This individual can provide initial access, but the inquirer must maintain that access.

Maintaining access requires establishing your competence to undertake the inquiry. A "know nothing" might be accepted as a tourist, but will not be given access to personal, potentially sensitive information. The inquirer must demonstrate "acceptable incompetence" (Lofland & Lofland, 1995, p. 53). The inquirer must know enough that participants can trust him or her to act knowledgeably, but not so much to suggest that teaching/learning is not possible. The inquirer must be nonthreatening and respectful about the people and the environment, but wise enough and persistent enough to manage the political undertow, or to move on when politics make it no longer possible.

If a team is used in data collection, securing team access will have its own challenges. Although team research has the advantage of more data collection and meaning makers, it is also more complicated. The team's sheer numbers may be overwhelming to the environment. Acceptance of the team will be based on acceptance of each individual in the team. Efforts to gain acceptance require assurance that the actions and behaviors of each individual is acceptable. The individual inquirer loses control of specific relationships in favor of a group effort to get along. From our perspective, the advantage of richer data gathering must far outweigh the access, social relationship, and data overload aspects of team research for it to be considered.[1]

Determining Focus and Structure

This discussion regarding focus assumes that the preliminary work of focusing the inquiry has been accomplished. The topic of the inquiry should be described succinctly enough to develop the direction of the research. In addition, it assumes that paradigm congruence has been established and that a constructivist perspective, using constructivist methods, has been determined to be most appropriate for pursuing the topic. Finally, the following discussion also assumes that, to some degree, feasibility has been determined. At a minimum, from the inquirer's position, there are sufficient time and resources to allow the final focus of the inquiry to emerge.

The foreshadowed questions based on the inquirer's personal intuitions, thoughts, and personal theories shape the original focus of the inquiry. This conceptualizing will give the initial impetus to the decisions about where to go, what to look for, from whom, and how to ask questions. However, this original focus must be tentative. Even the decision about whether the research will involve pure research, program evaluation, or policy analysis remains context dependent and evolves with the research.

Final focus, sampling, and site selection will be determined by how the working hypotheses develop in the context of the investigation. Because the process is ever emerging, all these decisions, including the shape of the working hypotheses, remain relatively unstable. All elements of the inquiry are in constant flux until stability is declared, when it becomes time to terminate the process and seek closure through the final report. This lack of predictability and the absolute need for all elements to emerge and be grounded in the context of the inquiry means that structure is achieved through the elements that are introduced to assure trustworthiness and authenticity. It is only through these efforts of assuring rigor that true, congruent structure emerges.

Using Standardized Instruments

Out of this and earlier discussions of emergence, it should be clear that a high degree of circumspection is necessary when deciding to use any standardized instrument as a constructivist data collection mechanism. Standardized instruments are built on assumptions and rigor needs that are contrary to the assumptions and needs in constructivist inquiry. Since any data collection technique should relate to the information sought, the use of standardized instruments should be minimal, because they are designed to eliminate the very type of information of interest to the constructivist. Standardized instruments are assumed to be stable across time and context and are interested in issues of distribution across a sample of a population, whereas constructivist inquiry seeks the in-the-moment uniqueness of perspective.

Questionnaires, surveys, projective techniques, and other standardized tools lose their power when they are used across paradigms. To be useful as a guide to conversations or observations, they will need to be changed to reflect the particulars of the setting. Validity and reliability for generalizability (the purpose for which they are designed) are destroyed when the instrument is changed or modified. In order to avoid the murk that develops when multiple paradigms are used to shape multiple expectations in a research project, predeveloped instruments should be avoided. The only exception might be, following Marx's suggestion (as cited in Silverman, 1985, p. 195), as a didactic and political instrument to generate dialogue rather than to provide researchers with packaged information.

Data Collection

The first step in developing the inquiry instrumentation is determining which type of word data collection method is most appropriate for the initial stages of the inquiry process. Because constructivism is intent on mutual shaping, conversations about the problem or subject of interest are preferred. The constructivist interview is the primary data collection mechanism, but other methods can be used interactively with interviews or as stand alone sources of information at different stages of the inquiry. The following provides a step-by-step discussion of how to implement each method. When important, the opportunities and challenges are also provided to aid the inquirer in later context-based decision making regarding how to collect data.

It is in the area of techniques that the new constructivist researcher will find many useful texts describing qualitative methods. Many will provide excellent ideas for approaches and processes of data collection. In fact, the appendix of annotated resources to this text has been developed to provide just such material for further reading. As the beginning researcher searches for details on techniques, attention should be given to ensure that the assumptions undergirding the techniques are compatible with constructivist assumptions.

The Interview

The constructivist interview is a context-embedded conversation with a purpose (Kahn & Cannell, 1957, p. 149). There is an agenda for the talk. Both the purpose and the context shape "what" will be said. The sampling and selection of the individual to be interviewed will determine "how" it will be said. The interview will generally be reciprocal, face-to-face, one-on-one, and in person.

Telephone interviews are possible but not preferred, due to the loss of important nonverbal information and visual cues essential for understanding and meaning making. Telephone interviews with unknown participants are not conducive to the relationship building necessary for honest co-construction, but may be useful for quick follow-up in an abbreviated member-checking procedure.

From time to time group processes may evolve when unexpected additional individuals include themselves in an interview session. Flexibility will be necessary to assure control of complexity and productivity when more than one person is engaged in an interview. Details of group interviews will be considered later in this section in the focus group discussion.

To be productive, the conversation should be in the context of a nurturing environment (everyone should be comfortable) and should involve a mutual search for shared meaning. The search will involve surfacing remembrances and reflections of the past; mutual revelations of ideas and information, combined with respectful listening, in a search for meaning in the present. None of these efforts can conclude productively in meaning making without a safe, respectful environment within which to converse.

INTERVIEW GUIDE   Most times this process is managed with what Rubin and Rubin (1995) call a "conversational guide" (p. 161) that has been customized for each interview and evolves throughout the emergent design. The structure of the guide really depends on the cognitive style and preferences of the interviewer. It can be a checklist of concepts to be covered; complete questions can be fully written; or an outline can be used with headings and subheadings that can serve to test concept relationships. Whatever is comfortable for the interviewer will work to aid in guiding the process. It also serves to record what was explored and what was not, from interview to interview. Experienced constructivists update their preferred conversational guide throughout the data collection. These updates tend to become themes for persistent observation. Table 6–1 shows the themes that evolved in a two-site study of neglect. They are presented in the order that they emerged in the two environments. These themes shaped the conversations with individuals, so that one respondent would define, shape, or reject a concept in relation to what the inquirer interjected based on prior information.

TABLE 6–1

Concepts Used in Persistent Observation

Site # 1	Site #2
Parents' responsibility factor	Culture
Culture	Chronicity
Chronicity	Safety
Safety	Resource availability
Willful neglect	Risk
Poverty	Intent
Minimum standards	Long-term vs. short-term placement
Societal neglect	Parents as cause—blaming
Emotional neglect	Emotional neglect
Resource availability	Societal neglect
Parents' rights	Professional liability
Parents as cause	Neglect with something else
Level of proof	Women and neglect
Danger	The decision to remove
Alcohol and neglect	Local protection system
Best interest	Middle-class neglect
Short-term vs. long-term placement	Poverty
	Parental attitude
	Making middle-class kids out of foster kids
	System's neglect
	Social worker's attitude
	Minimum standards
	Harm
	Child's responsibility

The guide, regardless of form, is always in flux. As the process moves toward more sophistication, some concepts and connections grow while others diminish in interest. As the collection process draws to a close, the guide becomes more and more focused, but is never rigidly applied.

ETHICS   Before considering the data collection aspects of this "truth-seeking," the ethical dimensions of the conversation should be established. Before the interview, a fully negotiated, fully informed consent is necessary. The fairness aspect of authenticity, in addition to the concern for ethical practice, requires that this is not simply a matter of the

ipant's reading and signing the consent form, but includes the in-
: ascertaining that the participant is fully aware of the potential and
in the process, is voluntarily participating, and is ready, willing, and
to provide the time and energy that the inquiry will require.

This negotiation of consent may occur at a different time than the
ial data collection. If it does, it will add to the inquirer's preparation
the interview. Prior to entering into data collection, the inquirer
should become as fully informed as possible about the participant. Why is
this individual important to the process? What might be his or her needs
in the process? Also important for new constructivists might be practicing the interview in order to sense how it might unfold and how best to
collect the data provided. Certainly, the inquirer should be clear about the
foreshadowed questions or the themes that should be the focus of the
time spent together.

STRUCTURE PREPARATION   should involve the general content and sequence of the questions in the context of the participants' language. This
becomes the individualization of the conversational guide. Knowledge
about general verbal capacity and language style of the participant is important in order to have real communication, but a skilled interviewer
who enters the interview without this information will soon make the
necessary adjustments to his or her own communication style or pattern.

Other logistical issues are important for stage setting and relationship building. They are also generally overlooked in social research. Social
workers familiar with standard social casework texts (see Carkhuff, 1969;
Cormier & Cormier, 1979; Fischer, 1978; Hepworth & Larsen, 1993;
Shulman, 1984) will recognize the importance of deciding on the inquirer's appropriate dress, the role to be assumed, and the level of formality to be maintained in order to really hear the participant and vice versa.
Confirming the time and place of the interview is a matter of courtesy
and respect. This should be done with each participant.

Setting the tone of the interview is important to assure productivity.
Broad, universal, overview questions, called "grand tour" by Spradley
(1979) should be used initially to give the respondent practice in the process. Using an inquiry about child neglect, for example, initial discussion
could begin with the idea that children require protection and the type of
protections that might be expected. Only after these preliminary questions were discussed would the interview begin to focus on what constitutes child neglect. The initial questions should also relax the atmosphere
and help the individual provide thoughtful information about his or her
view of the subject of the inquiry.

The inquirer is responsible for establishing the pace and managing the productivity of the interchange. More and more specific questions should occur as the interview moves along in order to gain clarity or to develop points. Probes and directed cues should be used for more information. For example, "pumps" like "tell me more about . . ." should be utilized to encourage the creation of more information. It is also important to ask for examples if they do not come spontaneously in order to be certain that the inquirer understands precise meaning. In addition, calls for reactions or questions to embellish or extend information should also occur. In short, the inquirer dialogues, inquires, sustains the conversation, becomes a partner in meaning generation, and finally, terminates and closes the activity.

Termination and closure occur when the interview has ceased to be productive or the information is redundant. Another time to terminate is when both the interviewer and the participant display fatigue, or when a response seems guarded or distracted. Closure should occur by the investigator summarizing what is believed to have been said while asking the participant to verify, amend, and extend the constructions of the inquirer. Before the interview is completed, each respondent should be asked to assess the precision and faithfulness of the interviewer's constructions (a member check). When necessary, he or she should add new or refined information. A record in the field journals and expanded field journals should be made of the participant's confirmation and verification of the data.

As a part of the hermeneutic activities, the participant may be asked to provide questions that might be asked of other specific participants or stakeholding groups. For the purposes of sampling, other nominations of potential inquiry participants should also be elicited from the participants.[2]

Nonverbal Data and Focused Observation

The major source of nonverbal data, that "listening with the eye and ear" (Kadushin, 1990), is the constructivist interview. Meaning of the words is enhanced by attention to timing, smell, touch, body language, and so forth. It is important to remember that information is contained in the silences. Often, nonverbal cues are the clues that further clarification is needed.

Nonverbal data are also available through organized efforts in observation. These observations range in type from complete participation with no data collection to complete observation with no participation and only data collection. In this range of observation, according to Denzin (1970), the inquirer, in greater or less formality, shares in the lives and experiences of the participants, while attempting to learn the symbolic world in which the problem is being investigated.

Complete participation and complete observation both focus on the viewpoint of the stakeholders and occur in the context of their interactions. Both are processes that should occur over time, but generally do not involve structured data gathering or recording. Either type of data collection can be a useful part of a field strategy. Either can triangulate with document analysis, and interviews, not for validation purposes, but as an extension of information.

Participant observation is preferred by constructivists over complete observation or complete participation. Participant observation is preferred because the data is created in relationship and the inquirer can check for meaning in the moment, a process not possible when complete observation is the activity. Complete participation, where the inquirer's role is concealed from the participants, is totally rejected on ethical grounds for constructivists. The complete observer, where the role of the researcher is not known, is also rejected on the same grounds. Complete observation is only acceptable when the observed know of the observation and have consented to it for specific information collection. An example of an acceptable complete observation might be during an evaluation of family preservation services when the inquirer, the home-based therapists, and the family agree to have the researcher "shadow" a session in the home to get a sense of what occurs and how it "feels."

Constructivist participant observation must be a many-sided, long-term relationship with those being observed. It includes weaving a process of looking, listening, watching, and asking into the natural context of the observation. Lofland and Lofland (1995) see a real mutuality between participant observations and interviewing because in many cases the details of the social situations that are being observed only make sense after an intensive interview.

The difficulty of meaning making when the inquirer is involved in the role of both a participant and an observer has been thoroughly discussed by Lincoln & Guba (1985). For them it is difficult to be both a legitimate member of an environment and an observer of it for logistical and balance reasons. If the act of data collection in the context of a face-to-face interview is daunting, imagine the challenges of data collecting while actually participating in the activities being observed.

Data should be collected in an observation in ways that parallel the interviews. There should be some sort of guide or purpose for the observation. It is important to remember that the observation may take different forms at different stages of the inquiry. As the process becomes more focused, so, too, will the observations. Whatever guide is used for data collection should be shaped by what is originally intended to be accomplished, while allowing for the collection of other interesting, surprising, or otherwise meaningful information. As in an interview, the nonverbal information is as important as the spoken data. Therefore, it, too, should be collected and recorded in some expanded form as soon as possible after the observation. Here, again, the tendency for a new constructivist will be to wish to audio- or videotape the activities. The same warnings apply for observations as with interviewing and relate to the logistics of transcriptions and the need to guard against data overload for the next stages of data deconstruction.

Actually, in most cases, the data from observations are not entered into the raw data that will be unitized for analysis. Instead, it will be used in "background" to extend depth and scope in the meaning making and reconstruction.[3]

Focus Groups

A natural relationship is hard to establish in a group. For this reason, focus groups in their purest form are difficult for constructivist data collection. In a traditional focus group, the inquirer acts as group leader and uses group dynamics and group communication skills to manage a conversation with from 6 to 12 participants for about an hour (Morgan, 1988). Focus groups were first developed in the private, commercial sector to enhance market research. They have now become a standard method of public and nonprofit sector research, since they allow for major "chunks" of data to be collected in a short time with little technical skills or resources needed.

STRUCTURE   With respect to structure, focus groups are consistent with emergence in that, according to Krueger (1994), there is no "right way" to conduct a focus group or analyze the data that results. Mutual shaping does occur as participants' ideas are sparked off one another. In this "sparking," communication and self-disclosure are stimulated. Participants do influence each other in meaning making. In this regard, focus-group processes are consistent with the hermeneutic dialectic of meaning making. It might be said that a well-developed focus group can actually become a face-to-face hermeneutic circle of the type described in Chapter 4.

Participants in the group should be selected in the same way as other samples in constructivist inquiry, with attention to maximum variation while enhancing fairness. The size should be small enough to allow everyone to have voice, but large enough to ensure diversity. The decision to use a focus group for data collection will be related, as are other data collection decisions, to the type of data that is desired. Due to the far-ranging data that tend to be produced in focus groups when the groups are not bounded by a focus on a program, a product, or an organizational context, the usefulness of such groups in program evaluation or policy analysis is more likely than in the "pure" investigation of a problem or concept. Focus groups in programs and policies can be used before, during, and after the program or policy has been implemented.

PLANNING   As with an interview, planning the focus group is critical for success. The purpose must be clear and consistent with the focus of the constructivist inquiry. Kreuger (1994, pp. 44–45), has identified two circumstances when focus groups are particularly congruent with constructivist inquiry. A focus group can be used when there is a communication or understanding gap between groups or categories of peoples, or when insight is needed about complicated topics with multifaceted concerns. He also suggests times when focus groups should not be selected, for example, when the environment is emotionally charged and more data collection is likely to intensify the conflict; when control over critical aspects of the study has been lost to such an extent that other agendas are being served by the inquiry; or when confidentiality of sensitive information cannot be ensured. From a constructivist perspective, we would add, when evenhanded treatment and equal chance at participation cannot be guaranteed.

Kreuger also provides a good discussion of the types of questions used in a focus group, including opening questions that break the ice and identify what commonalities exist in the group. These are followed by introductory questions that introduce the general topic of conversation, prepare the group for competent participation, and encourage conversation and interaction among the participants. Transition questions move the group to the question of interest by showing participants how others view the topic. Usually two to five key questions guide the data collection. Ending questions bring the process to closure by summing things up, asking for final positions if consensus has not been achieved, or asking for final questions. For a constructivist inquiry, these final questions might be used as working hypotheses for subsequent group or individual activities. It is during the final stage of the focus group that themes are tested and checked in a member checking process.

It should be clear that the role of the observer/moderator in focus groups is fraught with the same or greater challenges than with participant observations. In this case, data loss can be a problem without at least a second person to record field notes. When focus groups are selected as a data collection process, then it is likely that tape recordings will be necessary. The same caveats exist with recordings as in other environments where recording may be selected. Remember that permission to record is part of establishing fully informed consent.[4]

On-line Data Collection

A relatively new opportunity for data collection comes from cyberspace. In recent years, the Internet has been an excellent, rich, and quick resource for information collection for literature reviews. With the advent of on-line services like America On Line or Compuserve, "in the moment" conversations in "chat rooms" are now possible. For example, a recent experience of research about chronic wounds indicates that on-line participants are a very rich additional source of information for constructivist inquiry. In fact, stakeholders who might not ever be accessed by traditional means can make themselves available via a modem. This may also be a productive means of including the introverted or the fearful participant in a constructivist inquiry.

Clearly, this type of data collection faces the same challenges as telephone interviews. There is an absence of affective data. There is also an anonymity that might enhance or impede honest conversations. There is no real way to know that the participants are who they say they are. There is no real way to pursue indirect clues of subtle meaning. Certainly the inquirer will know that a participant is upset when he or she "flames" by printing in capital letters, but beyond this the subtleties end. On the other hand, stakeholders who might not be competent to engage in a face-to-face conversation can do so via computer. Those without voices to speak can type. Those who cannot use a keyboard can create words by blowing through a straw on the computer. However, one should not overlook a major bias of on-line inquiry. Access to participation remains heavily class based and limited to only those who can afford computers and Internet access.

This on-line data source is virtually untapped. At this stage of technique development, it is recommended that on-line information be used to extend data and understanding in the same way that observations might be used. At most, in a multisite investigation one site might be a Web site, while the others remain more traditionally defined contexts.

Nonhuman Data Sources

Records and documents present some of the same challenges for constructivist data collection as standardized instruments, but for different reasons. Rarely is a document or record an outgrowth of the constructivist inquiry. Instead, they are usually developed to serve another, and sometimes unknown, agenda. Because of this, they no more reflect the uniqueness of the inquiry than does a standardized instrument. On the other hand, both can supplement observations and interviews. They can be rich reflections of the values and beliefs of the participant stakeholders. They can be helpful to garner greater understanding of the people and the setting.

As such, they can serve as background to enrich or supplement the other constructivist methods. They can be content analyzed for the presence of material that can supplement information acquired through the conversational guides used in interviews or observations. For example, using the concept "willful neglect" from Table 6–1, the inquirer could refer to client records to see if protective service investigators have operationalized it in their assessment of a case. They might refer to the policies and procedures documents to check for the existence of a concept and to verify whether or not it matches what was found in the record. This is done, not as validation, but to further understand the relevant aspects of the concept.[5]

Audiovisual material use as a data source is taken from traditional anthropology. It is a means of capturing the daily life of the group under investigation. Again, with the exception of an audio- or videotape of a participant observation or a tape of a focus group, it will be rare that films, photographs, or audio- or videotapes are produced in the process and context of the inquiry. The same limits and opportunities apply with this material as with records and documents.

Methods of Data Enhancement

The iterative process of meaning making in constructivism also means that data can be enriched after its original creation or collection. There are several processes that can be used to complete this sensemaking process, either during data collection or during analysis. Five strategies particularly suited to constructivist inquiry will be discussed. The first strategy, *filling patterns,* is undertaken through further interviews or observation when something is missing in the logic of the category system as a whole. For example, if the inquirer is investigating the meaning of mentoring with an at risk child, and the analysis does not include any information that might be included in a category such as "self-esteem," then the inquirer might return to the data sources to see if that part of the pattern can be developed.

The other strategies actually extend or expand the data. *Extension* is a way of expanding the data set in which the inquirer uses personal knowledge to develop further questions, conversations, or guides for examining documents, or for further reading. *Bridging* can be undertaken when what has been constructed seems disconnected. Further inquiry is undertaken to make the connections in the cognitive map. *Surfacing* is chosen when the inquirer is able to propose what ought to have been found that was not. The inquirer then becomes involved in further inquiry to verify the information with the participants. Finally, *member checking* can be used as data extension when, in addition to checking key points in an interview, or data collection, or data analysis, it is also used to supply more data or revise existing data.

The Role and Use of Tacit Knowledge

Verbal and nonverbal data are not the only way of knowing in constructivist inquiry. Intuition and other instinctive ways of knowing are central to constructivist research, not only in understanding the outside world, but also in comprehending the inner world of the constructivist researcher.

In Data Collection

Tacit knowledge in data collection is just like practice wisdom in clinical practice. It operates when the inquirer knows the meaning of the unstated and understands the meaning of the nonverbal without need of verification. Intuition operates when the inquirer knows what next questions are and what next steps need to be taken to enhance co-construction. Clearly, the tacit is most useful when it can be articulated. Articulation occurs with the stakeholders when checking to be sure what the inquirer thinks is "true" is really "true." Articulation also occurs in conversation with the peer debriefer when vague feelings and senses get "figured out."

In Reflexivity

The major role of the tacit occurs in reflexivity. First discussed by Garfinkel (1967), it involves doing and understanding. It is in the doing of the data collection that the understanding of the subject of interest is achieved. This understanding comes from the meaning-based methods of data collection discussed above. Reflexivity demonstrated in the reflective musings and in discussions in peer debriefing shows the open, continuous communication with all that surrounds the researcher in the context of the inquiry.

Recording and Storage of Data

Emergence means never really knowing what is important and what is irrelevant data to the inquiry until it is focused. Therefore, in constructivism, "corralling" the data collected is in many ways as important as collecting it. Capturing this continuous communication is a challenge. If the process really develops a problem-bounded focus, then the inquirer will not know in advance what should be collected. Hence, plans for recording and storage of data should be the most flexible possible. They must also be feasible because data collection, analysis, and storage begin with the research idea and must continue systematically until the final product is returned to the context of the investigation or rigor documentation is lost.

Even without the requirements for trustworthiness and an outside audit, many research record systems have been recommended (see for example, Bogdan & Biklen, 1982; Corsaro, 1981; Schatzman & Strauss, 1973), mostly for qualitative research, but a few have been offered for alternative paradigm research such as constructivism (Lincoln & Guba, 1985; Schwandt & Halpern, 1988). Because in constructivism each project is different and each inquirer develops and manages information differently, the exact form and structure of a system to ensure and to document trustworthiness must fit the cognitive style and management preferences of each inquirer. The following is a discussion of how to develop the major dimensions of the collection, recording, and archiving system along with examples of some of the most important for auditing. They are offered as exemplars only, not as models for replication in each and every project.

Journals

Discussion in Chapter 5 should have made clear the necessity of several journals in monitoring the quality of the process and product for the purposes of auditing. Most of these journals are not just important for accountability. They are essential to the management of the context imbeddedness of the data collection and analysis. They aid the researcher in determining the appropriate focus and structure of all relevant research strategies. Together, they help the researcher determine reasonable next steps. The documentation that follows should be seen not as the unfortunate tedium of a complex process, but as excellent resources for sensemaking and meaning construction. Constructivist research cannot match its potential without serious attention to all the mechanisms that follow.

Reflexive journals seek the "aha" of making tacit knowledge propositional. Their focus is on the researcher's role in the emergent inquiry. The reflexive journal should be a diary of the inquirer's journey through the project. In keeping this record, the inquirer will enter into a personal dialogic conversation in which underlying assumptions about the problem, the people, the context, and so forth are uncovered. Implications in the formulation and implementation of the study of personal assumptions, biases, or prejudices will be probed and explored. What occurs is a reflective conversation with oneself that investigates possible meanings from what is happening in relation to one's own values and interests.

The journal is used on a daily basis, or as needed. Use will ebb and flow as the process ebbs and flows. It will be essential in easing into the orientation and overview phase of the inquiry and very helpful as the inquirer begins to manage the chaos of multiple perspectives. It is useful for review and for further considerations as the inquirer moves into data deconstruction and reconstruction. Many times the major elements of the investigation's findings are contained in early musings in this journal. Tacit information has early on taken tentative propositional form. Figure 6–1 provides snippets of reflexive journal entries throughout a constructivist process to provide a flavor for what one constructivist found useful in self-management during an investigation.

FIGURE 6–1

Reflexive Journal Entry Examples

1–16   So far, I have not been turned down by anyone I have asked to participate. Everyone seems much more interested in neglect than I expected. This is particularly true for the parents. They aren't professionals, but they are still interested. It is very refreshing. It gives me energy.

2–5   Two things are fascinating about the interviews. Almost everyone is using examples to define their concepts or positions. Native Americans also seem to be a focus of attention. Are there community biases or community sensitivities?

3–21   After my last talk with (subject 1) and the interview with the sheriff, it appears that, in order to get the full picture in (site 2), I need to go in two other directions. I need to get into the school system and into the reservation. This may mean another 10–15 interviews. This makes me very nervous. I may never finish this within the time frame.

4–21   I wonder what it means when in both sites there is continual intermixing of abuse and neglect discussion. It's clear to me that to the respondents there is a clear conceptual difference, but it's almost as if they throw into the discussion something about abuse because they are more sure about it or because it is easier to talk about. It really is no wonder that some researchers pile it all together into maltreatment. It gets us off the intellectual hook.

5–9   I am very frustrated. I have had no energy to work on data cards. I am not going to make my goal of returning to (site 2) by the 18th of May. I don't think I'll ever get finished with this, mostly because I'm afraid I'll have no good information.

6–5   I'm done! At least I've finished the beginning stage. A strange thing with the (site 2) data is that there seem to be very few cross-referenced cards. The idea that (site 2) perspective is much less complex than (site 1) seems to continue to hold. I guess I'll double check my view of this next week.

7–1   For the first time (peer reviewer) understood the scope of the difficulty with so much information. For the first time he realized part of the reason for me having so much difficulty getting started telling these two stories. He doesn't know either how to set the context, tell personal stories, and still deal with the research question at hand. But he knows I can do it!

9–2   I still cannot confront the basic conceptual problem I have with the case study.

11–24   The stories are finished and now I must arrange for the audit. Who knows if the audit trail is sufficient to withstand the outside inspection. I feel that just asking for an outsider may be setting myself up for criticism because of differing standards. I wonder if I have made sufficient progress to call this research finished.

The first entries should include everything the inquirer "knows" about the subject about to be investigated. Everything that the inquirer thinks will be important to know is useful to include as well. Reflections on how the inquirer feels about what has been included is also helpful in the conversation with self, because it serves as the beginning of the self-monitoring that will continue throughout the process. Generally, this initial self-talk will help in shaping the foreshadowed questions that give entry into the inquiry process. But, remember, a foreshadowed question is a methodological decision and should find its way into the journal related to methodological decisions. The point is that reflection and methods really are related.

Once clarity about the next steps has been achieved through reflection, then methodological decisions and their justifications are recorded in the *methodological log*. It should include research questions, purposive sampling elements and their serial selection, analytic decisions, coding mechanisms, decision rules, category labels, and tentative ideas about the relationship between categories. Information about decisions regarding management of the hermeneutic circle should also be recorded for auditing purposes. Though it is difficult to audit the circle, the auditor can at least attest to the attention that was paid in order to assure quality. Figure 6–2 provides an example of how methodological decisions can be recorded and justified. When data collection is actually under way, the activity and movement might preclude persistent attention to journaling, but if anything should warrant daily entries for close monitoring of emergence, the methodological journal should. It is absolutely essential for a successful audit.

For both the journals discussed above, it is important to select a medium that is comfortable. Some constructivists prefer small spiral notebooks that fit easily into a purse, backpack, or attaché case. Others like to color-code notebooks so that by color the inquirer knows what information is contained within. Many constructivists have difficulty distinguishing between a reflexive entry and a method entry, so instead of maintaining two journals, one is kept; but methodological decisions are highlighted in order to aid the auditor in later work. Finally, some constructivists do not use journals at all, preferring to keep separate computer files of reflexive and methodological issues. There is one caveat regarding computer usage. The new constructivist must have facility with composing at the computer in order for the computer to be a reasonable choice for reflexive work.[6]

Formal data collection from interviews and observations is recorded in a series of *field journals*. Our discussion here will focus on our preferred method of data collection, which involves note-taking in the field and expansion after the field experience. We encourage even the first-time constructivist to consider this "low-tech" method because of its lack of dependence on environments conducive to higher technology. No electricity or working batteries are necessary. Data can even be collected in low light and with sound distractions. But more importantly, note taking is a mechanism for assuring that the human instrument is working to its highest potential in the moment with all skills and tacit and propositional

---

FIGURE 6–2

Methodological Journal Entry Examples

1–15   I will vary the interview process to accommodate the wishes of participants. Preference will be to interview in their work or home environment, but I'll talk to them wherever they will meet me. Also preference will be for individual interviews when I'm working with couples, but if they are nervous about that I'll try at least to see each person separately first and then together afterwards.

1–29   An additional page will be added to each interview explaining why each was chosen and the person's link to others in the study or to myself.

2–4   The following convention will be used to accomplish unitizing:
1. In the expanded journal each unit will be underlined and numbered.
2. Each unit will be entered on a 3 x 5 card in full language as recorded in the journal.
3. Each card will be coded in the following manner:
    a. Site (1, 2, 3)
    b. Respondent type (SW; GAL; J; DA; LEO; P; PON; PN)
    c. Interview number with that respondent (1, 2, 3 . . .)
    d. Interview number out of the total (1 of . . .)
    e. Number of the unit in the interview

3–24   Sampling in (site 2) will be extended to include key people in the school system and social workers from the reservations. The school system is being included because there appears to be a real focus on lack of reporting from school as a major part of the system's problems around neglect. The judge is very interested in adding this perspective to the study. He feels that it will add to our understanding. The reservation-based social workers are being added because it appears that the formal system does not attend to Indian children. Because of this extended focus on (site 2), the third site will be dropped from the research design.

knowledge in action in the interchange. Separating the inquirer from the respondent through the use of recording devices may increase the fidelity of the concrete words, but will lose the richness and warmth of the holistic meaning achieved in the experience of mutual shaping. In this, only the trained human instrument will screen data to underscore meaning.

To create field notes, Lofland (1971a) suggests that the inquirer maintain a concrete running account of what is occurring as it is occurring. The emphasis here is on "concrete" in that no inferences or interpretations should be recorded, only that which is said by the inquirer, observed, or heard from the respondent. Impressions, analytic ideas, thoughts about the participant or the inquirer, resulting ideas about what might be a needed next step, or further needed information should be saved for either the reflexive journal or the methodological log. An example of a page from a field journal can be found in Figure 6–3 (pages 140–141) along with its expansion for the purposes of data analysis.

The idea of condensed and expanded field notes (Spradley, 1980) should be familiar to social work students and practitioners with experience in process recordings. You will recall that a few notes taken during an interview were enough to spark the memories of the encounter for later, when an expanded version was prepared for field instructor or field liaison review. As in process recordings, the "expanded" field journal is a record of the full interview or observation. It should be created within 24 hours of the experience in order to avoid, as much as possible, the natural reshaping that occurs when experiences become a part of memory. With time to think about what occurred, certain issues are highlighted and others recede. The inquirer wants to avoid this type of interpretation in favor of as complete a running account of what transpired as possible. Nonverbals should be recorded as well as areas where further information or clarification might be needed from this respondent or another.

Personal reactions, analysis, and other interpretive work should be recorded in the reflexive journal. In nonreflexive qualitative research, the general recommendations, as with Spradley (1979), have been to include the analytical ideas and thoughts about the information, potential categorization for data reduction, further data collection needs, and so forth, in this expanded field journal. It is our recommendation that all noninferential material be recorded in the expanded field notes and everything regarding sensemaking be either recorded in the reflexive journal (when it relates to insights and ideas about meaning) or in the methodological journal (when it relates to data inclusion, exclusion, or other methodological issues). This separation ensures that the inquirer's cognitive mapping of the emerging process remains clear for the outside audit. Removing interpretation from the field journals also aids in ensuring that the findings emerge from the data and its deconstruction and reconstruction, instead of from the perspectives of the inquirer.

As with the other journals, inquirer preference should determine what medium is used. Remember, however, that there must be a way to link data recorded in the field directly to the expanded material found in the expanded field notes. In Figure 6–3 the line numbers found in the field notes can be followed to the expanded conversation via the marginal numbers. Notice that the first example is from page 19 with each line labeled for A through Z and AA through DD. Note that 19–G to J is found on the left of the entry in the second example. This means that the raw source of the expanded narrative of "Pete" found in the middle of the expanded field notes can be found in the original field notes on page 19 lines G through J. With this tracking mechanism the auditor will be able to go from the data in the expanded form to the raw form to assess the reasonableness of the expansion.

Figure 6–4 (page 142) is provided as another model for data collection. In this case, material from these note sheets can be expanded and transferred directly to a computer-based text manager. Those wishing to gain more details in data recording are directed to Lofland and Lofland (1995). Many other texts on qualitative research are also available, but the reader should be warned that many methods suggest that interpretation begin as the data are expanded. In other words, for other methods of recording and analysis, choosing to expand only themes of interest, or only that information related to the research question is suggested (see for example, Spradley, 1980; Strauss & Corbin, 1990). The deconstruction/reconstruction demanded in constructivist analysis, however, requires that all information be retained and reported as close to the actual dialogue as possible. At this stage no effort at data reduction is desirable. Instead, if ideas emerge as the notes are expanded, these should be recorded in the reflexive journal and pursued in subsequent data collection processes. This form of data analysis is in keeping with the ongoing maintenance of the hermeneutic circle. Any further reduction or interpretation from the raw data at this stage of the inquiry will impact the quality of the confirmability audit.

If the inquirer must audio- or videotape in order to have confidence about either the quality of the participant/inquirer interaction or the quality of the data collection, there are a few things to keep in mind. First, transcriptions of the tapes should be made as quickly as possible after the data collection encounter to allow further management of the information and to avoid data management backup when data reduction time occurs. Sec-

FIGURE 6–3

Field Journal and Expanded Field Journal Entries

Field journal

	1:00		
	3:00		#23
clean		1-31-86 Pete & Anna R	
neat good	A	Ana followed Pete	
smell	B	get started with	
Paul 161/2	C	—asked me to ask them questions—	
Vincent 14	D	—money	
quiet	E		
voices	F	Med care—	
opinions	G	P	with make sure take medicine and
senior—	H		work with—
job after	I		easy to overlook—
school	J		catch it—
good student	K	A	see what they like—healthy
deduction on	L		being sure that they drink and
insurance	M		eat healthy—vitamins
Spanish	N		when don't like to take vitamins
influence	O		sick and sorry—make sure have
Family/	P		balanced meal
parental resp	Q		
Safety	R	P	We know one family
	S		what parents doing
	T		not taking care
	U		cold, running noses
	V		didn't seem to care
	W		
	X	A	Sometimes— know at what point
	Y		Concerned
	Z		two kids not same
	AA		
	BB		Vin—wants to be pampered
	CC		
	DD		Paul—leave alone

FIGURE 6–3 (*continued*)

Field Journal and Expanded Field Journal Entries

Expanded field journal entries

Vincent is very involved in Boy Scouts. He is away this weekend, skiing in Nebraska. They laughed about the idea, but say that Paul had been there before and it was fun.

Paul came in and was introduced. He asked if I was going to tape the interview. He had done interviewing for one of his classes and thinks that was easier.

He left saying he was going to visit a friend.

We began: What do you think are basic needs in medical care?

IV-19-G→J

Pete: With kids who are sick you need to make sure the kids take their medicine. You need to work with them. When they get older it's easier to overlook things. You need to catch it.

IV-19-K→Q

Ana: With my kids I watched to see what they like that's healthy. I work on being sure that they drink and eat healthy. I watch the vitamins when they don't like to take vitamins. I don't want them to be sick and sorry so I make sure they have balanced meals.

IV-19-R→W

Pete: We know one family where we don't know what the parents are doing. They don't take care of the kids. They always have colds and running noses.

---

ond, observation notes should be made on the transcription before a great deal of time elapses. Nonverbal, unobtrusive measures, or other types of information not available when sound is the only datum should be included to avoid loss of very important meaning enrichers. Third, the inquirer should be prepared to spend a good deal of time moving this information into a form amenable to the constant comparative method of data analysis. Due to the high fidelity, much information tangential to the research process will have been captured. That same material will have been screened

FIGURE 6–4

Data Collection Form

(From William Beverly, School of Social Work, Virginia Commonwealth University.)

Interview Field Notes Sheet *Study:* ———————————

Interviewer:	Date/Time/Place/Setting:	Page Number
Participant:		

Foreshadowed Problem(s):	Interviewer's Feelings . . . Senses

■ Observation Notes: Time, Nonverbals, etc. . .

1. _____

2. _____

3. _____

4. _____

5. _____

6. _____

7. _____

8. _____

9. _____

10. _____

11. _____

12. _____

13. _____

14. _____

15. _____

16.

out by the human instrument using field notes while in the field. Now the human instrument must perform the same sort of screening so that the data will be ready for subsequent analysis.

One final journal is of interest for data collection. Besides being the mechanism for documenting a persistent emergence, the *log of activities* may be a source of data. Through it other interesting data might emerge. In constructivism, what does not occur is as interesting as what does. In this process, lack of data is also data, so the chronology serves to capture interesting information like the type of people who tend to cancel appointments, or when appointments were changed in relation to other research or context-based occurrences.

Archiving

Many more details about the auditing process will be provided in Chapter 9. For now it is important to consider information storage for the purpose of protecting data and creating an audit trail (Guba & Lincoln, 1989; Lincoln & Guba, 1985; Schwandt & Halpern, 1988). The trail must delineate all methodological steps and decision points and give access to all data in their raw and analyzed forms. Clearly, any inquiry of normal magnitude will involve the creation of more than one of the reflexive and methodological journals. These should be trackable. Many field notes and expanded notes will need to be stored and organized for easy access. Thought should be given to how these journals and the documents and records, and so forth, that will emerge should be stored.

As the inquiry progresses, computer storage or low-tech storage of data, like 3 × 5 notecards in boxes, will also be important and should be determined very early in the process. Basically, the entire data collection, storage, and retrieval system should be determined before any data have been developed. The system may change and grow as the process emerges, but something must be in place in the beginning to avoid data overload and data loss disasters and to assure that trustworthiness can be documented.

Data Collection Links to Direct Social Work Practice

The structure and steps necessary to undertake a constructivist interview or a participant observation or to moderate a focus group might need to be learned. But the skills necessary to implement the steps are already available to a trained social worker. Quite some time ago Garrett (1949) identified the techniques that social workers use well. Her suggestions still apply to current-day social work practice. Trained social workers know how to observe and listen. They can start where the client is at in questioning, talking, and answering personal questions. They use leadership or direction in purposive processes, and they are capable of interpretation. These skills are constructivist research skills of listening, observing, personally interacting, question framing, and questioning. Gentle probing and managing conflict necessary in negotiation are also part of the skilled social worker's repertoire.

In sum, the skilled social worker trained in direct practice, with a firm understanding of the helping process, and in possession of the relationship-building skills needed to explore, assess, and plan a social work intervention, is also in possession of the basic skills necessary to undertake a constructivist inquiry. In fact, with their capacity to establish change-oriented strategies, skilled social workers will also have the capacity to move constructivist inquiry to its greatest change potential through the implementation of all dimensions of authenticity rigor. Some of the greatest challenges of constructivist research practice will not be new challenges for the trained social worker because they are a familiar dimension of the work of enhancing social functioning and promoting social justice basic to the purpose of the social work profession.

Notes

1. Readers interested in more discussion of access in qualitative research are directed to Bogdan & Biklen (1992), Eisner (1991), and Patton (1990).

2. For more information on interviewing from the social work literature see Carkhuff (1969), Hepworth & Larsen (1993), and Shulman (1984) and from the research literature see Fontana & Frey (1994), Rubin & Rubin (1995), and Spradley (1979).

3. For more information on observations and participant observations see Atkinson and Hammersley (1994), Reason (1993), and Adler and Adler (1993).

4. For further discussion about focus groups see Birn, Hague, and Vangelder (1990), Krueger (1994), and Morgan (1988).

5. Those interested in this type of data should refer to Hodder's (1993) thorough discussion of the interpretation of written texts and artifacts.

6. Those wishing to do further reading regarding journals will find that recent literature focuses on journals as data, not journals as documentary evidence of the research undertaking. See for example, Josselson & Leiblich (1995). For those wishing more information about the development and management of journals to document research, please refer to Lincoln (1981), Reinharz (1979), and Spradley (1979).

Discussion Questions

What follows will develop skills in data collection including observation, participant observation, interviewing, focus groups, and nonverbal and nonhuman data.

1. Select a location where human activity is occurring. Without participating in the activity in any way, spend 10 minutes observing what is happening. Take notes about the observation. Immediately following this experience of complete observation, expand your notes into complete statements about what you saw. Now try to determine what you "know" for sure about what you saw. What requires follow-up with those in the activity in order for you to fully understand what you observed? Discuss what you learned from this experience about yourself and the data you can collect.

2. Find another environment where you can be an observer, but this time make sure that you can also join in the activity. Attempt to record field notes as you participate. Once the activity ceases, expand the raw notes into a full discussion of what occurred and your participation in it. Compare this experience of data collection with that in the above exercise. What did you gain in this activity? What did you give up?

3. Choose an individual about whom you are curious. Engage him or her in a purposive conversation in which you try to learn something new about him or her. While you are engaged in the conversation, take notes including important words and phrases and any nonverbal communication that feels important. Immediately following the interview, expand your notes into field notes that include what you said, what he/she said in response to your questions or probes, and any nonverbal information that is useful to aid understanding.

4. Identify an area of research interest. Now identify a record, a document, or an unobtrusive measure you could look for to expand your understanding of your area of interest. What might be the problems with each regarding risks of misinterpretation?

5. Find a group of six to eight individuals who are willing to talk together on a topic of your choosing for about 20 minutes. Decide five questions that you would like them to discuss regarding the topic. Introduce the topic and ask the questions, allowing or

encouraging group discussion. Take notes of the interchange as you facilitate the first 10 minutes of the process. During the second 10 minutes, ask one of the participants to take notes for you. As soon as possible after the discussion, expand the notes from both data collection exercises. What was captured and what was overlooked in each strategy?

CHAPTER 7

Constructivist Data Analysis

Chapter Contents in Brief

Planning data analysis throughout the inquiry
The use of foreshadowed questions and working hypotheses
Detecting emerging themes for persistent observation
Data deconstruction including unitizing and categorizing
Grounded theory building
Negotiating results of data analysis

Since constructivist research is emergent research grounded in the particulars of the people and the setting in which the investigation is being undertaken, data analysis must be an ongoing process that begins with the first contact in the field and continues until the final report is returned to the setting. For meaning making, the results of the data analysis must be grounded in the context of the study. Much has been written about grounded theory building (see, for example: Charmaz, 1983; Corbin & Strauss, 1990; Glaser, 1978, 1992, 1993, 1994, 1995; Glaser & Strauss, 1967) and what will be accomplished in constructivist data analysis is a type of grounded theory building; but it will be theory building set in an interpretive paradigm.

The procedures discussed in most of the literature about grounded theory are designed to meet the criteria for doing good positivistic science with goals of generalizability, reproducibility, verification, and so forth. What will be discussed in this chapter is a type of grounded theory that is congruent with the standards of good constructivist practice with attention to trustworthiness and authenticity instead of control for generalizability. For those of you who are familiar with Glaser and Strauss and their followers, much of what follows will have a familiar ring, especially when we discuss techniques. But from the start, it is important to remember that what follows are procedures that are very different in intent and in the type of tentative, context-imbedded theory that is produced from the constructivist inquiry process.

Planning the Ongoing Data Analysis throughout the Inquiry

Data analysis must be a planned-for activity that is central to the early thinking about the design, the feasibility of the inquiry, and the resources necessary to undertake the investigation. Some of the decisions about the data analysis are conceptual, such as determinations of foreshadowed questions and working hypotheses. Other analysis decisions are more concrete and related to the decisions about data collection and storage covered in Chapter 6. All serve to focus and bound not only the research design and implementation, but also what is desired and possible in the process of analysis. This first section will discuss the more abstract issues that will lead the inquirer to the more concrete activities involved in "doing" analysis that make up the rest of the chapter.

Foreshadowed Questions That Grow into Working Hypotheses

Foreshadowed questions, those issues that the inquirer brings to the inquiry from his or her own experience, from study, or from general curiosity, really serve as the conceptual framework, not only for the initial design stages of constructivist research, but also for the data analysis that begins early on in the process. To develop the questions that lead the inquirer to begin a study, a good deal of data collection (at least in the form of words) and analysis has occurred. The inquirer has developed hunches about the main things that must be studied. There are suspicions about the key factors or variables and their relationships that shape the rudimentary beginnings of the constructivist process. From where does this information come? Basically, it has been collected from everywhere and has been analyzed either consciously or unconsciously as the inquirer's human instrument has become shaped in preparation for this particular inquiry.

The inquirer, starting with something that is puzzling, has reviewed the relevant literature and has selected themes and aspects of theory to drive the first steps of the inquiry. At this stage of the analysis, a type of rough data analysis is accomplished; first, reflexively in the reflexive journal in which the inquirer states as explicitly as possible what is "known" and what the next steps should be. From this should come a type of descriptive framework for the study. This framework may take the form of statements with the assumed linkages included, such as the following, developed to guide a study in housing policy:

- What do entitlement jurisdictions perceive as different about what now is required of them and about their relationship with HUD?
- How will spatial deconcentration and economic integration be understood at the local level and across jurisdictional boundaries and what is the role of race in that understanding?
- How far along the continuum of care will responses to homelessness be in each locality and metro wide?
- How will the requirements that each locality have plans to affirmatively further fair housing and to identify and eliminate regulatory barriers to affordable housing be met?
- How will the volatile environment at the federal level, especially with regard to level of funding, effect implementation of the new policies? (Crowley, 1995)

Each question is related to what the inquirer supposed would be important elements in the creation of a quality planning process that would respond to the social problem of homelessness in a metropolitan area. These questions were the basis of initial probing with the stakeholders in the planning district.

Using another strategy, the framework could take the shape of a figure that describes the major assumed dimensions of the study and what their relationships might be. For example, in the study of neglect, the entry "picture" about what constitutes neglect sufficient to warrant formal intervention might have been described graphically as in Figure 7–1. The current definition about neglect, in combination with who is deciding that neglect exists and the evidence that is available, provides

the material upon which to decide to intervene formally in cases of neglect.

In either strategy, prior analysis of available data has suggested a way
of focusing and bounding where to begin the inquiry. At the first stage of
the inquiry, foreshadowed questions help to determine who will be con-

---

FIGURE 7–1

Graphically Displayed Foreshadowed Questions

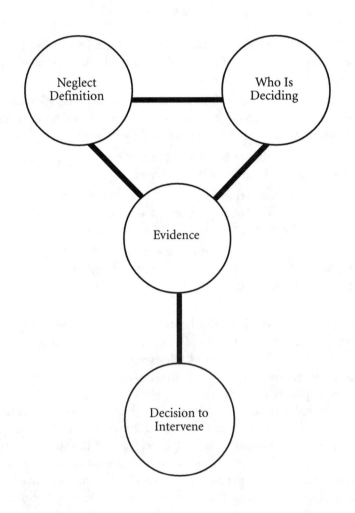

tacted initially and what will be the beginning exploration. Foreshadowed questions create the first parameters for limiting what is included and what is excluded as the inquiry starts.

From this stage of analysis come the first questions that will be asked in the inquiry Phase I of orientation and overview. For the neglect research framework described above, first questions would be about the dimensions of what constitutes neglect, who should/can determine what constitutes neglect, and what type of information is necessary to move to a decision that neglect exists. Guidance is developed for further data collection and analysis through tapping the initial participants about these questions and through analysis of their responses. Clarity develops from this refinement of what constitute the "real" questions and the functional interrelationships of interest in a context.

The analysis of initial responses to entry questions could still be considered informal, in that reflections in journals, rereading initial interviews, and attending to what is being observed in the orientation phase helps to refine what should be asked of whom later. This gets worked out in journaling, writing memos, or just thinking about the material. In some ways, this is a narrowing of the research. A degree of selectivity is developing about what will be the questions and who might have a stake in answering them. As this first stage is closing, the foreshadowed questions develop more sophistication to become working hypotheses. For example, the foreshadowed questions for the first phase of the neglect inquiry that grew out of the graphic in Figure 7–1 became the following working hypotheses that began the more focused exploration of neglect in the second phase of that inquiry:

- There are multiple levels of neglect.
- A consequence to the child helps to determine neglect.
- Minimum standards of parenting help to determine neglect.
- Neglect can be a single incident or a chronic condition.
- Culture and other aspects of context play a part in a neglect definition.
- Different disciplines have different definitions of neglect.
- Those investigating have different definitions from those being investigated.

A working hypothesis should not be confused with the type of hypothesis that drives positivistic studies. There, the hypothesis includes precise operational definitions, with all variables defined and assigned a type (dependent, independent, intervening, and so forth) so that they might be tested in the subsequently implemented research. "Working" hypotheses are not fashioned to be tested for confirmation or rejection to assess their generalizability. First suggested by Cronbach (1975), a working hypothesis is a mechanism to describe factors that are unique to a context or event. They are tentative descriptions about reality that can be investigated and said to be true only in a specific time, situation, or context. In constructivism, working hypotheses tentatively guide the data collection and are finally fashioned at the completion of the inquiry process in the form of the "lessons to be learned" developed in the case study report.

During the emergent process, these working hypotheses help to further shape and bound data collection and analysis by serving the function of a traditional research question. In a traditional research process, the research questions represent "the facts the researcher most wants to explore" (Miles & Huberman, 1994, p. 23). Because constructivist inquiry is almost totally an inductive process building on the particulars that are discovered, it should be assumed that the working hypotheses will be changing as the inquiry proceeds. In fact, a lack of change in the working hypotheses will put emergence, and, therefore, trustworthiness and authenticity rigor in question in the auditing that follows the completion of the case report.

The expected shaping and changing of the working hypotheses is iterative, based on analysis of new and old data. As new data sources are identified and tapped, new information shapes what constitutes the questions that should be covered in the investigation. The data analysis involved in the ongoing molding of the working hypotheses has some of the informal dimensions described in how foreshadowed questions move to become working hypotheses. There is also a more formal aspect described in the next section that considers emerging themes. These emerging themes, in fact, are dimensions of the working hypotheses.

Emerging Themes for Persistent Observation

As the inquirer moves data from field notes to expanded field notes, a type of inductive analysis begins. Reading and rereading the data in the various forms at early stages of the inquiry begin to provide ideas about major areas of interest to the participants. These areas of interest may strike the inquirer in the form of words, concepts, or statements. They may only "come to" the inquirer as reflexive recording is happening. This is a messy, ambiguous stage of the analysis process in which glimpses of relationships between concepts are beginning to emerge. These ideas of what might be important are used to shape the next cycle of more focused questioning.

In constructivist inquiry, no tightly structured interview protocol is designed, but a protocol of sorts emerges as the inquirer interacts with the already collected data. For example, after the interview with "Pete," whose field notes and expanded field notes were discussed in Chapter 6 (see Figure 6–3), certain ideas appeared to emerge related to medical neglect and how difficult it is to respond to the medical needs of very different children. A second theme concerned the challenges that working single parents have in guarding against neglect. Chronic neglect seemed to become linked with serious neglect that could warrant removal.

The inquirer had gone into the interview with the idea of investigating "cultural influences," "parental responsibility," and "safety" in determining neglect. This interview confirmed that, with these participants, there was a cultural consideration about what constituted good parenting and what were the dimensions of parental responsibility. As a result of the conversation, the concepts or themes for further investigation were expanded to include a chronic dimension of lack of safety and the possibility of the child being somehow accountable in neglect. The inquirer did not want to filter out information by simply sticking to the themes that guided the beginning of this interview.

Because data collection and analysis go hand in hand, the next interview was shaped by the major concepts that seemed to be confirmed and was expanded to include these two new dimensions that Pete provided. This is why the themes for persistent observation that were discussed in Chapter 6 and shown in Table 6–1 emerged in different ways in each inquiry site. It is important to note that many of the themes are the same in each of the sites, but they emerged at different times and, in some cases, had slightly different meanings. These themes constituted the dimensions of the working hypotheses about neglect. They were all the elements of what constituted serious neglect in the two sites of the investigation.

At this stage of analysis, important elements are being identified, but details of the elements and their relationship in the context have yet to be constructed totally. These themes are not the results of the inquiry. They are only what has shaped the data collection. These concepts or themes have served to define who participated in the inquiry and what sort of questions were asked of them. Formal data analysis has not begun. Themes for persistent observation or working hypotheses have only created the parameters for data collection. They are the parameters for the work of the hermeneutic dialectic. Once the entry of new information has slowed, or the allotted time for data collection has been reached, then the formal process of data deconstruction and reconstruction can begin. It is in this next stage of data analysis that the techniques of grounded theory building are most apparent.

Unitizing and Categorizing for Grounded Theory Building

For traditional grounded theory building, formal data analysis begins with the first collection of data and continues throughout with the goal to "generate a rich, tightly woven, explanatory theory that closely approximates the reality it represents" (Strauss & Corbin, 1990, p. 57). The analysis occurs through three types of coding: open, axial, and selective. Open coding labels "chunks" of data according to categories; axial coding places these categories in relationship within a framework of conditions, context, action/ interactional strategies, and consequences; and selective coding determines the core categories around which all the other categories are integrated in order to develop a clear analytic story line which is the precursor to a theory. The product will be an extended statement or a figure called a conditional matrix that shows: "under these conditions (listing them) this happens; whereas under these conditions, this is what occurs" (Strauss & Corbin, 1990, p. 131). For traditional grounded theory building this deconstruction and reconstruction occurs when the first interview has been completed, recorded, and expanded, and continues through constant comparison (Glaser & Strauss, 1967) until the conditional matrix is created. This means that formal data units and analysis categories are identified very early and these analytic decisions shape the subsequent data collection and analysis. This also means that the formal analysis procedure, computer based or low tech, begins with the first interview.

Constructivist analysis is keen on the creation of a grounded theory, but this is a theory only in that it is the final product of data reduction and interpretation, which is the framework to tentatively tell the story within the limits of the time and context of the investigation. Data units and categories are utilized for the creation of the grounded theory through the constant comparison method articulated by Glaser and Strauss. It is with the continuous and simultaneous collection and processing of data that the inductive analysis processes of constructivism are congruent. It is used as a means of processing data, not deriving theory for prediction and explanation. Therefore, the formal constant comparison of constructivist analysis only occurs when the majority of data collection has ceased. Subsequent, focused data collection might be necessary for filling in patterns after the deconstruction and reconstruction; but that will be guided by the results of the data processing, not the evolving working hypotheses, as was true in the rest of the emergent process.

UNITIZING   Units of data are identified as a result of a persistent look at the accumulated data to identify information that is relevant and applicable to the focus of the inquiry. If data have moved from raw field notes to expanded field notes, this can occur by referring to the expanded interviews. If data were recorded and then transcribed, the inquirer will perform one step in data reduction prior to unitizing. With transcribed data it is important to remove irrelevant "noise" in the data. This means eliminating all the "ums" and "ahs" and all tangential information that tends to accumulate in early and late stages of interviews, in which the inquirer is either setting the stage and making the participant comfortable, or terminating the interview and showing gratitude for the time the participant has given to the process. All this should be considered extraneous data, not linked to the inquiry per se. It should be eliminated before proceeding to the unitization stage of analysis.

Once data are prepared for unitizing, the inquirer identifies the smallest piece of information that can be understood by someone with minimal knowledge or experience with the phenomenon under investigation. This will be identified as a unit. Units can be as short as a word or as long as several paragraphs, but they must each stand alone and require no further explanation. "Pete's" first interview about what constitutes neglect can provide examples of how his interview was unitized:

> [It's too bad, but kids need somebody.] [Maybe the family needs to be talked to in order to realize what they are doing.] [Kids need somebody to take care of them.] [I guess you'd see some kinds of signs in order to take them away.] [If the kids are sick in school and no one cared and the kid is really run down something should be done.]

These five units can stand alone without need of further information. Each should be considered a separate "chunk" of information to be processed independently. This is the deconstruction process.

The first stage of processing involves assigning a code to each unit that will allow tracking to the original data source. This level of coding should also capture important aspects of stakeholders or context that might serve as a basis of later analysis. It might be important in later stages of analysis to compare father's and mother's perceptions or professional and parental perceptions on neglect. That will only be possible at the unit level if each data unit is coded at the onset with variables that might be of later interest.

Coding, like much of everything else with constructivist inquiry, will be determined by the style of the inquirer. Codes should build from the foreshadowed questions, the working hypotheses, and the sample frame. The code should make sense to the inquirer and be simple enough to be explained to the auditor. A typical coding system for data units might be:(site), (respondent type), (interview # with respondent), (data type), (data unit #). In Pete's case, he was the first male nonneglecting parent from one of two sites. The data were verbal and drawn from the first interview. Using the above statement, "It's too bad, but kids need somebody," as the first data unit, the code could be: 1.1NNP/M.1.V.1, meaning Site #1, first non neglecting parent/male, first interview, verbal data, first data unit. This code would somehow be attached to the unit. If cards were used it might be placed in the upper left-hand corner of the card. If a computer-based text manager is used, be sure that coding by source and type of data is possible, as well as coding by category.

All interviews should be unitized and prepared for data manipulation before moving to the next step in data processing. If cards are used, all units should be on cards and all cards should have the initial code allowing tracking to the original source. If the computer is used, all lines of text that will be used for analysis should be identified, separated, and coded according to the instructions of the data analysis package.

For planning purposes, keep in mind that this stage of data preparation is likely to be the most time consuming of all parts of the inquiry. An hour interview will produce between 30 and 150 data units, depending upon how verbal and eloquent the respondent. This means that with 60 participants, the inquirer could be managing upwards of 9,000 data units in computer files or on cards. Whatever time you think you will need for identifying and preparing units should at least be doubled to ensure adequate time for thorough, constant comparison.

CATEGORIZING   Once all data units are prepared, each is compared with all other data units to identify relevant themes or categories. This is a process called *sorting* (Lincoln & Guba, 1985). The units that seem similar are brought together into provisional categories. This operation is called *lumping* (Lincoln & Guba, 1985). Using the units from Pete's interview and a few other units from the same inquiry should give the idea of the sorting and lumping process.

Imagine the inquirer starts with the following ten data units to be sorted and lumped:

1. It's too bad, but kids need somebody.
2. Maybe the family needs to be talked to in order to realize what they are doing.
3. Kids need somebody to take care of them.
4. I guess you'd see some kinds of signs in order to take them away.
5. If the kids are sick in school and no one cared and the kid is really run down something should be done.
6. The older child can cope better with things.
7. With the younger child, you have to look at safety features.
8. In neglect, if parents don't teach a child to get along in the system, there is a problem in school, with schedules . . . There are minimum standards for cleanliness that society expects.
9. If kids really live in two worlds they can't get along. This is a form of neglect.
10. With neglect and the young child there is an emphasis on the home environment more than with the older child.

Starting with the first data unit, create a pile. Compare the second with the first. They seem to have something in common, so they remain together. Add number three, which also seems related. Number four is different, so create another "lump." Number five feels like number four, so it remains in that pile. Number six does not appear to be similar to either the first or second "lump," so a third one is created. Number seven can be placed with six, while numbers eight and nine seem to have something in common with four and five. Finally unit number ten seems similar to units six and seven. By comparing each unit with the other it is possible to bring them together into three provisional categories. The rest of the units in the inquiry would be compared to these and brought together into these and other categories. This is the reconstruction phase of analysis.

For the purpose of the example, each of the three "lumps" becomes a category that could be named: "need for protection," "age and neglect," and "measuring neglect." Data units 1, 2, and 3 could fit under the concept, "need for protection"; 6, 7, and 10 under "age and neglect"; and 4, 5,

8, and 9 under "measuring neglect." Naming the lumps is the second step in data processing, but the actual labeling of categories will happen throughout the constant comparison. Whenever a new data unit does not seem to fit with any of the provisionally established categories, form and name a new category. As the constant comparison proceeds, some units will not appear to relate to any of the emerging categories. Do not discard these units, but place them in a miscellaneous pile for later review.

Once 50 or 60 units have been gathered into six to eight categories, the inquirer should move to the next step of data processing. Each category label should be defined. The definition should capture the properties of the units contained in that category. This definition will serve as a *decision rule*. It describes the category properties and justifies unit assignment to that category. The definition is most important, not only for unit assignment, but for later tests of internal consistency and the logic of the analysis by the outside auditor. Each category and its definition must be nonredundant and exhaustive. Categories should not overlap, though units might reasonably be assigned to more than one category, particularly if the card contains more than one thought. If a data unit could appear in more than one category, just repeat the unit and cross reference the category assignment for later interpretation.

With our lumping and sorting above, the category "need for protection" might be defined as all that refers to meeting children's health and safety needs. "Age and neglect" could include all that refers to the age of the child experiencing neglect. Finally, "measuring neglect" could refer to all references to evidence for determining if neglect exists. The inquirer working with this data set would continue to sort and lump, label and define until no data units remain unassigned.

Next, the inquirer returns to the "miscellaneous" category to see if some of the units placed there can now be fit in other categories. Most will. At this stage, look closely at the remaining unassigned units to determine if any could be discarded as clearly irrelevant. Some may remain unassigned, but may still be relevant to the inquiry. Lincoln and Guba (1985, p. 349) suggest that no more than five to seven percent should remain unassigned without risking a serious deficiency in the category set. For a data set of 9,500 units this would mean 400 to 600 units, which seems to be unreasonably high; our experience in numerous inquiries has ranged from 5 to 30 units unassigned in various-sized data sets. A more conservative measure of one percent of units assigned a "miscellaneous" category would assure a solid effort in conceptually capturing the data.

Once the units have been assigned to defined categories, return to the categories themselves to be certain that there is no overlap. Categories must continue to be nonredundant and exclusive. If overlap exists, relabel, redefine, and reassign units. Next, look at the categories to be certain that they are all on the same conceptual level. In many cases categories are really subsets of one another. In our example the category "age and neglect" could be a subset of both "need for protection" and "measuring neglect" in that the need for protection depends on the child's age and, therefore, the evidence in a neglect situation will also relate to the age of the child. In this case, "age and neglect" could be eliminated as a stand-alone category and unit 6 could be assigned to "need for protection" and 7 and 10 could go to "measuring neglect." These two units will serve as a catalyst to create a subcategory under "measuring neglect" related to age.

Besides different levels of abstraction, sometimes a category is just too unwieldy. If a large percentage of units are in one category, then there is a good chance that the category can be usefully subdivided to more precisely reflect the properties of the units that have been included. Once the categories and subcategories have been identified in a first round of analysis, return to the data units to test the categorical assignments. Using the decision rules, determine if every unit belongs where it was originally assigned. Continue this with all data, adding or eliminating categories and subcategories as needed. The same rules regarding nonredundancy and detailing decision rules apply at this level of analysis.

This process continues until possible relationships between the categories begin to emerge. Data have been deconstructed into units and are being reconstructed into categories with greater and greater degrees of abstraction. Overarching categories with clear relationships is the goal of the reconstruction. Before this is possible, some categories may be missing. If this occurs, using the techniques described in Chapter 6 for extending data, subsequent data collection may be necessary. These new data are analyzed in the same manner as earlier rounds of data collection and become part of the category and subcategory sets. Category management, subdivision, and reconstruction continues until no more than nine major categories capture the whole of the data set. In most cases good data reduction will result in less than nine major categories. Nine sets of disparate information appears to be the largest heuristic possible for human sensemaking (Kahneman & Tversky, 1979), meaning that more information than this will either go unassimilated, be forgotten, or otherwise not be included in meaning construction in the minds of the individuals concerned with meaning making. Concluding analysis before this level of reduction is accomplished will mean great difficulty in telling a clear story with easily identified lessons. Table 7–1 shows a partial category set and level of subcategories that finally captured the data from one site in the neglect inquiry. Note that each level of category has been numbered or coded. All relevant codes will be recorded with each data unit to allow tracking of the unit through the deconstruction/reconstruction process.

TABLE 7–1

Example of a Category Set with Decision Rules and Codes

I. Stage setting category includes all background factors that establish the parameters for recognizing neglect.

1. Law subcategory includes all interpretations of state statutes regarding neglect.

2. Neglect definition subcategory includes all aspects of components of neglect.

2.1 Physical neglect sub-subcategory includes all that relates to environment or physical care.

2.2 Educational neglect sub-subcategory includes all that relates to lack of intellectual formation.

2.3 Emotional neglect includes all that relates to lack of caregiver warmth and affection.

2.4 Medical neglect includes all that relates to lack of health maintenance or care.

2.5 Latch key includes all that relates to lack of supervision while caregivers are away from home.

2.6 Spiritual neglect includes all that relates to lack of religious/ spiritual formation.

2.7 Societal neglect includes all that relates to lack of responsibility to family on the part of the larger society.

2.8 Neglect with something else includes all that refers to neglect in combination with another type of child maltreatment.

continued on next page

Using data unit 6 from our example (The older child can cope better with things), in addition to the code that links the unit to its source, in the other corner of the card, another code should link the unit to its place in the analysis categories. In this case the analysis code for unit 6 would be I.2.2.9, meaning that it was assigned to the sub-sub category "age of child in relation to neglect" within the subcategory of "neglect definition" which was in the major category of "stage setting."

TABLE 7–1 (*continued*)

2.9 Age of child in relation to neglect includes all that refers to the age of the child experiencing neglect.

2.10 Child's role in neglect includes all that refers to the neglected child's role in a neglect incidence.

2.11 Effects of neglect includes all measurable consequences of neglect.

2.12 Personal reflection on child care includes all references to personal child-caring practices.

2.13 Abuse includes references to child battery.

2.14 General includes miscellaneous definitional issues.

3. Standards subcategory includes all aspects of expectations for parental care.

3.1 General sub-subcategory includes miscellaneous expectation issues.

3.2 Educational sub-subcategory includes all references to expectations for intellectual development.

3.3 Shelter includes all references to expectations for housing.

3.4 Nutritional includes all references to expectations for nutrition or feeding.

3.5 Medical includes all references to expectations for medical care.

3.6 Clothing includes expectations for clothing children.

3.7 Emotional includes expectations for the family emotional environment.

This additional coding is particularly important for low-tech analysis. When you are managing hundreds and thousands of cards, it will be easy for them to get out of order even in the most well-contained situation. One time dropping the box containing 500 cards and their category labels that have simply served as dividers between units without being transferred to each card by way of code will convince you of the necessity of taking this extra step. Placing a code on the card that links the unit to its categories will save the need to reanalyze if an accident occurs. It is also essential to enable the auditor to check for confirmability. This extra, and sometimes aggravating, step can be eliminated in computer-based analysis, because this type of coding will happen automatically.

Allowing Theory to Grow from the Data

New constructivists will think that with the unitizing, categorizing, ordering, and coding of all data, data analysis is complete. If real meaning construction is the goal of constructivist inquiry, then two additional steps must be undertaken for this stage to be complete. What has been constructed so far by the inquirer must be checked with the participants. At issue is whether or not the reconstructions have successfully captured the participants' constructions. Do the concepts and their definitions make sense? Does the ordering of categories and subcategories also seem reasonable? Participant examination and reaction, if positive, is a good sign that meaning construction is on track. If negative reactions occur, then further data collection and negotiation will mean that the final product will make sense to all, not just to the inquirer. Serious attention to this level of member checking enhances trustworthiness and will also increase the quality of the hermeneutic circle, thus increasing authenticity potential. Aside from aiding the inquirer in the audit, this further inductive/deductive process may put the last elements in place for the cognitive mapping of the data.

The theory that grows from these data is really the inquirer's cognitive map (Miles & Huberman, 1994; Morine-Dershimer, 1991) of the data. It is the inquirer's way of organizing mountains of data so that sense can be made in a nonhierarchical network form. The final stage of data analysis is not just reducing the data to major categories, but positing a relationship between and among these categories. The goal of constructivism is understanding the network of relationships involved with the phenomenon under investigation. The analysis is not complete unless and until this sort of structural relationship can be designed or described. Figure 7–2 shows the matrix that was used to describe determining neglect sufficient to warrant formal intervention in the first site of the ne-

FIGURE 7–2

Site One Neglect Decision Matrix

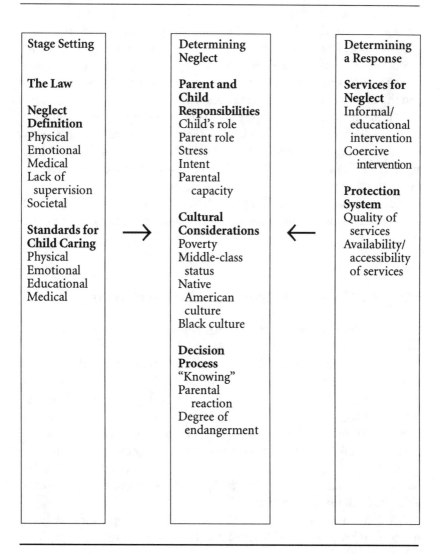

Stage Setting	Determining Neglect	Determining a Response
The Law	**Parent and Child Responsibilities**	**Services for Neglect**
Neglect Definition	Child's role	Informal/ educational intervention
Physical	Parent role	Coercive intervention
Emotional	Stress	
Medical	Intent	
Lack of supervision	Parental capacity	**Protection System**
Societal		Quality of services
	Cultural Considerations	Availability/ accessibility of services
Standards for Child Caring	Poverty	
Physical	Middle-class status	
Emotional	Native American culture	
Educational	Black culture	
Medical		
	Decision Process	
	"Knowing"	
	Parental reaction	
	Degree of endangerment	

glect inquiry. In that case, neglect could not be determined without taking into consideration contextual issues of stage setting and possible responses. Basically the law, the currently understood definition of neglect in all its forms, and locally accepted standards of child care in all its dimensions serve as the basis for decision making. But, in addition, the decision that might involve removal of a child takes into account both the available services in the community for the child and the quality of the system of protection. A better option must be available for the child before the decision to remove can be considered a viable option. Only with these dimensions in background will the decision be made that includes consideration of the parent's and the child's responsibility and the special cultural considerations in the circumstance being investigated. Finally, the decision relates to a combination of the child protective service investigator's tacit knowledge, the parent's reaction to the investigation, and the degree of risk that is being observed.

Until the inquirer can display the results in a simple graphic, illustration, or table, and until the results can be stated in no more than a paragraph, meaning has not been constructed. Readers are referred to Miles and Huberman's work (1994) for their coverage of data display. Keep in mind, though, that the authors are coming from a positivist perspective, so their focus will be on replicability whereas the constructivist focus will be on whether or not all stakeholders can understand the results as displayed.

Negotiating the Results of Data Analysis

It is at this level of analysis that formal negotiation of results can begin. To this point issues have been checked in ongoing member checking and further expanded through the use of the hermeneutic circle. Perhaps the emerging categories have also been declared to make sense by participants. Now, following the empowerment tradition of both constructivism and social work, the inquirer takes steps in aiding the powerless to gain control of their lives (Simon, 1994) by making sure that all voices have been heard in the way the meaning has been constructed by the inquirer. Do participants see themselves in the graphic and the short explanation of the findings? Are the graphic and the statement understandable? Do both make sense to them?

If their voices are not accurately reflected at this stage, and if they do not comprehend what has been produced so far, then it makes no sense to move on to the construction of the final case report. In most cases where there has been ongoing member checking and careful attention to meaning, this stage of negotiation only serves to further validate the inquirer's work.

This is an important aspect of this stage of the analysis, because most researchers suffer from serious data overload and may not be fully recovered from overload before taking the results of the analytic process back to the field. Data overload occurs when the inquirer becomes unable to receive, process, or remember anything else. The inquirer is so immersed in the murkiness that there is no way to achieve cognitive removal for refocusing. In some cases, it becomes necessary to remove oneself from the analysis process and take a "breather" of several days or weeks to be able to reengage with energy and acuity. Even if data overload does not occur, the inquirer has been in the midst of an ever emergent process where fixed standards of quality, are, by necessity, lacking.

Negotiation in the field will occur at about the time that convergence and divergence have stalled. The inquirer may be acutely conscious of what Berreth (1986) called a constant, rhythmic loss of focus in which internal standards of quality are lost and great uncertainty reigns. The inquirer will not be certain that what has been produced is clear or even worth the time it took to produce it. He or she may be overwhelmed with the wealth of information, even if time has been taken to distance from the information. Receiving confirmation from the field at this stage will serve an empowerment function for the inquirer at the same time that the participants are being empowered. Fear of negative criticism should not prevent this circling back to the participants. The benefits in a well constructed process are very much greater than the fears that this testing of results will engender.

Clearly, if problems are identified, they must be negotiated and resolved prior to case report writing. This would seem to be relatively straightforward in a "pure" research undertaking. All participants will have a relatively equal stake and will have been protected against unequal power inhibiting the process, so individual negotiations with all participants or representatives of stakeholding groups should be able to proceed without difficulty. General communication standards will guide the quality of this effort.

In the case of policy or evaluation research, politics may make this negotiation a bit more challenging. If important stakeholders to the policy or the program under investigation are not pleased with these products of analysis, problems in negotiation may ensue. If the results do not represent unequivocally their perspective, but are reflective of an assumed consensus model, the inquirer will quickly realize that what was thought to be full consensus was really only partial consensus. The research contract will determine what will be the next step in resolving the objections. If the objecting stakeholder is also the principal recipient of the case study report, due to his or her role in contracting for your services, then serious, focused negotiation as described in Chapter 4 must be undertaken until the objections are resolved. If objections are of a more minor nature, then creation of a minority report in the final document should serve to satisfy objections. Again, serious, persistent attention to the quality of the emergent process and the development of a true hermeneutic circle will help to avoid such tricky situations. In most cases, the return to the field in policy analysis or program evaluation will be an exciting and exhilarating process for all involved.

Constructivist Data Analysis Skills and Social Work

Knowledge and skills related to assessment, the critical social work practice process, prepare the social work inquirer to perform most dimensions of data analysis, at least from a philosophical, if not technical perspective. Our review of the assessment literature (see Briar, 1964; Cormier & Cormier, 1979; Douglas, 1991; Freeman, Pretzer, Fleming & Simon, 1990; Garvin, 1986; Granvold, 1994; Griffin, 1991; Hepworth & Larsen, 1993; Kopp, 1989; Prager, 1980) indicates that, aside from material related to computer-assisted assessment (Hudson, 1992; Nurius & Hudson, 1988, 1993), no detailed guidance about managing and processing assessment data for analysis is readily available. The same is true for constructivist data processing. For example, assessment, just as in constructivist data analysis, involves gathering, analyzing, and synthesizing data. Assessment in social work, as in analysis in constructivist inquiry, is an ongoing process, beginning with the first contact with the client and continuing throughout the helping process.

Assessment in social work is an interactive process that includes data gathering through the procedures of interviews, reports, and observations, and validating this information for affirmation or disconfirmation with clients and other major actors in the client's systems. As in constructivism, social work assessment focuses on meaning attribution (Hepworth & Larsen, 1993), that takes into account the client's perceptions and definitions, which are considered and compared with the views of other stakeholders to enhance the social worker's understanding of the situation that is being assessed.

The assessment process is iterative, interactive, and emergent as the social worker weighs the significance of client and system behaviors, thoughts, beliefs, emotions, and other information to determine what is important to explore in depth. Assessment, like constructivist analysis, requires involvement of the client in the synthesis that occurs with the information gained in assessment exploration. The client is asked to validate the social worker's impressions and is given encouragement to disconfirm erroneous material and to provide additional input as necessary. These steps are congruent with the formal member checking processes and the intent of the creation of the hermeneutic circle for verification and consciousness raising about the subject of interest in the constructivist investigation.

Finally, the goal of social work assessment is accurate analysis of a problem in the context of needs, strengths, and limitations, in order to determine appropriate goals and techniques for intervention. The goal of constructivist inquiry is accurate reconstruction of the needs, strengths, and limitations of the context and the phenomena under investigation to provide a holistic understanding that might serve to promote effective change. Interestingly, assessment in social work, like constructivist inquiry, is a process and a product. In includes the fluid dynamism of receiving, analyzing, and synthesizing information that appears throughout the duration of a case. It is an actual statement of the "working definition of the problem that identifies various associated factors and clarifies how they interact to produce and maintain the problem" (Hepworth & Larsen, 1993, p. 193). For Hepworth and Larsen, assessment is a "complex working hypothesis based on the most current data" (p. 193), which looks to us to be a good definition of a case study report. In fact, from our perspective, the processes of social work assessment and constructivist inquiry are so akin, that the new social worker, in search of a way to manage the collected assessment information, might be well served to seek the assistance of the material in this chapter, not for the purposes of research in the traditional sense, but to perform a well-grounded assessment.

Discussion Questions

The following exercises will provide opportunities in unitizing, categorizing, and problem solving related to data reduction, **induction**, and negotiating results. The following is a short section from an expanded field journal of the inquiry into what constitutes neglect sufficient to warrant formal intervention. Please read it and then respond to the questions that follow.

Interviewer: *I explained the research and asked her to start in whatever way she wished.*

Respondent: First of all, when doing a neglect investigation, don't go to the police, go to the sheriff for support.

Actually, questions from you would be helpful because I do work with neglect so seldom. Most of my work is with teenagers where the court has determined when they should be removed. You are aware that with truancy they are removing kids now.

For example: I have a girl who attended school only 17 days since the beginning of school She was only removed January 26. I'm amazed at how slow the system is. I think the law says a child is a truant after 3 consecutive days of nonattendance or maybe it's 5 days. But here, to get action it was in connection with something else. She was running to her boyfriend. He's 21 and has been charged with contributing to the misconduct of a minor. She has run three times while in foster care. Her mother has no control. In fact, her mom condones the relationship.

I: *Is that neglect?*

R: Yes.

I: *Why?*

R: This kid is not getting her basic needs met in any sense. There's no education. There's no preparation for the future.

Her father is not in the picture. Parents must be responsible for seeing that kids get to school.

This kid is brighter than anyone in the family. You might want to talk to XX. He's her guardian ad litem. This girl is neat and clean. She comes from the worst home XXX (another worker) has ever seen. The school social worker says it's the worst situation she's ever seen.

She has risen above it. She agreed to go to school in November when she was seen in court the first time. She knew the alternative was foster care. She agreed, but she didn't attend school. Forty days later she was placed in foster care. Right now she is being evaluated in a partial program. The court hearing is today. The return home is the recommendation for the hospital. I talked to them. The psychologist is saying "go home." The program coordinator is saying "no." The psychologist said, though, if I thought the home was unfit that he'd recommend foster care, first, and then return home.

I: *What is fit to live in?*
R: With neglect and the young child, there is an emphasis on the home environment, more than with the older child.

I: *Why?*
R: Whooo. . . . It might be my own biases or prejudices, but I feel the older child can cope better with things. With the younger child, you have to look at safety features. Also, in neglect, if parents don't teach a child to get along in the system, there is a problem in school, with schedules. There are minimum standards for cleanliness that society expects. If kids really live in two worlds they can't get along. This is a form of neglect.

I: *Would you remove for any of this?*
R: Well, it would have to be pretty gross.

I: *How gross?*
R: What age? Well, let's say if we had a case where the family has adequate income to live. There are three kids preschool aged. They receive SSI, ADC, and medical care; but there are no clothes, no food, and the parents are always fighting. Head Start reports that the kids are extremely dirty. The hospital says they saw one of the children in the cold of winter in only a diaper. They recommended removal on this home.

We did a study at the time. The family obtained appropriate living arrangements. The parents are using their income.

Because the parents wouldn't work, the idea was foster care—not the first time, but the second time we had to deal with them.

Before any action, they left town. On follow-up in another town we found out that the children were removed to long-term foster care. I really felt good about that. I thought the kids should be removed.

When I make a decision about removal, I look at the effects and the kinds and the cooperation of the parents. I take into account if parents accept offers to change their circumstances. . . .

1. Return to the interview and identify all respondent data units. Remember that a unit can be as small as one word or as large as several paragraphs. Transfer these units to 3 × 5 cards. Depending upon how you make sense of the information, you will have somewhere between 17 and 40 units.

2. When all units have been transferred to cards, compare each unit with each other unit, lumping units in piles when there seems to be a connection between units. When all units have been sorted into a pile, label each pile. Return to each unit in each pile to be sure that it can still be included under the category label. Rearrange units and create new categories as needed to accurately capture the information. Now return to each category and define what you mean by the words you used to label each pile of data units. Return once more to each lump of data to be sure that, given the definition (or decision rule) the unit should still remain associated with the category. Make changes as necessary.

3. Review each category to be certain that they are all at the same level of abstraction. Try to bring related categories into subcategory sets under more overarching categories. This mapping of the categories will be complete when seven, plus or minus two, major categories have been identified. Now draw a picture or write a paragraph describing the relationship between these categories.

4. Imagine that you now must take this picture or the paragraph back to inquiry participants in a member checking effort. What specific questions would you ask of stakeholders to be certain that the categories and their association make sense or work for them? How would you record the results of this member checking for the audit trail?

The Results of Constructivist Inquiry

The last substantive section brings together all the material from the other sections for a thorough discussion of research quality. The focus continues on both the research process and the product, but the emphasis is on what must be done to warrant quality.

Chapter 8 covers the challenges of preparing a reductionist report of a holistic process. It includes the steps for developing the case study and criteria for assessing the "thickness" and the other dimensions of quality of the description. Chapter 9 develops the functions of research oversight in constructivism including peer review, peer debriefing, and trustworthiness and authenticity audits. All relevant processes, roles, and tasks will be covered, so that the reader will have enough information either to select a peer reviewer and auditor for his or her own research or to act as a peer review or auditor for another's constructivist effort. This section closes in Chapter 10 with a frank discussion of the major issues in constructivist research in social work. It will cover the paradoxes for the profession of social work, including involving research participants while being pulled into objective assessment; the need for power and control related to expertise while developing an emancipatory process for participants; and the politics and social justice issues of alternative frameworks within the traditional expectations of good science in social work. Ethics, relativity, and other potential costs and benefits are underscored in order to prepare the reader for informed consent in undertaking a powerful, alternative process for knowledge building for practice.

Discussion questions and exercises at the conclusions of Chapters 8 and 9 will facilitate more time savings, in that major errors related to peer review, auditing, and reporting results will be uncovered and managed prior to conducing a full-scale constructivist process. The discussion following Chapter 10 will help to solidify the reader's decision making regarding whether or not to undertake a constructivist inquiry.

CHAPTER 8

Presenting Constructivist Research Results

Chapter Contents in Brief

Creating the case study report
Grounding the data for interpretation and for the audit trail
Criteria for assessing the quality of the report
The challenges of a thick description and holism

The final stage in data processing for meaning construction is the preparation of the case report. The case study or case report is the primary reporting vehicle for constructivism, and most other forms of emic inquiry. The primary goal of the case study is to create understanding. It is the product, not a record of the research that was undertaken. The case study builds on the reader's tacit knowledge. It can demonstrate the interplay between the inquirer and the participants. It allows readers to do their own probing for internal consistency regarding the process, the inferences, and the product. It also provides material to allow readers to make their own assessment of the context of the inquiry. Finally, the well-written case study provides the thick description (Geertz, 1973) necessary for judgments about the inquiry results' transferability.

The Process of Creating the Case Study Report

Generally speaking, the case study report should be prepared in transparent, easily understandable language. The language should be directed toward the primary consumers of the information, the stakeholders in the process. They must be comfortable with the communication style and terminology, or the authenticity dimensions of the entire process may be called into question. On the other hand, the writing style should not be so informal as to negate the seriousness with which all engaged in co-constructing meaning. The reading level of the narrative should be pitched at about the fifth grade, which is the same level as most public service announcements and brochures. The issue here is that anyone with higher reading and comprehension will easily comprehend without having their intelligence insulted, while also allowing those with lesser skills to make their way through the material comfortably. Though not written in standard scientific language, that which is formal and distancing for both the inquirer and participants, pitching the writing to this reading level will still offer sufficient sophistication for those periodicals that might consider publishing material that is slightly out of the mainstream. The point is to avoid having to write one version of the case study for consumption by participants and another version for consumption by the reading public who had no involvement in the inquiry process.

The writing technique should be narration. The inquirer is telling a story, not objectifying the situation. It is a process of conquering a mountain of material. Because of this, it is impossible for the inquirer to dispense totally with interpreting what is discovered. In simply ordering the information, the inquirer is interpreting relationships and hierarchies. But when constructing the case report, the inquirer must not allow his or her own editorial interpretations or evaluations to enter into the narrative other than in the sections where it is intended, such as the section regarding lessons learned. Granted, this is an effort of co-construction in which the inquirer is one of the constructors. But to ensure that this is truly a reconstruction of the many realities of the multiple stakeholders, including the inquirer, his or her voice must not be represented more prominently than the rest.

Remember, the inquirer must scrupulously honor promises of confidentiality and anonymity, while not misrepresenting meaning. Also, the inquirer should establish a firm termination date for the inquiry, past which events reported can no longer be changed. If this is not accomplished, the report will never get written because one more "essential" element for meaning making will be available next week, next month, or next year. Finally, to avoid real hassles with the audit, all elements of journaling and maintenance of the audit trail should be continued. As writing proceeds, those things that the inquirer "knew" at the point of completing the data analysis may change. These changes in ordering concepts, relationships, or constructing meaning must become a part of the methodological history of the inquiry. The peer reviewer can be of immeasurable help in monitoring these aspects of the report construction.

While maintaining the integrity of the inquiry and the anonymity of the persons needing protection, the case report can take many forms. The most commonly used, and easiest to construct, but probably not the richest for allowing visceral reactions, is a report bounded by the theory or conceptual framework graphic constructed in the last stage of the data analysis (see Chapter 7). In this format, the story is framed by the major categories or concepts derived from the analysis and their supposed relationships. The relationships serve as headings for sections of the story. Most researchers with reasonable writing skills can construct this type of case report.

Other conventions that are more reflective of nonfiction novels or journalistic renderings are also acceptable. The story could be a scene-by-scene reconstruction of the research process showing the inquirer's engagement with stakeholders in their surroundings over time. It could involve character development through dialogue or be told through a third person, from a subjectivist point of view, like discussing the meaning of constructivist education through the eyes and words of a child who is being educated constructivistically. Or the story could be told through the full detailing of a major scene in the context in which the phenomenon gets its meaning; like telling the story of making public policy concerning the homeless through the final meeting where the vote was taken to establish the policy. These more creative means of relaying a story, known as figurative or rhetorical renditions (Miles & Huberman, 1994; Zeller, 1991), may require creative writing skills, not necessarily part of a social worker's repertoire. An option to acquire such skills would be to take a creative writing class prior to or during a constructivist research process.

Basically, the convention used should be determined by the general purpose of the report and the inquirer should develop the necessary skills to tell the story in the required manner. The inquirer should select strategies and techniques for story telling that are consistent with the purpose, not simply to reflect the skill level of the writer. For example, if the purpose of the inquiry is an evaluation to be used by a board of directors to further develop programs, then will it be more useful for them to gain understanding from a metaphorical story told in the voice of a "typical" client? Or would it be more useful for them to receive the reconstruction guided by the conceptual framework or theory that grew out of the data that details all important dimensions of their service delivery? The inquirer with solid familiarity with the context will have a good idea about what strategy of story construction will be both most useful and most acceptable. In constructivist reporting, just as in reporting of qualitative data using other methods and paradigms, there are no fixed formats. However, Miles & Huberman (1994) provide some good guidance about various important choices including: the audience and desired effect; the "voice" of the report; and issues of style and format. We direct you to their work with the reminder that it is set in a positivistic perspective.

In writing the constructivist story, an informative style is preferred. This should not necessarily be a persuasive style, since that would be more likely to reveal the ideology of the writer instead of the co-construction of the participants. As a last stage in the interaction of constructionism, the readers must come to their own conclusions/reconstructions of the material. As an aid to the reader's personal connection with the material, persuading the reader to accept the writer's perspective is not desired.

To ease the storytelling challenge, it is also good to define a potential reader. Who will be a likely consumer of this material? Schatzman and Strauss (1973) call this "audience conjuring." Once a potential reader is identified, evoke a role for the reader to play. Is the reader a recipient of didactic information? Is he or she participating in a Socratic process of consciousness raising while reading? Whatever the role assigned, a more engaging narrative will result if the reader becomes real in the mind of the storyteller.

Sources for the Provisional Outline

Once the purpose and the consumers of the report are clear, the inquirer should first return to the reflexive journal, in order to review all that emerged during the inquiry. Hidden in this material may be central notions of the lessons to be learned, which should be consciously a part of the story development process. Lessons to be learned must grow out of the data reconstruction that is finalized in the case report, but they may be known in advance of the story construction because of tacit knowledge development. If they are known, to some degree, then they can also serve to aid in conceptualizing the structure of the story. If you know where you want to end, then the story can be structured with that end in mind.

What is certainly available to the inquirer are the data categories, data units, the index of documents, and a graphic representation or theory of the results. Together, these can serve to create a provisional outline for writing the story. Categories can serve as main headings, and subcategories can be subheadings that provide guidance for the content of each paragraph or so in each section. In this way data units can be easily identified and used as quotations. They must also be used to justify any assertions made in each paragraph.

An example from the study of neglect may be helpful here to demonstrate how a category set can serve as a provisional outline. What follows in Table 8–1, taken from the category set created in the constant comparison in the neglect inquiry, could be developed into one section of the case report, the section discussing how neglect is determined. The narrative could cover the decision process, including the identified dimensions, by following an outline created by the ordered subcategories. The inquirer could discuss the "whys" by using the direct quotes that had been lumped in the why category. This could be followed by what participants said about "case-by-case" decision making and so on. It has been our experience that if a solid, clear category set has been created, the outline for the story has also been created so that the story virtually tells itself.

TABLE 8–1

Portion of a Provisional Outline Created from the Category Set

II. Determining Neglect

   1. Decision Process

      1.1 Why

      1.2 Case-by-Case

      1.3 Fear

      1.4 "Knowing"

      1.5 Difficulties

      1.6 Holistic Process

      1.7 Questions

      1.8 Values

      1.9 Chronicity

      1.10 View of Parents

      1.11 View of Child

      1.12 Scores

      1.13 Karma

Grounding in Data and Idiographic Interpretations

For the purposes of the audit trail, every assertion made in the story should be supported by data or it should not be included in the reconstruction. Further, *all* data must be included in the story. Nothing should be left out, even if certain categories create conceptual difficulties for storytelling. This is grounding the story in the data.

Think of all the data units within categories as reference points. They should be handled and regarded in the same fashion as you would when using the work of others to support your written work. Whenever another's work has shaped your own, the original work is cited. Besides honoring the other's work, it also allows for verification of whether or not you have correctly interpreted the other's work in your own. It sets your work in an intellectual tradition. The audit trail that links assertions in the text to data units and then to the original raw data, anchors the work of the case study in much the same way.

As an example of how this is accomplished, a small section of the case study in Chapter 11 has been reproduced here.

> During the time these families were together, they had difficulty with SRS about getting financial support. Having three separate households living in one house created problems with determining each family's eligibility for welfare. [12] Gina had been receiving unemployment and then General Assistance, pending eligibility determination for disability payments. The family of five was receiving ADC when Lilly, Rose, and Oscar moved in. They remember fighting the SRS system. Gina feels that even before the child protection problems, SRS was already prejudiced against her for confronting the procedures related to the family of five, showing she was "well able to fight for her rights and loudly!" "We are not unknown." [13]
>
> Lilly thinks the county considers Gina a possible problem to the "status quo" due to her tattoo, openness, and straightforwardness. [14] Gina says, "the problem is being different and the ability to stand my ground where the rights of an individual are concerned. Being an admitted smoker of marijuana and not a drinker, nor taker of hard drugs is hard for others to cope with." They both agree that small town attitudes were responsible for what subsequently happened to Rose. (Marijuana was never mentioned by SRS, the court or any agency connected with Rose's protective service case.)[15]

Four supports for assertions were provided in these two paragraphs in the form of the bracketed numbers: [12], [13], [14], [15]. Referring to the audit trail attached to this case study will allow you to see that for each of these numbers there is a corresponding number with coded information attached. The coded information for [13] is V-L(1)-35; V-L(1)-16; V-L(1)-15. Readers having access to the expanded field journal would find that these codes identify data unit numbers 35, 16, and 15 that would be found in the first interview with "Lilly," one of the study's participants. The reader would also find that everything that was asserted after [12] could be supported by the units provided in [13]. Every time there is a bracketed number in the text, the material from one bracket to the next is supported by identifiable data units. This should demonstrate the importance of remaining close to the original data in the story construction, not just for ensuring that the story is grounded in the data, but also in order to allow for outside auditing for confirmability. The auditor will make confirmability verification by tracing assertions in the case study to their original raw data.

In keeping with the idea that all data must be included, which means that all categories and subcategories must find their way into the story, the writer should err on the side of overinclusion in the first draft of the report. Only by including everything will the inquirer be certain that the ideology and values of the context, not his or her own preferences or passions, are determining what is included or excluded as the story takes shape. As another means of bounding subjectivity, the inquirer should continue the journalling process while preparing the report. Harris (1990) suggests that the writer start with an "interior text" that moves into a draft "generative text" and finally to the public text of the final report. The journal should be continued to show this process and to capture how interpretations and perspectives change along the way. For it is in the writing itself that the categories and relationships will finally have meaning.

To have meaning in keeping with the assumptions of constructivism, the following elements are necessary:

- The case report should establish no causation. At most, a tentative assertion of the form and process of simultaneous mutual shaping should be put forward.
- Everything should be seen to influence everything else. The manner of this influence should be the meat of the story.
- These findings should be reported based on interactions. There should be no directionality ascribed.

- All elements discussed should be seen as contingently necessary.
- All elements should be constructed as situationally determined and context imbedded.

The "meat" of the story must be reflective of the values that have influenced the inquiry. Aside from the values of constructivism, the research perspective, the values that dictated the choice of the problem to be investigated, must also be clear. Those of the inquiry site must predominate with all stakeholders' values also apparent. The inquirer's values should be clear as well. To that end, it is important that the reader can tell when the narration is in the voice of the inquirer and when it is in the voice of participants. In addition, the study should also include some discussion and reflection on the inquirer's personal experience in the intense process.

Beyond these few areas for standards, little more control or management is possible or desirable. Trying to control the case study by enabling, blocking, or masking findings to create a more powerful story or to produce interesting effects are contrary to the goals of constructivism. What you will find is that the factors introduced in the story may leave your control just as they do in novel construction. Side effects may occur that are important, but uncontrolled. Do not thwart these occurrences. Simply record them reflexively and methodologically for auditing purposes and go where the narrative takes you.

Since you, the inquirer, will probably not know what there is to know until the first draft is completed, allow plenty of time for the case study writing. This will help the interior text move to the generative, exterior text. But time must also be allowed for the public text to develop. There is nothing more frustrating for a writer than to have to share a flat, dull report (that interior text that hasn't even moved to a generative text) with a peer reviewer, participants, and the auditor because time does not allow the refinement in a second or third draft that the writer knows should be made before it "goes public." The report is such an important element in the final stages of the hermeneutic dialectic and so central for the future potential of the process that began with the inquiry, it would be a shame to allow time to limit its quality and impact.

Content

There is no fixed format for the story, but it should include several content dimensions. These dimensions are also guided by the assumptions of constructivism. The content should include a thick description of the site of the inquiry, the problem/issues under investigation, and the lessons that might be learned from this investigation

Denzin (1989), in discussing interpretive interactionism, gives some ideas about what thick description should *not* be. For him it should *not* offer inscription in the place of description. It should *not* romanticize the human actors or obscure, decontextualize, or overtheorize the presentation of the lived experience of the participants. The story should be a rich one that provides a powerful vicarious experience that would at least be a reflection of the power of the inquiry process itself, not simply facts independent of intentions or circumstances (Denzin, 1993). The goal, then, is a "thick description" (Geertz, 1973) that can lead to "thick interpretation" (Denzin, 1989). What constitutes thickness is controversial (see Maxwell, 1992; Zeller, 1987), but the idea is to provide richness and meaningfulness of detail in the context and situation of the investigation.

This richness should include a full site description. What constitutes the context of the study will differ. Some sites will have geographic, agency, or conceptual boundaries that will determine what constitutes the "site" to be described. This description should focus on all aspects of the context that are important for meaning making. An example of this idea can be found in Chapter 11, in which the location of the major interviews is thoroughly described in order to let the reader feel what the lifestyle and priorities of the family appeared to be, based on what could be observed. This type of description was important in telling a story about a family that was consistently investigated by protective services. First impressions, even to professionals, will set the stage for how a family is engaged. These impressions, without real attention to contextual detail, would provide the wrong idea about how this poor family cared for its children. This is central to their story. The inquirer will find that site description will always be central to a constructivist story.

Another area needing thick description is the discussion of the problem or issue that was investigated. One should think of this aspect of the case report as the "findings" section in a traditional research report. Here, however, parsimony is not desired. Full, rich details are necessary for meaning construction. The reader must be given a window into the research experience by hearing the voices of the participants in full detail, including that which is provided nonverbally. While using the structure provided by the category sets, the inquirer will elect to include less abstract details found in the data units in order to "fill out" meaning.

The final area with a "thickness" focus is with lessons to be learned. If thick descriptions have been fashioned related to the context and the focus of the inquiry, then thick interpretation will also be possible. These lessons should be fully described and clearly related to the major elements of the story. As in other reporting of results, the constructivist inquirer should not go beyond the data, even if generalizations are not the goal. Rich, detailed descriptions are an aid for the reader to determine if the insights represented therein can be of use in another context. Just as clear detailing of the problem and the context for transferability is important, so, too, is it important for outsiders. Well wrought lessons can also serve as a capstone of the research process. In addition, this is the "so what" dimension of the inquiry, that, when returned to the context, will continue to reverberate as new ideas and actions are derived from the information. A few examples of lessons learned from one site of the neglect inquiry follow:

- If intense criticism is common in well-developed, highly specialized protection systems, then those who appear more sophisticated about articulating what constitutes neglect are not necessarily more satisfied with the operating system. This is true from the point of those who deliver service, those who receive services, or ordinary citizens who watch service results from a distance.

- If the process of determining neglect is as uncertain, complex, unstable, unique, and value conflicted as portrayed in (site 1), then parents provide a perspective in determining neglect given by no other participants: that is, the need to know the family intimately in order to understand the "whys" of what is being observed. Believing that being objective is the mark of a true profession, professionals' efforts may tend to remove them from the intimacy called for by parents. Professionals seem to struggle daily with a perceived conflict between the intuitive and the scientific: "If we cannot measure it, it does not exist."

- If participants' fears about emotional neglect and the difficulties in capturing and predicting consequences in the affective realm are accurate, then the physical aspects and consequences of the neglectful environment may be less important than the emotional environment and consequences from a long-term individual and societal perspective, but removal is easiest in physical neglect because it is measurable.

- If there are such undifferentiated beliefs about types and context of neglect and if there are no agreed upon levels of minimal parenting, then there is no one definition of neglect, as there is no one standard for acceptable parenting.

These and other lessons from the inquiry process were useful in the recycling of the report to both inquiry sites. They were the basis of further discussion about the protection system in both sites. They could also serve as the propellant for further investigations in other sites.

Because the case report is not journalistic reporting or nonfictional writing, but a research report, attention must also be directed toward the structure and methods used in the process. Just having the warrant of good quality provided by a successful audit will not be sufficient. Since most consumers of the case study will be unfamiliar with auditing, they may wish to make their own judgments about the quality of the process, as well as the richness and usefulness of the product. A full record of the research reported in the case study is not necessary, but minimal discussion should include why the inquirer became interested in the focus of the inquiry; the importance of that interest; the foreshadowed questions and examples of working hypotheses; and methodological aspects for trustworthiness and authenticity.

Criteria for Assessing the Quality of the Final Report

Just as multiple realities and multiple stakeholders are central to constructivist inquiry, multiple measures of inquiry quality are also important. Since judgments about quality and viability depend on standpoint, several levels of quality assessment must be considered.

Peer Reviewer Assessment

The first assessment of the quality of the case study should be made by the peer reviewer. It is the reviewer in the role of debriefer who has accompanied the full process from a distance and should have the ability to determine if the draft of the case report actually captures what has come to be known and understood about the focus of the inquiry. There are several aspects that should be assessed prior to sharing the report more publicly. The feedback from the peer reviewer should move the product from a generative one to one that is public.

The peer reviewer reads the report to determine the adequacy of representation of sites. The rendering should allow the reviewer to picture clearly the important dimensions of the context of the inquiry. The reviewer also checks for existence of errors in fact or interpretation based on what has been shared by the inquirer during the unfolding of the inquiry process. It should be clear that there are no omissions, especially of salient aspects. As the reviewer is reading, there should be a clarity in voice. The writer's interpretations should be distinguishable from those of the participants.

As a measure of conforming with the ethical dimensions of the process and product, the reviewer checks to determine the degree of confidentiality and anonymity. Identities should be protected without changing meaning. Finally, the reviewer can be involved in editing to suggest elimination of irrelevant or controversial language. In this regard, the reviewer should help the writer to select unloaded or neutral language so that the language does not act as a barrier to consumer's engagement with the material. For example, instead of exact quotes where nasty name calling occurred, the peer reviewer can help to shape the discussion so that meaning can be derived without causing pain or anger. Here, again, changing or eliminating language should improve the potential for communication, not change the meaning.

Changes to the case report as a result or reviewer feedback should be recorded reflexively. They should also become part of the audit trail. These changes will be treated in the same way as the changes that result from the final member check to be discussed in the next section.

Participant Assessment

The draft of the case study should be shown to respondents in a comprehensive member check "to obtain confirmation that the report has captured the data as constructed by the informants, or to correct, amend, or extend it, that is, to establish the credibility of the case" (Lincoln & Guba, 1985, p. 236). This opportunity is provided to allow the participants to correct the data, challenge the interpretations, provide new data, assess overall adequacy of the story, and confirm the inquirer's reconstruction of their constructions.

A full member check would involve showing the draft of the case study to all participants in the process. Time limits, logistics, and other limits may mean that only representatives of each stakeholding group may be able to offer feedback at this stage. Determination of how the final member check will be conducted—with all participants individually or in groups, with a selection of participants, and so forth—should be based on the respondents' capacity to respond in needed ways. They should be able to respond verbally, in writing, or in a group, depending upon the strictures of the inquiry process at the time of the final member check. Care should be given, if representatives are selected, that those chosen are legitimate representatives of the stakeholding groups, capable of assessing whether or not accurate reconstruction occurred.

Participants have a right to correct error of fact. To do this they should read to find their own constructions in order to assess the adequacy and accuracy of the portrayal. Participants can only alter their material. They cannot alter other constructions, including those of the inquirer. To be satisfied with the reconstruction, they must see that their perspective is accurately represented. They must see their voice. Their feedback, particularly related to revisions, any further action that should be taken, or comments about the feedback process must become part of the audit trail. Figure 8–1 is a model for recording feedback and revision decisions. When a data unit is changed based on feedback, that new data unit should become a part of the audit trail alongside the original data unit and be included in the original coding scheme. The use of "R" in front of the original code should be sufficient detail to allow audit recon-

---

FIGURE 8–1

Example of Case Study Revisions Document

CODE

Site:_____2_____

Date of revision:___6-23-88___

Type 1=Notes
2=New Documents
3=Draft
4=Questions
5=Qualifiers (none, some, many, most, etc.)
0=Other

Source PR=Peer Reviewer
PA=Participant
O=Other

R#	Type	Page	Lines	Source	Action	Comments
1	3	3	8	PR	add	document reference
		27	15	PR	change	language used change meaning

struction. For example, if based on feedback from Lilly, the family of five, discussed in the case study snippet above was really a family of six, then data unit V-L(1)-15 would become RV-L(1)-15, with family of six being recorded on the new data card. Both data units would continue in the process and both would be reported in the audit trail.

If the inquirer disagrees with the feedback or the requested change, negotiation should occur. This will be another time the hermeneutic circle might be invoked. The issue might be large enough to warrant a full-blown consensus-building process. If negotiation does not resolve the problem, then the objecting participant's perspective must be reflected in a minority report, which becomes a permanent addendum to the case report.

This final member checking is one of the last interventive and empowerment aspects of the inquiry. All aspects of authenticity can be enhanced when sufficient time is allowed for thorough consideration of the case report content, for feedback, and for any negotiation that might be required. The most important aspect is the power redistribution that occurs when participants are certain that the data they provided belong to them, not to the inquirer, or anyone else. When the inquirer honors participant input by either making changes or negotiating until all are satisfied, it may be the first time that they really realize how different constructivist research is. Their ultimate power is with the continued ability to withdraw from the process, even at this late stage. Their data will go with them, not to be recorded in the final report, except when two or more participants have said the same thing.

Auditor Assessment

The auditor will be working with the revised case report that includes the feedback from the peer reviewer, the final member check, and any revisions that have occurred as a result of the prior reviews of the material. The auditor's review of the case report is central to the confirmability audit in which the auditor will trace assertions to the original raw data. It is also important in the transferability assessment because the auditor will be assessing its thickness.

The first level of quality assessment involves judging the case report's congruence with constructivism. Are multiple realities and mutual shaping reflected in the story? Are relationship patterns instead of generalizability evident? Are the values influencing the inquiry congruent with those of constructivism?

Lincoln and Guba (1990) have suggested four additional criteria for judging the quality of case reports that should be helpful in determining how well the case is done. *Resonance* relates to value congruence in all its dimensions. Is the case study congruent with the assumptions of constructivism? Are the values that influenced all aspects of the inquiry reflected? The **rhetoric** criterion allows assessment of the form, structure, and characteristics of the case study. Is unity exhibited by the story advancing well-organized, central ideas? Is the story simple and clear? Is the story well crafted? *Empowerment* assesses the degree to which the case study can facilitate action on the part of the readers. Is the story clear and powerful enough for the reader to be propelled to take some action about the circumstances reported, or other similar circumstances? Finally, Guba and Lincoln offer an *applicability* criterion to judge the potential for readers to draw inferences and linkages to his or her own experience. This is not to be confused with generalizability. The question is about whether the meaning is clear enough that readers might draw out applications to their own experiences even if they are dissimilar from what is reported in the case study.

Zeller (1987, 1991) has also provided guidance about determining if the case study is thick enough. Does it have *power* and *elegance*? Is it precise and graceful? Is the story *creative*? Does it go beyond the concrete reporting of the "he said/she said" to new ideas? Is it playful? Does it challenge the reader to explore unexplored grounds? Is the case study *open* and focused on *problematic qualities*? Is it open to negotiation by being tentative and exploratory in its conclusions, such as the lessons to be learned about the problem under investigation? Is the story *independent*? Zeller (1987) asks, does the writing demonstrate the intellectual wrestling that the writer went through to get beyond his or her own constructions while also being able to honor the other, different constructions in the story? Does it *demonstrate the writer's commitment to craftsmanship*? Has care been given to the construction of the story so that the story does not appear to be thrown together at the last minute through typos, sentence structure, and other details? An emotional and intellectual connection between the writer and the case should be apparent. Does the story display *courage*? Is there any risk-taking exhibited, or has the status quo been supported? Finally, is *egalitarianism* represented so that all constructions are respected and presented, even if they are not all equally informed and sophisticated?

As a final check for quality, the auditor should also determine the quality of the document as a research report. Certainly, the majority of the quality of the methodology will be determined through other aspects of the audit to be discussed in Chapter 9, but in a general sense the case should provide sufficient information for those other than the auditor who will be interested in the quality of the research process. To make this type of methodological judgment, the following should be noted.

- Is there a formal problem statement about a dilemma or an unsatisfactory state related to an action, a value, or a perception?
- Is there a review of the literature that places the problem in a historical context?
- Is there attention to multiple perspectives and meanings that imbed the issue in ongoing history?
- Are the research questions discussed as they emerged?
- Is the inquiry strategy detailed including the setting, how the research was undertaken, and who participated?
- Was what occurred to seek alternative constructions and limit the context, made clear?

Consideration of these different aspects of quality should provide a thorough outsider's assessment of the quality of the case report. The final outsider perspective of interest is that of the uninvolved reader.

Reader Assessment

Though little attention has been focused on the uninvolved consumer of the case report, some recognition should be given to individual readers other than those directly or indirectly involved in the research process. Generalizability is not a goal of a constructivist process, but empowerment is. All types of empowerment potential should be considered, including whether or not an uninvolved reader might become empowered as a result of exposure to the story. The quality case report will do just that.

For the outside reader, the first question is whether a vicarious experience was enabled. There is an assumption here that a powerful experience will evoke or facilitate action, just as it can for participants; that an evocative story will serve to create consciousness raising. This consciousness may not be as thorough and complete as for those who have had a persistent participation in hermeneutic dialectic; but clarity about the issues, a potential for reconstruction of long held constructions, should be possible. If this occurs, then action should not be far behind.

If the reader is as interested in a report of the research process as in the story that the inquiry has produced, certain other issues should be judged.

- Was methodology reported, including the participants, the interview protocol, the confidentiality protections, the research process?
- Were the constructions well-drawn with coherence, a thick description, and a balanced view?

Judgments along these dimensions allow the reader, in addition to the auditor, to make an independent decision about the quality of the constructivist inquiry. In keeping with the assumptions and goals of constructivism, the role of the consumer of the research shifts to include another very important aspect of knowledge utilization.

Thick Descriptions and the Responsibility of the Reader

In Chapters 6 and 7 we detailed the responsibility of the inquirer or the sending agent in the creation of a research product. We also suggested elsewhere that the major responsibility regarding the subsequent use of the case study rests with the receiving agent. The following section will detail the responsibilities of the outside reader in relation to the case report.

The reader should try to engage seriously with the story. This means that full attention should be placed on the written word. This engagement should be as focused as with a novel that is too good to put down. No other thoughts or realizations should occur, except those related to the story line. True engagement may even result in loss of time and space orientation. The reader should allow himself or herself to be carried away by the story. If this happens, then the reader has reached a metaphorical (approximate) or real understanding of the material.

When the reader works on understanding, he or she is also open to the possibility of being stretched through new learning. The reader can test his or her own knowledge so that it can actually be challenged by what is being read. It is important that readers allow and accept the potential challenges to their own current constructions. It is through this challenge that new constructions grow from the experience. In this way, the reader participates in the hermeneutic dialectic. Most importantly, the reader should enjoy the vicarious experience and be willing to learn from it.

The reader is also responsible for whatever subsequent applications of the findings might occur in another setting. The reader should use the ideas from the case report to determine what is relevant to another particular situation. Even by comparing very different constructions, new ideas may emerge about what might be relevant in another context. New working hypotheses will emerge to be tested in another setting. Remember, the only requirement with the sending context, the work of the inquirer, is to fashion as thick a description as possible. The receiving context, the reader, needs to determine if inferences can be drawn that may have applicability in their own context or situation

The Challenges of Creating a Holistic Report

Case reports can rarely be reduced to the normal article size of 12 to 20 pages; but the intense long-term experience of the inquiry must be reduced to be manageable for all stakeholders. The goal is a holistic report that captures all salient variables in a network of relationships embedded in the complexities of a specified time and setting. It is not an easy task to report an all-encompassing process with sufficient detail to allow vicarious understanding of the meaning that has been co-constructed. Some reduction will occur, though a holistic picture is ever the goal.

Since holism is the goal, there is a tendency for case reports to run into tens to hundreds of pages. This places the consumer of the report at risk of the data overload that plagues even the most experienced constructivist researcher. If the reader is overwhelmed with detail, then it will be virtually impossible to enter the case in a sensemaking fashion. Providing a very thick, rich, holistic story may make the story essentially unconsumable except to the most diehard readers, such as those who have a vested interest in the results; those who commissioned the research; or those who approved the research proposal. Care should be given in the second or third drafting to allow for reader engagement. The story should be crisp and clear, warm and detailed, but it should not overwhelm.

Though concise presentation is necessary to avoid overwhelming the consumer, it is a rare case report that will be shorter than 30 pages. In less than that length it is difficult to provide sufficient, rich detail. This length will automatically limit the range of publishing possibilities. Few professional journals can afford to publish lengthy research reports. This will probably mean that, aside from monographs like those prepared as a final research report for a funder, the major option for publication of findings will be in book chapters. Only book chapters allow sufficient lengths to guard against reductionism that could spoil the thickness the inquirer has worked so hard to achieve.

Clearly, case studies have limits as a holistic report of an engagement that occurred on many levels over a long period. Real feelings may be lost. The sites and subtle sounds may not be captured well enough to record their impact. Smells and subtle feelings are also generally absent from the reconstructed co-construction. Many times meaning comes from much more than the words. Unfortunately, the nonverbals generally are not so finely recorded so that they serve as well constructed, stand-alone data units. In short, the case study, while portraying the "meat" of the story, may lose the "heat" of the process.

Just as much experimentation is occurring in the development of authenticity standards, in standards for the quality of a case report, and in the auditing process, so, too, is some experimenting being undertaken to find alternative ways to report this alternative process and product. Though there is recognition that the case report is the manner most likely to be able to cross paradigmatic perspectives for acceptance and appreciation, some researchers are looking for reporting methods that are uniquely congruent with the constructivist process.

The politics of research (see Diesing, 1991) has necessarily limited this search. Most dissertation committees and research funders are not interested in supporting new and potentially "fringe" reporting methods. Therefore, this experimentation has tended to occur in the classroom setting, where the newest scholars to encounter constructivism, the students, are pushing the limits of the process and product vision. Such ideas as art work, films, interactive videos, and other multidimensional renderings of results are being developed. The reader is encouraged to take up this challenge as well. Experiment with ways to give voice to the process and product of constructivist inquiry by trying new ways to capture the reconstruction. Your help is needed to develop a method of reporting that can capture the holistic intensity of the constructivist inquiry process.

Discussion Questions

These questions focus on determining the appropriate means to reporting results and of evaluating the quality of the case study report.

1. What elements should be considered in determining the focus of a report? Who should have final say in how the case report is focused?

2. What are the various forms that a case report can take? Given your experience and skills, what form will probably be your preference? Why?

3. Why is it virtually impossible to reduce a case report to 12 to 20 pages? What are the risks involved in attempting this sort of reduction?

4. Discuss the various ways to evaluate the quality of the research report? In doing so, look at the responsibilities of the peer reviewer, the auditor, the research participant, and the uninvolved outside reader in assessing case report quality.

CHAPTER 9

Peer Debriefing, Peer Review, and the Audit

Chapter Contents in Brief

The tasks of peer review and debriefing
The audit process and the tasks of the auditor

There is a very big risk that emergent design research with an intersubjective, mutual-shaping focus will be dismissed as nonrigorous knowledge building. Many, mostly from a more traditional, positivist perspective, will doubt that this type of process can be called research, let alone scientific research. As a response to the concerns that constructivist inquiry is more art and intervention than science, various elements of research oversight have been developed. Outside observation and monitoring of the process and product attempt to warrant the rigor of the constructivist process and product. The challenges to prove quality in constructivist research are a bit different than with traditional research. In traditional research, if the results are either generalizable or reproducible, there is agreement that the research has merit. In alternative research such as constructivism, generalizability and reproducibility are neither of interest, nor are they possible. Therefore, warranted assertibility (Lincoln & Guba, 1985; Schwandt & Halpern, 1988) is the goal of research oversight in alternative paradigm research. Here, the researcher must put into place sufficient safeguards and reviews to suggest that the findings are reasonable, given the assumptions, the processes, and the context of the inquiry.

What follows in this chapter are details regarding tools and techniques whereby the rigor of a constructivist process can be procedurally assured and assessed both in process and in retrospect. All that is contained in this chapter will aid the constructivist inquirer in establishing the merit of the research work that is being undertaken. In addition, there should be sufficient detail to allow the reader to participate competently in all aspects of quality judgments of another's constructivist inquiry, either as a peer reviewer or as an auditor.

Peer Review and Debriefing

In Chapter 5 the function of the peer review was discussed. Peer review establishes a connection between the investigator and a peer who is not a part of the inquiry process but has knowledge and skills to support the inquiry as it unfolds. In this section the focus will be on selecting a peer reviewer and undertaking peer review and debriefing. The peer review process begins the possibility of warranted assertibility, but it is much, much more.

The debriefing aspect of peer review will sustain and support the inquirer through the most difficult stages of this essentially uncontrollable, knowledge-building process. The peer reviewer gains an intimate knowledge about the inquirer and the inquiry that is being undertaken in order to facilitate the quality of the inquiry. In essence, the peer reviewer becomes another partner in the inquiry. This partner focuses more on the process and methods of inquiry, rather than on meaning construction, as do the other participant stakeholding partners.

The decision about whether or not to engage a peer reviewer is clear cut. If one wants to conduct a constructivist inquiry, a peer reviewer must persistently accompany the process from its initial steps to the completion of the negotiation for the final case study report. Who is selected to be the peer reviewer is of central importance to the affective and intellectual dimensions of the inquiry, because who performs the review and debriefing functions will have marked impact on the inquirer and how information and feelings are managed. The selection of the peer reviewer should be as serious a decision as where to begin the inquiry.

The peer reviewer should be selected based on several requirements. The reviewer must be an individual with whom the inquirer can develop trust. The inquirer must be able to risk being vulnerable with this person and must respect the individual sufficiently to allow his or her advice to be considered seriously. The reviewer must know the methodology of constructivism. Without this competence, a major function of the peer review relationship, that of research oversight, will be lost. The peer reviewer must be technically able to undertake a constructivist inquiry of his or her own in order to act in the role of reviewer.

Peer debriefing is not just oversight of the technical aspects of the emerging design. There is an aspect of research supervision as well. The reviewer will be called on to act much like a clinical supervisor would in a case conference, only here the conference will be regarding the whole of the inquiry. To competently serve in this regard, it is essential that the reviewer have some substantive competence in the subject being investigated. If substantive competence is missing, then the inquirer will either reject suggestions or have the capacity to fool the reviewer and, in doing so, may end up fooling himself or herself and the rest of the inquiry participants with ill-conceived results.

The reviewer must also have time available to serve in the capacity of reviewer and debriefer. Contact will be frequent and persistent throughout the life of the project. Meetings will average once every other week for at least one hour. At different stages of the inquiry, particularly at the very beginning and during the analysis, these meetings may occur more often and be of longer duration. In most cases, these will be face-to-face encounters, but sometimes just a quick contact by phone or e-mail will be all that is necessary.

Not only should the reviewer be able to respond when needed while acting in the role of supervisor, he or she must also be able to actively pursue meetings. If the inquirer decreases contact, the peer reviewer can help the quality of the process by facilitating continued contact, even when the inquirer does not seem to need support or assurance. The reviewer, to be of real assistance, must have an eye on all aspects of the research as it unfolds. Less than that will limit the auditor's capacity to provide warrants of the oversight, the emergence, the bounded subjectivity, or the methodological decisions.

Finally, the reviewer must agree to make a consistent record of the debriefing activities. The *peer reviewer journal* serves as a type of triangulation to the process and to the progressive subjectivity of the inquirer. The peer reviewer should record the material addressed in any debriefing session and any recommendations, advice, or other support that was provided. The auditor will refer to these entries in a cross-referencing process during the audit to see that what was discussed during debriefing found its way into the reflections of the inquirer or into methodological decisions. Lack of a full peer review journal may effect the auditor's assessment of confirmability, dependability, and credibility. Figure 9–1 provides an example of a peer reviewer's entry after a session with an inquirer.

The Tasks of Peer Review

There are four major tasks of peer debriefing and peer review. The results of all the tasks should be part of the journal. Absence of evidence of any of these tasks could place the auditor's warranting of quality in jeopardy.

The first, and most important, task is *asking difficult questions.* Whenever the reviewer senses the development of a potential problem in any aspect of the inquiry, the question must be asked. If it appears that the inquirer is leading respondents in the questioning; if the inquirer seems to be prematurely closing off discussion because he or she has found what she wanted and does not seem to want to pursue disconfirmation; or if the inquirer seems to be rationalizing a decision, instead of it being based on real, not imagined information, then the reviewer is obligated to force a serious look at that aspect through direct questioning. In many cases, the inquirer "knows" that the question must be posed and answered; it may just be easier to avoid working out the problem. The peer reviewer serves to keep the inquirer honest.

This type of questioning may be a bit uncomfortable from time to time, but the reviewer should not necessarily strive to make the inquirer comfortable. This process should be envisioned as yet another dimension of the hermeneutic circle. Therefore, the discomfort of a dialectic should be expected and embraced. It will make for a sturdier relationship between the inquirer and the reviewer and will assure a better process and product in the inquiry.

With the inquirer, the reviewer should also engage in *exploration of methodological next steps.* What should happen next in the development of the research design, data collection, or analysis? The inquirer is certainly in charge of the methodological decisions, but, in many cases, needs to talk about what the steps should be and what should be expected. At other times, the researcher may be so close to the process that he or she does not "see" what should be done. Here the technical competence in constructivism is essential. The reviewer will be far enough removed from the process to have a more holistic view of what has occurred and what should happen next. The reviewer then can serve as a technical consultant. The inquirer and reviewer, together, can explore what to do and how to do it, because the reviewer has no vested interest in the outcome of the inquiry.

The inquirer will desperately need the next task at various critical junctures in the process. *Sympathetic listening* is central in helping the inquirer to bound his or her own emotions and biases as the inquiry proceeds. Frustration about inaccessible participants; fear about what effect the questions might have on certain types of participants; worry about technical aspects such as disguising identity, or finding meaning, all require someone with whom to process the worry, tension, or fear. No advice or consultation is necessary, just unconditional support. Sometimes important breakthroughs in meaning occur as the inquirer works out his

---

FIGURE 9–1

Peer Reviewer Journal Entry

2–26   With her knowledge about neglect, there is a question that she is setting too much structure in the interviews. We looked at several expanded field notes and found lots of triangulation. We tested for the types of questions . . . not many closed questions.

It would seem that she is able to build trust from prior knowledge. This helps relationships.

Looked also at site 1 categories. The cards seem to fit the categories and the categories make sense to me.

We talked about the next steps in analysis and how to keep the richness. At issue are conceptual/theoretical issues like urban vs. rural, long-term neglect, parental intent.

3–18   (phone) We keep missing each other. The question is how to deal with the judge in evaluating whether or not he is having too much influence in the process and how participants are reacting. Data do not suggest a problem.

4–20   Given the entry of new participants, she will drop site 3. The differences between site 1 and site 2 seems to be able to provide enough diversity.

Much worry about how case studies can come from all this data. I don't really know, nor does she; but I told her not to worry!

4–22   Read all the interviews from site 2. There are open and represent a qualitative difference from site 1. Some themes are emerging that are not surprising, but validating. Next step is to unitize site 2 data. We will meet again once she has completed initial categorization.

---

or her own feelings and intuitions with the reviewer present. Most inquirers are not blessed with a sympathetic partner or spouse who is willing or able to process the intellectual and emotional baggage that accrues in such an intense experience. The reviewer needs to be available for this or the quality of the inquiry will be threatened by an inquirer without energy, focus, commitment, or distance. Sympathetic listening helps the inquirer to do this for himself or herself. In this regard, peer debriefing can have a cathartic effect.

Social workers familiar with either administrative or clinical supervision will recognize the final function of the peer reviewer, *research supervision and documentation*. New social workers know that the most effective way to develop skills in practice is when good supervision is available. The reviewer, who is also an experienced constructivist researcher, can help the inquirer to hone his or her skills during the investigation. The reviewer can help the inquirer to practice needed skills like role playing interviewing an expert or a particularly difficult participant, or developing conceptual schemas for understanding the data. The reviewer can help the inquirer to focus on specific problem situations, so that the inquirer can feel more competent and confident. As in other supervision, the reviewer should not only focus on conceptualizational skills and data management techniques, but should also be alert to any "blind spots" the inquirer might have.

The reviewer should never take on the role of therapist. The goal of peer review is to facilitate skills development in constructivist research. Any interpersonal issues that might interfere with a successful implementation of an inquiry should be addressed in other venues outside of the peer review relationship. As with administrative supervision documentation, all results of these communications must be reported in the peer review journal for the reviewer to comply with the peer debriefing accountability expectations.

Finally, in specific situations such as when an inquirer crosses race, class, or gender boundaries, it may be helpful to call on the services of one or more additional peer reviewers. The task of these reviewers would be to serve as cultural interpreters, monitoring inquirer sensemaking and the conduct of the inquiry to assure cultural or ethnic competence. For example, when an Anglo male inquirer was investigating young African-American male self-esteem building programs, it was essential to count on a second peer reviewer who was African-American and who knew the context and philosophy of these types of programs. The second reviewer advised about communications styles and on appropriate next steps to guarantee appropriate engagement with legitimate stakeholders. This reviewer also monitored the development of the category set for cultural sensitivity. Finally, he reviewed the draft of the case report prior to its return to the field for insensitive or controversial issues. This additional support enabled the inquirer to effectively cross boundaries that had been almost impossible to bridge in the past.

Auditing

As the major warrant of the quality and rigor of the constuctivist research process and product, Lincoln and Guba (1985) and Schwandt and Halpern (1988) recommend an audit approach, and we recommend their work for many useful details about planning and conducting a constructivist audit. Fashioned on the fiscal auditing metaphor, the audit looks at the research practices and the findings to assure the integrity and quality of the inquiry.

The auditor is responsible for the examination of the methodological processes, the data collected, and the subsequent reconstructions derived from the analysis in order to attest to the trustworthiness and authenticity of the constructivist process and product. The audit involves a formal examination of the records to assess evident inquirer bias and to verify consistency, appropriateness, and accuracy of the content and the procedures for analysis (Lincoln & Guba, 1985; Skrtic, 1985a). Reports in the literature of such audits are few (See Chelimsky, 1985; Green, et al., 1988; Halpern, 1983; Hudson & McRoberts, 1984; Skrtic, 1985a), but auditing is an important dimension of constructivist inquiry. This section will discuss the "doing" of auditing from the perspective of both the auditor and the inquirer, so that the reader will have information about two important skill packages, that of auditee and auditor, to create the framework for a very new idea in peer criticism.

The Audit Process

Schwandt and Halpern (1988) have developed a reasonable procedure for conducting an audit that runs from preparing for the audit to the completion of the audit report. This framework (see Table 9–1) will structure this discussion because it can serve as a useful guide for trustworthiness and authenticity audits. This discussion is also built on the assumption that a full audit trail has been developed and maintained by the inquirer and that it is available for all aspects of the audit. This is done on the belief that the purposiveness necessary to create a thorough and complete audit trail, rather than leading to possible deception and bias as Green et al. (1988) suggest, introduces more reflexivity into the inquiry and more sophisticated searches for meaning.

Preparing for the Audit. In the first stage of the audit, Schwandt and Halpern note that inquiries may be audited for a variety of reasons based on the needs and desires of the inquirer or other parties interested in demonstrating the rigor of the study. It may be a requirement of a research contract or it may result from a decision on the part of the inquirer. Once a decision has been made to engage in the auditing process, a potential auditor must be contacted.

As with peer review, the choice of auditor is a critical decision for the inquirer. To assure that no one questions the integrity of the audit, an independent, external agent should be selected. The process is too intense and fraught with subjectivity, which could impinge upon outside acceptance of the audit results without the distance created by an independent outsider. Even if the inquirer is an insider in the context of the inquiry, an outsider is necessary to assure accountability to all consumers of the inquiry product and to all who feel the impact of the inquiry process.

Content and methodological expertise are needed to address competently all aspects of trustworthiness and authenticity. Without familiarity

---

TABLE 9–1

Auditing Procedure

Step	Goal	Product
Preparing for the audit	Identifying audit needs	
	Explore auditor/auditee fit	
Assessing auditability	Assessment of audit trail	
Negotiation and contracting	Set audit scope and objectives	Contract
Preparing the audit work	Determine how to achieve audit objectives	Audit work plan
Implementing the audit	Gather and evaluate evidence to test assertions	Audit work papers
Preparing the audit report	Form an audit opinion	Final audit report

This material is based on the work of T. Schwandt and E. Halpern (1988). *Linking auditing and metaevaluation: Enhancing quality in applied inquiry.* Newbury Park, CA: Sage.

with the substantive issues embedded in the entity being studied, there is little likelihood that an auditor can determine if the findings are logically based on the data for a confirmability audit. Although a naive auditor could trace data clumps back to the original data source, that auditor would be challenged to assess the quality of the logic of the category systems that emerged without some familiarity with the internal logic, assumptions, and understandings already reached in the field of study.

Though a dependability audit would not be much of a challenge for auditors unfamiliar with the content area, some of the methodological decisions based on the political issues that might emerge in the context may be beyond their ability to assess without a concomitant familiarity with the subject matter. Credibility and all dimensions of the authenticity assessment are also substantially dependent upon content as well as method expertise. Knowledge about the subject is central in determining if credible findings were produced. This knowledge is also essential in determining if all important voices have been included in the process and if the inquiry has resulted in education and new sophistication about the subject. Finally, content expertise is essential in facilitating the development of inquirer trust in the auditing process and product. Without that trust, the inquirer remains perfectly able to stonewall or otherwise manipulate the content and process of the audit.

Because of the anxiety produced by laying open one's complete data files and reflexive journals to an outsider, the development of a trusting relationship is critical to a collaborative audit process with potential for reasonable warrants of quality. Like the constructivist inquiry and the peer review, the audit can produce dynamic tensions and conflict. These also can be a part of a hermeneutic dialectic (Guba & Lincoln, 1989) leading to intense, powerful insights about the inquiry, or this dynamism can be what constrains collaboration and limits a true auditing process.

Shared substantive and methodological expertise are a beginning basis for mutual respect. The intensity of the process, in combination with this mutual respect, can facilitate trust. But caution must also be taken regarding the trusting bond between auditor and auditee, for such resonance may compromise rigor. Overidentification between inquirer and auditor, and the interactive nature of the audit may create a sense of power about the inquiry and a reassurance about its quality that are unwarranted, given the data. The collaboration and the informality that tend to grow may subtly adjust the expectations about the quality of the work, compromising standards, and thus jeopardizing a rigorous audit and solid judgments about quality.

The audit has its own power, but it is not without risk. There is the potential for such a strong bond to develop that the auditor becomes co-opted and/or blinded to potential inquirer biases, much like the potential for inquirer blindness to participant bias and manipulation in an inquiry. Shared mind-sets and possible overidentification raise questions about the rigor of the audit that are similar to the standard questions about constructivist inquiry rigor. Without having to resort to auditing the audit, accepted constructivist inquiry methods can be used as safeguards to enhance the trustworthiness of the audit. The audit process should be documented both methodologically and reflexively. The auditor must address issues of expectations and common values orientations during the process and in the audit report. Bounded subjectivity should be evident. A complete description of all audit activities should be part of the report in order to allow the reader to assess the rigor of the audit to be certain that compromised standards are not part of the warrant of quality.

After locating a possible auditor, the inquirer must describe the study and the scope and goals of the proposed audit in sufficient detail for the potential auditor to make an initial decision of whether or not to undertake the audit. This description may be in verbal or written form and should include a description of the context and purpose of the inquiry, why an audit is desired, the proposed scope and goals of the audit, and the dimensions of the audit trail that has been laid down. This should serve as an orientation to the study and will be the first decision point in the audit. Both parties must feel comfortable enough with all dimensions of what is available for audit and the goals of the audit to proceed to the next stage of auditing.

The second stage of auditing involves *assessing auditability, negotiating, and contracting the audit.* An initial, direct examination of the audit trail is recommended to determine if the study is truly auditable. The trail should consist of raw data, data reduction and analysis material, data reconstruction and synthesis information, process notes, and journals. It should also include records of intentions, dispositions, and instrument development, if they exist. The auditor must become familiar enough with the trail material to determine its completeness and comprehensibility. If the audit trail is seen to have utility, then the audit process can proceed. If there are gaps in the trail, the inquirer must decide to revise the audit trail as necessary and/or decide whether to proceed with the audit.

If this auditability assessment is satisfactory for both parties, they move to a formal agreement phase in which negotiation of an audit contract is undertaken. This contract details the scope and objectives of the audit as well as such procedural details as timelines, deadlines, and fees. Mechanisms for renegotiation should also be spelled out in detail.

Regarding the negotiated timeline, Green et al. (1988) suggest that limiting the time frame of the audit allows the auditor to become immersed in the study and thereby gain a holistic understanding of the inquiry. This familiarity with the content under investigation will enhance the auditor's capacity to manage any efforts on the part of the inquirer to limit the scope and depth of the audit. Intimate knowledge will help the auditor maximize the effort to validate methodological considerations and research implications, because the difference between limits for personal self-protection and limits to cover or obfuscate will be apparent. With content familiarity, it is possible to determine if the time limits imposed will impinge on the auditor's ability to attest to the quality of the process and the product.

To further mitigate against potential inquirer manipulation, another logistical issue, on-site audits, should be considered and built into the contract. On-site work not only minimizes the distractions for the auditor (just as is found in financial audits), it also ensures the availability of all necessary documents and records. When information is not available, the auditor on-site will be more likely to recognize this either as a real gap or as something not essential to the logic of the reconstructions being audited. In addition, the intensity of an on-site effort creates an environment within which trust can develop rapidly. With the details in writing regarding timing, location, format of the final report, and mechanisms for renegotiation, the formal agreement phase ends.

In the third stage, *preparing the audit work program*, the auditor develops a preliminary plan for the audit based upon the scope of the audit and the standards to be used, including the constraints of agreed-upon timelines. Plans should be made to audit for both trustworthiness and authenticity. Schwandt and Halpern (1988) provide guidance about assessing confirmability, dependability, and credibility. The auditor must plan on how to assess whether findings are grounded in data, whether inferences are logical, whether the category structure is useful for confirmability. For dependability, plans should be made about how to assess the appropriateness of inquiry decisions and methodological shifts. Credibility assessment plans should include ways to assess design and implementation of inquiry strategies and their integration with outcomes. Also, the assessment of congruence between the descriptions of methodological choices, data sources, findings, and the audit trail should be planned.

To develop the trustworthiness audit plan, the auditor can rely on background material (research proposal, case studies, etc.) supplied by the inquirer to suggest specific steps in document examination. In reviewing materials, the auditor should take notes about the content, issues raised, questions that need clarification, and specific claims made to pursue later in the auditing process. From this work, he or she can also become familiar with the case report, so the time on-site can be devoted exclusively to audit trail review. In reading the case report, it is good to note particular statements or questions that seemed surprising or otherwise interesting to serve as material for backtracking to the original data sources on site.

Schwandt and Halpern (1988) provide no guidelines for an authenticity audit, but our experience indicates that this type of audit is possible without the need to create new tools or documents for the audit trail. This is not to say that auditing for authenticity is not without its own special challenges that must be addressed if this aspect or rigor is to become fully developed. We refer you to Chapter 5 for a detailed discussion of the current challenges in this type of audit.

At this stage of authenticity development, plans to assess fairness should focus on how to measure the degree to which stakeholding voices are heard and protected in the emergent design, data collection, and member checks. Two major warrants of fairness include the product of the process and the voices of the participants regarding the process. If the auditor can find evenhanded representation of all viewpoints in the case study, and if testimonials of the participants indicate that they felt included, respected, and heard, then there is a good chance that the process was fair.

Short of observing the hermeneutic dialectic in action, plans to warrant ontological authentication should include assessing data from member checks and testimony of participants. Participant responses, including those of the researcher, should show an appreciation of how complex the issue under investigation is. Statements about possession of a better understanding of self and others are adequate warrants that consciousness raising has occurred.

Educative authenticity assessment should be planned to include measuring a continual circling of communication in the dialectic hermeneutic. But without the possibility of observing this process, plans to assess educative authentication should include the assessment of reflexive and methodological journals, expanded field notes, and the series of member checks. Evidence that the inquirer has incorporated ideas from one perspective into the conversation with individuals from another perspective as demonstrated in the field notes is a beginning measure of educative authenticity. When these field notes also demonstrate that other participants are forging accommodations, full educative authenticity is apparent. If these accommodations are not apparent in the moment of data collections, they may be present as testimonials as the process is terminating, so authenticity assessment plans should include the ending stages of the inquiry.

Because of follow-up needs, catalytic and tactical authenticity are more difficult to document and, therefore, assess at the point of an audit. From our perspective, without the possibility of direct observation of the hermeneutic dialectic and further follow-up to judge social change, planning for assessing true warrants of the quality of the process is close to impossible.

The last substantive stage of the audit is *implementing the audit work program.* Schwandt and Halpern (1988) have provided focusing questions for specific audit trail material to assess confirmability, dependability, and credibility. We refer you to their work for a more complete discussion. For trustworthiness, the auditor should institute procedures and focusing questions to determine whether findings were credible, dependable, and confirmable to participants in the study. Below are examples of some focusing questions that were used in a trustworthiness audit of the inquiry on the multiple meanings of neglect. They are provided to demonstrate the degree of specificity that should be pursued in auditing:

- What appeared to be the reason for the difference between the two sites in terms of the average number of data units per contact?

- Is there evidence of bias in the selection of five people from each site to participate in the final member check process?

- Do the categories for each site emerge from the data or is there evidence of any imposition of a category system or premature closure on category development?

Unfortunately, there are currently no clear guidelines for an authenticity audit, though Manning (1997) has developed some useful direction about overcoming mistrust and overdirection, and in producing mutuality in the inquiry project and its interpretations. What remains clear is that decisions about authenticity "must be based on the context of the study and the respondents' needs and viewpoints" (Manning, 1997, p. 100). In addition, because of the relationship between the quality of a research product and the quality of a research process, it stands to reason that, at least to some degree, demonstration of elements of trustworthiness will also serve to demonstrate dimensions of authenticity. For authenticity, the auditor looks for evidence of multiple perspectives, negotiation, fully informed consent, demonstrations of an increase in participant appreciation of the complexities of the subject under investigation, and a gain in appreciation of the challenges and opportunities of each stakeholding group in the focus of the inquiry. In most cases, because of the time lapse needed between inquiry and assessment of catalytic and tactical authenticity, the other aspects of authenticity are rarely assessed.

Below you will find examples of focusing questions used for an authenticity audit that occurred in conjunction with the trustworthiness audit discussed earlier.

- *To assess fairness.* Are all important stakeholders' perspectives tapped and present in the final report? Are the voices of parents and children as powerfully heard as those of the judges? Is there evidence of stakeholder opportunity to criticize, amend, or negotiate findings through various levels of member checking?
- *To assess ontological authenticity.* Is there evidence in interviews or member checking material that participants were learning about neglect and the system of child protection? Is there evidence of growing insight about different standpoints on neglect and child protection? Is there evidence of improved understanding of personal perspectives?
- *To assess educative authenticity.* Is there growing evidence of stakeholder sensitivity to alternative views in interviews and member checks? Do interviews and member checks show that participants seem to better understand views differing from their own?

Though Lincoln and Guba (1986) and Schwandt and Halpern (1988) discuss the need for documenting methodological decisions and insights about the inquiry process, as well as emerging reconstructions throughout data collection and data analysis, we would urge the extension of that documentation to include case study writing and the audit. New insights about the meaning of the data emerge during the drafting of the case study. Continued journaling during case report construction forces continued analysis, possibly resulting in shifts in category systems and in the emergence of new relationships in the data. Documenting these shifts is important to allow the tracing back to the raw data from the finished written product that will be undertaken in the audit. Documenting the shifts also aids the auditor in tracking inquirer biases.

The auditing process, when done well, emerges as an extension of data analysis. As the outsider becomes quickly and intimately immersed in the study and asks the "naive" or critical question, or comments on a relationship, usually the inquirer will be able to respond by clarifying and articulating his or her tacit knowledge. Though different from what might be expected in a financial audit, our experience with auditing seems congruent with the authenticity dimensions of the constructivist inquiry and the hermeneutic dialectic (Guba & Lincoln, 1989). This congruence seems desirable in an interactive process that may be as unending as the inquiry itself. Just as feedback into the inquiry environment creates opportunities for new insights and observations among participants, the questions, clarifications, and feedback during audit produces new insights not possible without the intensely personal, intimate audit process that can develop with a supportive auditor. New propositional insights then can be reflected in the final product as a result of the audit. For this reason, the audit should be timed before the inquirer has achieved final closure on the inquiry report.

Once all the questions have been answered by what has been made available in the audit trail, the last stage of the audit can be undertaken. In *preparing the audit report* the auditor has a responsibility to both the inquirer and the other consumers of this evaluative report. The auditor owns the responsibility for conducting the audit, though the inquirer sets its parameters. The auditor is, however, neither responsible for uncovering unethical behavior, nor for agreeing completely with the choice of the practices used in the inquiry process. The auditor's purpose is to attest independently to the fact that the practices used are (or are not) within the boundaries of sound, ethical, constructivist practices. The auditor, in the form of an audit report, offers an opinion, not a guarantee of quality.

This attention to research practices without guaranteeing quality should not move in a direction contrary to the constructivist assumptions to what might be seen as pseudo-objectivity in the audit report. A dry, at-a-distance reporting on standards of quality and performance fails to reflect accurately the power and the intimacy of an audit. Instead, re-

straint should be replaced with enthusiasm whenever it is warranted as a
first step in the development of an audit report that has the same spirit of
richness as the goal of a constructivist case report.

Tasks of the Auditor

As with peer review, there are four major tasks that are the responsibility
of the auditor. Completion of each of the tasks is essential in order to assure the auditor's capacity to complete the required dimensions of the
audit report.

The first and most tedious aspect of the audit is a *systematic review of
the evidence*. The auditor must physically observe or read all aspects of
the audit trail including raw data, journals, documents, records, and any
other evidence provided by the inquirer. Review for the existence of the
materials is an important first step in the audit, but not sufficient to produce a meaningful audit report. Assessment of the quality of what was
produced in the audit trail and the research process is also needed.

Quality assessment will first involve *assessment of degree that methodological procedures fall within acceptable constructivist practices*. The auditor is concerned with the appropriateness of inquiry decisions and methodological shifts. Not only should these be identified, explained, and
supported, but they should be in keeping with the assumptions of
constructivism. Inquirer bias should be tested in data collection regarding premature closure, and the degree of exploration of all aspects, both
positive and negative, of the phenomena under investigation. Member
checks, peer debriefing, and triangulation should be apparent. The decisions about how to conduct the investigation, including sampling and triangulation, should be reviewed to assure that logistical challenges did not
unduly influence the process. Instances of co-optation, in which the inquirer "folds" to power or is otherwise "bought in" to a particular perspective, and premature judgments resulting from this or inquirer biases
should be identified. Finally, the overall design as it emerged should be
evaluated for consistent compliance with the assumptions of constructivist inquiry.

Reconstruction of data must be undertaken to ensure that the category sets and the case report are grounded in the data. Samples of findings, such as the most unusual or most interesting, should be traced back
via the audit trail to the raw data found in the field notes and the expanded field journals. If assertions are directly connected to the data, the
same assessment should be undertaken to test if the assertions are logical

and if the categories also make sense. The category structure should also be investigated for its utility, clarity, and fit with the data. The goal of data reconstruction is to assure that the data and interpretations in the report are grounded in the experience of the inquiry and not just the inquirer's personal constructions.

The final task prior to report writing is *the examination of the inquiry process for full and productive stakeholder involvement.* Both trustworthiness and authenticity depend on this. Evidence should be available through the methodological journals, peer review, reflexive journals, expanded field notes, and participant testimony. It is not sufficient to simply have various participants providing their own constructions about the focus of the inquiry. Instead, focus should be on the productive dimension of involvement in the investigation. Evidence should be present that the participants' own constructions have been improved or expanded, developed, or elaborated as a result of the maturation gained from the dialectic of the hermeneutic circle. Stakeholders should be "smarter" because of their involvement in the inquiry. They should possess more information and be more sophisticated. Consciousness raising and empowerment should be documented by noting participant comments regarding new or modified thoughts, or feelings of capacity or power regarding the phenomenon under investigation.

Based on the completion of the above tasks, the auditor should be able to fashion a detailed audit report. The audit report, aside from the elements agreed to in the audit contract, should include specific statements regarding trustworthiness and authenticity. The auditor should give the evidence upon which he or she bases the ability to attest to the degree of rigor and technical accuracy. The auditor should also, upon assessment of audit trail data, attest to the authentic quality among participants in the process and product of the inquiry. Once completed, this written report is provided to the inquirer or any other individuals agreed to in the audit contract, and the audit process is drawn to a close.

Future Challenges

Constructivist inquiry, though not focusing on establishing certitude or universally valid judgments, is directed at deriving meaning from experience. The accuracy of the inquirer's meaning reconstruction is what the trustworthiness criteria of credibility, transferability, confirmability, and dependability are testing. Constructivist inquiry is not simply an interpretive reflection of reality, it is a mutual construction of reality. Authenticity documents the quality of this interventive dimension. Even in alternative research, despite what some may assert (Smith, 1984), there is a difference between well-constructed or sloppy inquiry, between good and poor logic, between accurate and inaccurate reflections of multiple perspective, between respectful, empowering research and insensitive, oppressive research. The criteria and the processes described here provide sufficient information to make judgments about the quality of a constructivist process and product. But much more development is needed if auditing for trustworthiness and authenticity is to become a consistently implemented part of a constructivist inquiry. Further development is also needed if nonconstructivists are to recognize the audit for its potential, instead of diminishing the practice as "misplaced rigor." The following are the challenges for future constructivist researchers.

Generally speaking, both the trustworthiness and the authenticity dimensions of the audit require further development. More guidance is needed for both the inquirer and the auditor. The inquirer should be provided with more information about the degree of control that should be maintained in the audit. Because the inquirer has been involved in an emergent, almost uncontrollable and certainly unpredictable process, insecurities will be present about the quality of the structure of the inquiry including the audit trail. With this will come a tendency to wish to bound and limit auditor access to material. Guidelines or important questions about the degree of control appropriate for the auditee should be developed and included in auditing expectations.

This need for control on the part of the auditee might be moderated if standards were developed to indicate what is sufficient documentation of trustworthiness and authenticity on all dimensions. However, the basic assumptions of constructivism suggest that fixed standards are impossible in research that is unique and ever emerging. Perhaps the best we can expect are "methodological considerations without prescription," such as those provided by scholars such as Kathleen Manning (1997, p. 93). But more is needed. For practical reasons of implementation, focusing questions and issues for the auditee and auditor should be developed for the assessment of authenticity, just as Schwandt and Halpern (1988) have developed them for trustworthiness.

Given the delicate balance needed in assessing the quality of an interpretive process in which different perspectives are compared and contrasted in an attempt to reach mutual understanding, if not consensus, direct observation may never be possible. Perhaps we must be satisfied with serious attention to the ideals of authenticity, in the short term. In the long term, support for follow-up must be developed for true assessment of the quality of the constructivist inquiry process. Only through evaluation of effective change can judgments be made about the appropriate use of power and the degree of openness and empowering practices that are assumed to be central to quality constructivist inquiry.

Standards are needed against which to judge the appropriateness of categories and the logic used to link these categories for meaning making. Auditors should be helped to know when it is appropriate to draw conclusions about the meaning of data. We join Green et al. (1988) in calling for further development of standards for judging the emergent nature of the inquiry.

There is also the need for standards in developing the auditing relationship. Much guidance is possible from the expectations regarding relationships with respondents in the inquiry process; but until this audit takes on the character of constructivist inquiry instead of financial auditing, the auditor's role will continue to be unclear and potentially conflict laden. Guidance is necessary to assist the auditor in determining the degree of support to offer during the audit interaction.

This chapter must end with a call to those of you who may undertake constructivist inquiry to participate in the development of the principles to guide the quality of an emergent research model. Much more thought and work is needed to produce suggestions to aid the researcher to think through ways to support a high-quality research process and product. No prescriptions will be possible, but more ideas about considerations and questions that should be raised and thought about during constructivist inquiry will be a welcome addition to the development of the model.

Discussion Questions

These questions cover preparing for and determining auditability, selecting and managing an auditor, and the auditing process.

1. You have taken notes in the field and have expanded them in expanded field journals that include both verbal and nonverbal data. You have unitized and categorized the data. How will you link all this to the case report? Design an audit trail that allows the auditor to go from the final case report to the raw data collected in the field?

2. You have been asked to serve as auditor of an inquiry about which you have substantive competence. What information will you look for to determine if the inquiry can be audited for trustworthiness and authenticity?

3. What elements must be considered for you to determine who can function as an auditor of your constructivist research? In negotiation with the auditor, what questions will be most important to you to be certain that an evenhanded audit will be accomplished?

5. Why is an audit an important conclusion of a constructivist inquiry? What are the ways in which an audit report can be used?

CHAPTER 10

Challenges for the Future of Constructivist Research in Social Work

Chapter Contents in Brief

Developing a central role for the hermeneutic process
Managing paradoxes
Managing power and control
Constructivist research's relationship to social justice
Politics, ethics, and relativity in emergent research

Constructivist research is an intensely personal, introspective experience that provides a fit between the science and art of inquiry and the goals and values of social work. A social work inquirer in a well-managed constructivist inquiry should never experience a lack of fit between social work values and the research question, the people, the process, and the interpretations that result from the co-construction product. There should be a congruence in the effort of sensemaking that is generally only felt during a well-targeted clinical intervention.

This is not meant to imply that this type of research is not without unique challenges. These challenges are the subject of this chapter. Now that the reader has been exposed to the assumptions and mechanics of constructivism, we come full circle to the meaning of the constructivist research experience in social work by highlighting some of the thorniest issues in constructivist research practice.

Berreth (1986) captured the challenges of the constructivist research experience well in her report on constructivist inquirers engaged in constructivist inquiry. Constructivist investigation is an intellectual process of convergence, punctuated by periods of divergence. Along with this ebb and flow, there is a constant, rhythmic loss of focus, causing the process to be permeated with feelings of uncertainty, and loss of an internal standard by which to judge the work. Because there are no easily identifiable outside standards and because the process is ever emerging, there is a consistent lack of clarity. At the same time that focus and meaning are unclear, the inquirer can be overwhelmed and frustrated by the wealth of information, while also being comforted and blanketed by it. Often there will be a need for distance from such an enveloping experience in order to accomplish sensemaking. This will usually result in markedly expanded time frames, which will feel like a total loss of control.

In addition, the necessary attention to details, both for understanding and for substantiation of rigor, is tedious and time consuming. This may even devolve to a question of rigor over relevance. Those inquirers who easily attend to details will have a much better experience with audit trail development and maintenance, but this part of the effort is never fun. At best, all the documentation can make for a sense of secure, documented decision making. At worst, it allows for almost mindless motions through documentation of details.

For trained social workers, it will not be the hermeneutic process, but the audit that will be the stage of the inquiry most filled with tension. Social workers know how to overcome resistance, to establish a forum for communication and respect, and to deal with conflict among people with whom they are working. All of these skills are essential for a productive hermeneutic process. The more personal side of constructivism may provide stress and tension. An outsider's assessment of an inquirer's competence through the audit impacts the inquirer at the level of his or her personal/professional self. It is at this stage of the process that social workers may feel the most threatened. Generally speaking, preliminary negotiations of an audit contract are not threatening. It will be helpful in providing a context for new insights because positions and thought processes will be articulated with the auditor, when before they might only have been held tacitly. But the process of verifying the soundness of the research decision making and the thoroughness of the documentation can be more threatening than ever imagined. An outsider will get closer to your inner workings and intellectual capacity than has ever happened in normal evaluations at work or in school. There will be a level of intimacy required and a level of trust needed for a successful audit that probably mirror the intimacy and trust that develop between the inquirer and the participants in a constructivist investigation. This risk taking, necessary to expose one's work to outside audit, serves as a metric for sensitivity with participants in subsequent inquiries. It is also a great power equalizer during the final stages of the constructivist investigation.

Because of the unsettling nature of the audit experience and the needed development in the audit technology, both content and methodological expertise on the part of the auditor are essential. Clearly, this is important in making informed judgments regarding the sufficiency of the audit trail, the quality of the inquiry process, and the logical linkages between the data and how the results are presented. It is also necessary in order for the inquirer to trust the results of the auditing process, regardless of other evaluative measures.

The Central Role of the Hermeneutic Process

The inquiry process and product are full, live entities that continue to grow at every stage of the inquiry, including the final member check and revision. Every stage allows for new insights and meaning that move to a profound sophistication about the subject under investigation. The hermeneutic process and the products of the dialectic within that process provide a mechanism for the inquirer to tease out the various constructions being held at the time of the inquiry, and bring them together into a coherent whole that also includes whatever other information is found to be salient in the process.

Though this is not an easy process, the give and take of the hermeneutic circle, in which sensemaking evolves as information is shared, evaluated, excluded, or incorporated, is essential in the development of a more sophisticated understanding of the phenomena. The circle can only come about through the interaction of the various constructors with information, contexts, settings, situations, and other constructors (Guba & Lincoln, 1989). Agreement is generally not possible or desirable in the beginning stages because the tension, the dialectic, that comes from disagreement is central to avoiding incomplete, simplistic, uninformed, or just "wrong" constructions. So both the tension and the possibilities inherent in the hermeneutic process are desired products of the dialectic.

To get to real mutual meaning making, all constructions of participants must be challenged in the constructivist process. Four types of new information will be open to challenge: that which expands an existing construction; is inconsistent with the existing construction; is consistent with the existing construction, but requires growth to understand, appreciate, or apply it; and finally, that which presents both an information and a sophistication disjunction in which the information just does not make sense in view of the developing understandings. The last requires the most change and the most skill on the part of the inquirer in opening participants to the possibility of considering alternative constructions and the concomitant changes necessary to embrace the alternative. This is the process of consensus building. This is the hermeneutic dialectic. No meaning making is really possible without the interpretive comparison and contrast of divergent views that include the goal of a higher level synthesis of all perspectives. No results will be possible to report unless all parties, including the inquirer, have, at least to some degree, reconstructed their constructions with which they started the inquiry. Even when true consensus is not achieved, all parties have participated in mutual education. All parties have become empowered because of the careful, considerate critique of each perspective. This is what makes constructivism a knowledge-building intervention like no other model of research.

For social workers engaged in social work research, the hermeneutic circle should also help in identifying and recognizing the web of relationships in professional life. New insights will be possible about how the inquirer's professional life is a very personal experience. It should underscore the complexities of communication and relationships in the professional arena, particularly if it is a focus of investigation. But even if the social worker's professional associations are not part of the context of inquiry, an unintended consequence of constructivist inquiry may be improved capacity to negotiate or mediate controversial issues. As a by-product of the constructivist experience, the social worker, as well as other constructivist inquirers, will be able to transfer these negotiation skills to other contexts. The inquirer becomes a skilled mediator, able to facilitate the consideration of other issues in which consensus is necessary to move forward to decisionmaking.

Managing Paradoxes

Consensus-based decision making when entering the world of multiple perspectives in constructivist research means being propelled into the paradoxical. Our natural tendency is to assume that something cannot be two (or three or more) different things at the same time, which is the assumption of multiple perspectives. Further, it goes against all our training to assume that contradictory perspectives could all be true. Within constructed realities, paradoxes reign because such impossible circumstances fill the constructivist inquiry process.

If truth depends on perspective, and if every stakeholder in an inquiry can speak to his or her individual truth, then everything about constructivist research is paradoxical. Is welfare reform good or bad? Did this family neglect or not? Is this program efficient or wasteful? The answer is yes and no. The details are in the perspectives. Reaching a higher level of sophistication about a subject is becoming able to understand how contradictory interpretations can be held to be true.

It is in the context of the hermeneutic circle with the dialectic conversations that paradoxical thinking becomes possible. It is within the circle of information that the struggle over ideas occurs and where shared meaning is achieved, which can even be "more powerful than money and votes and guns" (Stone, 1988). Within the dialectic that is composed of struggles over the criteria for classification, the boundaries of categories, and definitions, shared meaning is achieved. Meaning is co-constructed.

Central to constructivism is the belief that there are multiple understandings of what appears to be a single concept. The focus of the hermeneutic circle is understanding how these understandings are created and manipulated. Within the hermeneutic dialectic, it becomes possible for all to see that constructing meaning is not nearly so simple as knowing something is true. Co-construction occurs when all involved recognize the paradoxical and realize that the dialectic is simply a conflict between or among equally plausible conceptions. This meaning making, managed by the inquirer, is about the temporary resolution of the conflict. The resolution, by way of co-constructed meaning, holds only as long as one dimension of a paradox is preferred over another in constructing the shared meaning and shared reality. Nothing is ever static. Instead, negotiation about the preferred plausible conception is ongoing. This means that maneuvering within paradoxes is also ongoing.

Power and Control in Constructivism

It would be naïve to overlook the sociopolitical implications of the methodology. The participants are real people, not a data set. The findings have real contextual meaning and, therefore, real political consequences. The methodology redistributes power, not only in the context, but also in the inquiry process. The participants own their data, and as a result of consciousness raising in the hermeneutic circle, they know it. This aspect of knowledge-as-power creates a more active and reactive interchange during the data gathering and interpretation phases. In fact, this kind of research is never finished because the consequences of the process itself continue to reverberate with personal and contextual development even after the inquirer disengages.

The methodology produces change. It is developmental and educational for all involved. Further, for the social work practitioner, constructivist inquiry can capture how professionals think in action (Schön, 1983). It can add to the worker's capacity in conscious use of self. The worker will sense more personal/professional power at the same time that the power in the research process is being shared.

This naturally resulting shift or growth in power presents a special challenge unique to constructivist research. The researcher, whether or not he or she is involved in pure, evaluative, or policy research, will only be in charge at the beginning of the first interview. From that point forward, the inquiry takes on a life and power of its own. The researcher is merely an orchestrator of a negotiation process that aims to culminate in consensus on better informed and more sophisticated constructions about the meanings of situations. The researcher becomes a subjective partner with other stakeholders in the literal creation of data, which means the inquirer becomes entirely dependent upon the people and context for the results of the inquiry.

This asks a lot of the professional who has spent a great effort to develop independent expertise. But it also requires a good deal from the context and participants in the investigation. The context must be "amenable to the unpredictable sociopolitical outcomes that will result from the emergent, uncontrollable power-redistributing nature of the constructivist process" (Rodwell & Woody, 1994, p. 318). Attention to the human/political interaction must be ever present. Recognition of power dynamics are important in preparing adequate, appropriate responses to the emerging political dynamics that will develop as stakeholders grasp the true meaning of a hermeneutic dialectic. When participants see the possibilities within the context of an emergent research design, change occurs. Relationships will be changed in uncontrollable ways. Unfortunately, some contexts and individuals will not have the capacity to absorb what will be perceived as assaults on their control or positions.

To ensure a successful completion of a full constructivist investigation the inquirer must be prepared for and attentive to the mix of rational and nonrational responses of the political forces in the context. Some participants will not trust emergence. Their need for certainty and control may result in efforts to prevent a free flow of information. The inquirer will wish to counter these reactions even when the process appears to have taken on a life of its own. Loss of control by the inquirer can never lead to efforts on the part of the inquirer to maintain control over information. If information is controlled for political reasons, the political barriers to this type of research will be so great as to prevent the dialogue and change central to constructivist inquiry.

Social Justice and Constructivism

Constructivist inquiry is a robust individual and contextual educational intervention. Participant experience with the research process will be empowering and, if managed well, will contribute to positive change. The research also impacts professional skills and decision making in ways different from traditional research. The intensity of the hermeneutic process all but guarantees that all participants, including the researcher, will be forever changed as a result of the experience. Some of these changes will be personal and some will be professional. New insights will uncover new resources and new dimensions in all participants that are deserving of respect and nurturance. The personal power within will be unlocked in unexpected ways for all concerned. This will lead to true, internally driven empowerment, which is generally considered an important redistributive dimension of social justice (Rawls, 1971; Wakefield, 1988).

Empowerment will result, not only from the collaboration and mutual education that the process produces, but also from the changes that should result. The status quo of belief systems or contexts will not be maintained in a constructivist study. Researchers, sponsors, and funders must be aware of this prior to undertaking this type of research. Recycling of information is a natural result of the constructivist process. Returning to a prior question with new information or greater sophistication because of the research is not just a possibility, it is an expectation. Once the researcher leaves, the inquiry is not over. According to Guba and Lincoln (1989), constructivist processes never stop; they merely pause. Our experience has been that at every pause, new developments emerge that can result in changes in the direction of a more just society. Access to service is improved, decisions become more ethnically competent, and individual competence is recognized and rewarded.

Politics of Constructivist Research

The methodology by its very nature seems to prevent escape into "pure" research, because it practically and theoretically eliminates the distinction between a phenomenon and the context within which it is found. This is not at-a-distance or "cool" investigation. The methodology, including the hermeneutic aspect, forces attention to the issues of the implications of that which is being understood by the inquirer and participants. This means that the results of an inquiry will probably always have evaluative and policy implications for both the inquirer and the participants.

The power of the process and the power of the politics will be primarily internal to the process. At some level, what outsiders think will feel irrelevant. Participants will not tend to concern themselves with outsiders' assessment of the quality of the inquiry. Instead, what stakeholders think will be important. Therefore, internal expectations about the inquiry product and process will be shaped in ways not seen before.

But to get to this sense of self-contained capacity to assess practical relevance of the research, participants must be willing to share personal, professional, and political power. Organizations and communities that are not collegial will not support the collaborative, teaching/learning nature of the constructivist process. Settings that cannot withstand the consequences of a shared responsibility and empowerment that constructivist inquiry can engender will not be amenable to the inquiry process. In addition, those contexts uncomfortable with continual evolution will not benefit from a constructivist process that is continuous, ambiguous, divergent, and essentially unending. The contexts that benefit most from constructivist inquiry are those that can allow and support mutual respect among all stakeholding groups and can take the actions that this type of research will inspire. In these environments the power shifts that move to real collaboration will have palpable political consequences.

Ethics and Relativity in Emergent Research

These power and political consequences in the midst of a recognition of no "real" truth, just relative truth, will have ethical consequences. The nature of a constructivist inquiry, where nothing is ever certain, will naturally focus on the ethics involved in the multilevel roles and relationships in the context of the inquiry in order to monitor research developments. The ethical complexity of the research undertaking has always been an important dimension of knowledge building, but it is made explicit in and by the constructivist process. Role challenges, competing perspectives, and the difficulties in ethical decision making will be an apparent part of meaning making. Consciousness about the value-based nature of all dimensions of the context of the inquiry will place ethical considerations in a central position in dialogue and consensus building.

To assure a productive hermeneutic circle in which stakeholders honestly and openly enter the negotiation of co-construction, a constant attention to ethical behavior will be important on the part of the inquirer. Because of this constant attention, not only to research ethics, but also to contextual ethics, a fascinating consequence of constructivist inquiry develops. The social work researcher/practitioner will become even more attentive to use of self in a professional sense. The focused attention to managing paradoxes and the potential for ethical dilemmas in the research process adds another level to the researcher's practice sophistication. The practitioner becomes more "conscious" in his or her conscious use of self in practice as a result of constructivist inquiry experience.

Change does occur as a result of the process, but the intervention is not stable. The ethical problems can manifest themselves when constructivist research practices are introduced into a particular setting. The practices are at least as much affected or changed by the context as they are likely to affect the context; therefore, what constitutes good ethical practices or an ethical dilemma will be just as contextually determined. For example, what is ethical is relative to the process. Absolute informed consent and a research accountability that attends to rights of privacy, confidentiality, and freedom from coercion (Fetterman et al., 1996) must be central, but to guarantee these issues is impossible in an emergent design.

This means that accountability is a relative matter and impacts all interacting parties equally. No one has a "lock" on what is right. Determining the "right" approach is almost impossible because facts and values are inextricably linked. Valuing is an essential part of the process and provides the basis for an attributed meaning about that which is under investigation. But it does little to establish the parameters of inquirer ethical behavior. That must be negotiated among and between all stakeholders. This is both the advantage and disadvantage of constructivism.

In addition, this sense of relativity means change cannot be engineered. It is a nonlinear process that involves the introduction of new information and increasing sophistication in the use of that information until the people involved create constructions of reality, which continually change. In the final analysis, ethical behavior, effectiveness, or failure is shared by a conglomerate of mutual and simultaneous shapers. In constructivism, no one can be uniquely singled out for praise or blame.

Other Potential Costs and Benefits with Constructivism

Constructivism will attract the same criticism that tends to plague both quantitative research and other forms of qualitative research. It will be seen to lack rigor and generalizability. At the same time that rigor is criticized, the peer review and auditing processes will be criticized for misplaced rigor because qualitative methods, by their very nature, are not objectively rigorous. Because these criticisms will rarely affect the usefulness of the process and product for the stakeholders in the inquiry, only the inquirer will be forced to face the consequences of these criticisms.

The consequences on this line of critique are very serious for social workers in academic or consultative settings. Work will not be published as easily as traditional reports on quantitative or even qualitative work done in a traditional paradigm. Difficulty in publishing will impact peer acceptance of the professional's competence, which can affect both tenure and hiring decisions. Constructivist consultants dependent upon research contracts for their livelihood may need to market skills in quite different ways than traditional researchers who can cite multiple published articles. Though research can be published, it tends to appear as book chapters instead of in peer reviewed journals. Sometimes the lack of peer review with books is a concern, since peer review has traditionally served as an outside warrant of the competence of the researcher and the quality of the products produced. For constructivists, sharing audit reports may provide sufficient evidence of inquirer competence to undertake the research in question.

Another challenge to acceptable scholarship is that the data derived from constructivist inquiry have neither special status nor legitimization. They represent simply another "construction" to be taken into account in the move toward consensus. The inquirer can never be an expert because there is nothing stable to become an expert in. Everything is a matter of negotiation toward consensus among informed and sophisticated participants in a specific time and context. Every context and situation will produce a different format and structure for consensus and co-construction. The most a social work academic or consultant can do is build inquiry processes upon the lessons learned in other contexts, because generalized knowledge building is not possible.

If these challenges to scholarship were not enough, it is also important to underscore the idea that constructivist research is not for the fainthearted. Do not underestimate the tasks involved in constructivist research. Managing the emergent design, assuring a productive hermeneutic circle, and processing mountains of information in order to create a meaningful construction is tedious, time-consuming, hard work. On the other hand, while it may not be for every researcher, nor for every context, when it is successful, it can be as personally and professionally powerful and gratifying as any social work intervention. It is powerful because the findings have real contextual meaning and political consequences. It is gratifying because this type of research can make a difference in a given context even if the report goes no further than the stakeholders involved.

If public and professional acceptance is central to a decision to undertake a research project, then a constructivist investigation may not be an appropriate choice. The risks involved in entering into alternative research must be substantially balanced by the potential that a constructivist inquiry can achieve. The information likely to be derived must be sufficiently weighty to overcome questions from the scientific or professional community and objections from the context of the investigation.

In addition, access to data will be dependent upon the inquirer's ability to manage risk. The research is essentially uncontrollable, with almost guaranteed resultant political upset. On the other hand, the process may be the most meaningful activity that the stakeholders have ever engaged in. They must be helped to let go of control so that all can have a gain in relevance.

The constructivist report is not expected to contain a rational explanation of social affairs as in the normal expectation from the traditional scientific perspective. Instead, the goal is an understanding of the nature of the social world at the level of intersubjectively shared meaning of experience. The results will have contextual relevance, or the process will not have complied with the quality expectations of both trustworthiness and authenticity. Once involved, legitimate stakeholders will be converted to this type of knowledge building because of the warmth, importance, and immediacy of the process and the product.

Now it is for you the social work researcher to decide if this type of research approach has potential. Can it move knowledge building to higher levels of sophistication and utility? Can it overcome the major criticisms that tend to come from those practicing from a more traditional scientific perspective? Can constructivist inquiry make a difference for social work practice and research? Is it worth the effort?

Discussion Questions

These end-of-chapter exercises include real dilemmas that highlight the very real challenges encountered by social work constructivist researchers.

1. You have negotiated access to a community-based children's mental health agency in order to conduct a constructivist evaluation. The director is interested in assessing effectiveness of program services. As you proceed with the inquiry, it is clear that in the minds of other stakeholders, the more important question is one of ethnic competence. The clinicians wish to look at the possibility of racism when Anglo professionals are dealing with African-American families. In your effort to create a hermeneutic circle of information, you share this emerging perspective of what the real question is with the director, who is absolutely unwilling to pursue this line of inquiry. What do you do next? Can you complete the constructivist inquiry? If you do not, what might be the consequences for the other stakeholders, including the families served by the agency?

2. You are involved in an investigation of recidivism in juvenile justice. You have received all the appropriate approvals from human-subjects review committees, but the director of research at the state level of juvenile justice has told you whom you can interview in her agency. You note that all potential participants are known to share her particular perspective on the subject. The director has made it clear that choosing other participants will bar you from collecting data in the state system. What should you do?

3. You are in the midst of an investigation of child neglect when you visit a home of a family known to the child welfare agency as a potentially neglecting family. When you arrive at the home around midday, it is clear that you have just awakened Mom. Three children under five are in the living room watching

television. They seem to have been up for quite a while because there is cereal, bread, and milk in the chairs, on their T-shirts, and on the floor. The children appear lethargic. Mom has no affect and very little energy as she asks you to come into the living room. You note that the shades are drawn and the whole house is dark, stale, and not very well kept. Mom begins the interview by telling you that she really thinks that caring for her kids is beyond her capacity right now and that she is very worried about their well-being. She says that since you are researching child neglect you must know a lot about it. She wants to know if you think she is neglecting her children. As a constructivist researcher, what should you do? As a mandated reporter for child abuse and neglect, what should you do? What are the issues that must be considered regarding the ethics of intervening while involved in research?

4. In an investigation of intimacy you happen to include individuals who are currently in an intimate relationship together. You are aware of the need to freely and openly share information in the hermeneutic circle. But in the process of sharing elements of intimacy that you have gained from other inquiry participants, one of the individuals in the relationship shares with you a very different version of their relationship than what you heard from the other. To complete the hermeneutic circle, should you share this information? What are the consequences of not sharing to the quality of the hermeneutic circle and the co-construction of meaning regarding intimacy?

SECTION IV
A Research Example

This last section was developed because of the paucity of examples of constructivist research products in the literature. It is offered not as *the* model, but simply as *a* model of constructivist inquiry. It is a reflection of the author's cognitive mapping of a study on protective services and foster care. It should be encountered as an exemplar open to criticism and modification, particularly related to coding, data analysis, and report construction. At the minimum, the reader will see how an audit trail is incorporated into a story.

Because this research was successfully audited, it should also provide an idea about the minimum sufficient evidence necessary to establish a trustworthiness and authenticity audit trail for outside assessment of quality. Discussion questions at the conclusion of the example will guide you, the reader, through an assessment of the strengths and weaknesses of the research as a means of creating your own "words to the wise" when you undertake your own constructivist process. As a result of work with this research exemplar, you should see common mistakes and develop ideas about how to avoid them in subsequent research activities.

CHAPTER 11

An Example of a Constructivist Case Report

What follows is a constructivist case report entitled "How are we protecting our children: A constructivist study of one family's experience with protective services and foster care." Audit trail material is included at the conclusion of the case report. This study, as presented, does not have the type of methodological introduction that would be necessary for reporting these results in a professional journal or as a part of an edited text. There is no description of the methods used in the inquiry process, including analysis and rigor. However, this inquiry did undergo a successful audit, so there is evidence that the constructivist process was within the bounds of acceptable constructivist practice. Instead of serving as an example of rigor, the case study is provided as an example of how data collected and analyzed at various levels can be deconstructed and reconstructed to create a story with some lessons learned.

The reader is reminded to judge the quality of the case study report along the dimensions discussed in Chapter 8. The audit trail and a coding system have been included to demonstrate a straightforward way to link the story to raw data from the field. In the body of the story, you will find bracketed numbers, such as [4], that will allow you to trace the assertions in the story to coded data.

One Family's Story

My interest in what happens to a family while under investigation by protective services and while their child is in foster care comes as a result of my many years of work in public child welfare. Unfortunately, my commitment to children has not always included an equal commitment to their families. As I was preparing three statewide symposia on child welfare law for midwestern professionals involved in the public system of child protection, it struck me that the perspective of the greatest protectors of children, their parents, was missing. I knew much about how the various professionals experienced the results of the mandates of the law and the limits of their particular system; but I knew little about how families experienced the professionals doing their jobs. This inquiry, then, grew out of a need to understand the linking of the law (policy-in-intent) to professional action (policy-in-implementation) and this action to a real instance of child protection (policy-in-experience). The goal is to provide a better understanding of the parents' perspective and, in doing so, to create another forum for more appropriate child protective practice.

Legal Background: Policy-in-Intent

Public Law 96–272, the Adoption Assistance and Child Welfare Act of 1980, was remedial legislation designed to rectify specific problems existing in state foster care programs throughout the United States. The act was markedly different from prior federal legislation governing state foster care programs because it included many detailed requirements and incentives intended to create fundamental changes in state foster care practice (Pecora et al., 1992). Its goal was to overcome the pervasive pattern of *foster care drift*, the haphazard and unplanned use of foster care by child welfare agencies.

The basic areas of intended reform under P.L. 96–272 were: (1) improvement in services to avoid unnecessary removal of children from their homes; (2) more careful placement of children to address their special needs and to facilitate visitation and communication between parent and child; (3) more efficient case planning and efforts to reunify families; and (4) more decisive and timely action to secure permanent homes for foster children, including return home when possible, or placements in another permanent, legally secure home [1]. In short, P.L. 96–272 was intended to provide protections for children to ensure that they enter care only when necessary, are placed appropriately, receive quality care, are reviewed periodically, and are placed in permanent families in a timely fashion.

In mid-1981 the Juvenile Code in Kansas was modified to become the Kansas Code for Care of Children. The "Child in Need of Care" section of this code was designed to comply with the mandates of P.L. 96–272 by detailing the specific behaviors of several stakeholders in protective services. The professionals included were: social workers from the State Department of Social and Rehabilitation Services (SRS), law enforcement officers, the courts, county and district attorneys, and guardians ad litem. It specifies who is responsible for investigation of reports of child abuse or neglect, who can remove a child from his or her home, and under what conditions. It establishes timelines for the inquiry and the court proceedings, and for review of the situation and treatment plans if a child is placed out of the home. It outlines the documentation required to ensure equal treatment and due process for both the parents and the child. It details conditions under which the district attorney may file petitions to the court for hearing the allegations, and instructs the court as to receipt and determinations in proceedings under the code. Finally, it establishes the guardian ad litem function, including independent investigation of the facts upon which the petition is based, appearance for the child, representation of the child during all court proceedings, and following the treatment of the child, until the situation is stabilized and the child is returned home, or placed in an alternative permanent placement [2].

Mandated Actors' Perspective: Policy-in-Implementation

Interviews were conducted with professionals who represented the mandated actors under the code: district attorneys, guardians ad litem, SRS social workers, law enforcement officers, and a district court judge, in order to compare their perceptions of expected performance with the performance expectations that resulted from the content analysis of the federal and state laws. The discussions produced a consensus opinion about the activities each must perform to comply with the code. In all cases the professionals reached agreement about what should be done; however, they were quick to point out that in practice, the system and its processes do not always work the way they should [3].

In order to locate a parent who had experienced a protective service investigation and the subsequent removal of a child from home since the change in the code, I made 11 contacts during a three-month period with private agencies, SRS, a mental health center, and private practitioners. In all instances, I was told that my idea was a good one and the information to be gained was important; but for various reasons, ranging from lack of time to conflicts with confidentiality, I was denied access to clients [4]. Finally, a contact with a lawyer who defends parents in "Child in Need of Care" proceedings produced a family who was not only willing to participate in the inquiry, but grateful for the opportunity to tell their story [5]. If the story that follows mirrors what generally happens, it will be clear why directly reaching a family was so difficult.

The primary stakeholders in this story are Lilly, the mother; Rose and Oscar, her children; Gina, Lilly's housemate; and Gina's daughter, Nancy. Their names have been changed to protect their identities. The professionals in the story will go unnamed, also to protect their identities.

A Family's Perspective: Policy-in-Experience

My initial contact with the family was by phone. Lilly called me within 15 minutes of my conversation with her lawyer. Arrangements were made to meet in her home [6]. The house is a small one, set far back from the rest of the homes in a tree-lined, older middle-class neighborhood. The pink stucco home was smaller than the rest of the houses with a motorcycle, chopped wood, and yard furniture haphazardly sitting in the yard near the front door.

I was greeted warmly by Rose and asked in as soon as three very large black dogs were put away. Inside it was very dark, even though the sun had not yet set. The only lamp in the living room was lit. The living area felt closed-in, with hundreds of books on shelves lining the walls and acting as a room divider. A few liquor bottles, glasses, boxes (still unpacked from a recent move), hunting bows, and several aquariums added to the clutter. There was space for five people to sit on two well-worn love seats and a chair. It was here that most of our subsequent visits occurred [7].

Lilly, a neatly dressed woman of about 40, with long sandy hair, and an intelligent, intent look had just returned from work. Rose, Lilly's daughter, a large girl for her 12 years, cute, with curly red hair and sparkling eyes, was dirty and sweaty from playing with the young children next door. Lilly had prepared for our meeting and had several boxes of documents at her side [8]. Gina, Lilly's housemate, came in without formal introductions and settled in a chair. Gina is an older woman, with long, graying hair, whose most noticeable feature is a tattoo, "LOVE," running vertically down the middle of her forehead. The tattoo is generally concealed by long, wispy bangs. Lilly's son, Oscar, a handsome 16-

year-old, was introduced and then asked permission to go to a party with friends. He was seen just as briefly in subsequent visits. Due to Gina's recent hearing loss, the discussions were conducted in very loud voices [9].

The History

The first official contact from SRS occurred in August 1981, 23 months after Lilly and her children arrived from Las Vegas. They had moved because Las Vegas was "no place to raise kids." Gina, who had been their neighbor in Las Vegas, had arrived eight months earlier than Lilly. They both had apartments in the El Rancho motel, a place that later was condemned and destroyed. On first arriving, Lilly was employed at the Ramada Inn as a maid. She was laid off and told to move to a better location before coming back to work, because she had contracted fleas at the El Rancho. This happened even though she had paid to have her quarters fumigated. Lilly was supporting her children through garage sales of junk she had collected from the garbage dumpsters at the apartment complex nearby. During one of these sales, two women "from the welfare" arrived saying they "wanted to help." They had received information that Lilly and her family needed help and they were investigating to see what SRS could do. They looked at the family's living area, looked at the children, and then left. Shortly afterward, Lilly received a letter from SRS saying her case was "closed" [10].

Several weeks later Lilly moved from the motel to a home on the north side of town with a woman who was recently separated from her husband. This woman was investigated for an abuse allegation by protective services while Lilly was living with her, but no formal actions occurred. After four months and a "conflict of lifestyles," Lilly moved into a large, 10-room home with Gina and another family composed of a disabled husband, his pregnant wife, and their three children [11].

During the time these families were together, they had difficulty with SRS about getting financial support. Having three separate households living in one house created problems with determining each family's eligibility for welfare [12]. Gina had been receiving unemployment and then General Assistance pending eligibility determination for disability payments. The family of five was receiving ADC when Lilly, Rose, and Oscar moved in. They remember fighting the SRS system. Gina feels that even before the child protection problems, SRS was already prejudiced against her for confronting the procedures related to the family of five, showing she was "well able to fight for her rights and loudly!" "We are not unknown" [13].

Lilly thinks the county considers Gina a possible problem to the "status quo" due to her tattoo, openness, and straightforwardness [14]. Gina says, "the problem is being different and the ability to stand my ground where the rights of an individual are concerned. Being an admitted smoker of marijuana and not a drinker, nor taker of hard drugs, is hard for others to cope with." They both agree that small-town attitudes were responsible for what subsequently happened to Rose. (Marijuana was never mentioned by SRS, the court or any agency connected with Rose's protective service case) [15].

Serious involvement with protective services apparently began after conversations between Rose and some friends were overheard by their mothers. In what Lilly called "an attention-getting device," Rose told the children that she was being abused and that she was not being allowed to comb her hair or take a bath. Rose now says none of what she said was true.

Shortly after those conversations, the two mothers who had overheard Rose visited Lilly, claiming an interest in astrology and numerology (Gina is an astrologist and Lilly, a numerologist). They visited two times, once in the foyer and once on the porch. A few days later, a protective service worker came to the house to talk to Lilly. As he left, he informed Lilly that "the abuse allegations" he was investigating were unfounded. This visit by the worker was the first indication that any abuse allegations had ever been made or that SRS was investigating anything. The worker did not ask to see Rose, who was in another room [16].

Several months later the family of five moved and Gina's daughter, Nancy, with her husband and son, were visiting while they found their own house. Nancy and Rose had an argument about where to store a Tupperware bowl. (Rose knew where it belonged.) Gina intervened. In the heat of the argument, Gina knocked Rose in the head with the bowl and ordered Rose to put it away. She did. Gina saw Rose's behavior as "manipulative and needing strong response in order for Rose to understand." This was the third time Rose had "pulled this" with the same bowl. Nancy thought her mother's behavior was abusive and threatened to call the police [17].

Gina sees her role with Rose as that of a "father figure." She says she is direct and steadfast. She uses intelligent analysis, caring, and knowledge of astrology to provide the necessary guidance. Because of Rose's sign (Aries in the first house), Gina feels she has no sense of logic; she has to be taught. Gina acts as Rose's "reality" mother and disciplinarian. Lilly acts as her "biological" mother and disciplinarian. Rose is not confused with two mothers. Gina said, "Rose understands I'm not her mother, but I will reprimand her as such." Rose supported the perspective, in both words and actions, during my time with the family [18].

At the time of the Tupperware incident, Rose was having trouble in school. She was spending her days in the principal's office due to disruptive behavior. Lilly had been offered a big sister for Rose, but she felt that Rose had sufficient female influences. She did not see the need to create another situation Rose could manipulate to get what she wanted. She felt Rose needed a "this-is-the-way-it-is" type of person to guide her and Gina was filling that role well.

Gina and Lilly see Gina's daughter, Nancy, as a troublemaker during this period. Nancy wanted Rose parented differently. She did not feel that her mother had raised her the way she had wanted and she did not want the same thing to happen to Rose, even though it appeared that Rose was improving and growing out of the stage she was in. Of Gina's five children, Nancy is the only one with a police record, assault and battery, and a child with a history of school behavior problems [19].

Because of the earlier investigation, and knowing that Nancy would make a report, Lilly and Gina went to see the investigator who had been to their home. They told him what had occurred and asked for advice about how to deal with Rose. He recommended a visit to the mental health center. The family (Lilly, Gina, and Rose) went for one visit. Because of limited finances for cab fare and bad weather, they did not return for the next appointment.

Sometime later, Rose was spanked with a belt for lying. A report of this was given by Nancy to the same protective service worker. According to Lilly, he visited to remind her of the "law against physical punishment" and told her to find another method of dealing with misbehavior. Nothing more occurred [20].

About five or six weeks before Rose was removed from her home, she started arriving home from school at five or six o'clock with stories about being chased by dogs and other reasons for being late. Restrictions were imposed. But she stole money from Lilly and Nancy and was again spanked with a belt (this time with Nancy's approval). Nothing seemed to work. As a remedy, Lilly began walking Rose to and from school. Money was hidden and Rose was constantly watched.

This continued until Lilly was called away to care for Nancy, who by now had moved to a house of her own, and was recovering from a cesarean section. Gina, because of an ankle disability, could not walk Rose to and from school When Rose arrived home after dark again, Gina kept

Rose out of school for the next three days. Lilly agreed to this plan, because denying Rose a wanted privilege such as school, which she like very much, seemed the only workable discipline for her behavior. Lilly arrived home from her stay with Nancy on Saturday. Rose was placed in foster care on the following Wednesday [21].

The Investigation and Rose's Removal from Home

It was only after Lilly was served with the papers which allowed the police officer and the protective service worker to take Rose that she realized that a case had been built against her since the first visit by SRS at the motel, August 6, 1981. Each contact had been recorded as a part of an ongoing investigation.

The second time a protective service worker made contact, May 28, 1982, unlike what Gina and Lilly had understood, he had been "investigating an allegation of Rose being kept out of school as punishment." This was shortly after the visits with Rose's friends' mothers. For this investigation, and without Lilly knowing, the worker had gone to school to assess Rose's condition. When he visited Lilly to inform her of the allegation and to state that the report was unsubstantiated, the records show a note asserting "lack of familial support." When Lilly and Gina had gone to him to report the bowl incident and to seek help, he had recorded the incident as "abusive behavior," but had not come to the house to investigate. After his visit related to the belt incident, it was recorded as "no affection in the home, just discipline for lying." Lilly says she thought that with each visit the worker had really understood and really cared about how seriously they were trying to do what was right for Rose's needs. In retrospect, she sees that he was building a case. She says, "he was two-faced and just stringing us along. Later, in court papers and in court he turned around words and twisted meanings" [22].

Apparently the "last straw" in the protective service case occurred when a school counselor visited the home and asked Lilly when Rose would return to school. Gina told the woman, "She ain't going to school 'til she gets her head space straight. She doesn't deserve the privilege of school until then." The next day the same protective service worker came to the home, informing Lilly that he had received a complaint and that "they are going to do something." Within two hours a policeman and the worker returned, "playing the role of the total SRS official" to serve Lilly and remove Rose. Both professionals were quiet, calm, and cool. Lilly followed instructions for preparing Rose. She tried to explain what was happening to Rose, but feels she did not do a good job because she, herself, was in shock. The worker left with Rose, who was by this time crying very hard. He said that Rose should be home the next day. She was returned 21 months later. Rose was removed five days after her 10th birthday, a birthday she never celebrated because the family had put off celebrating until the next weekend when Lilly would have some money [23].

The Court Process

Both Lilly and Gina feel that they were "tried on their belief system." At the first hearing, records show their lawyer suggesting that their constitutional rights were being abridged because of their beliefs in astrology and numerology. Lilly felt that Gina was on trial, but she was not called to testify. Gina said, "I can be loud, dramatic, and embarrassing. Except in the court room, I was on my quiet behavior because I wanted that kid back. Belief system differences about the way to raise a child were the basis of why the state should keep Rose and that is why Rose was away so long" [24].

The records included incorrect information. They listed Gina and Lilly as "companions." The innuendo was that they were lesbians. They are not. They maintained separate households and continued to struggle with welfare eligibility because of it. Gina states, "Damned if any system is making me lie" [25].

They both say the protective services worker lied on the stand. It was not just a different understanding of the situation for Lilly, because she feels that his lies could be proven by the SRS documents that were never a part of the court's evidence. He asserted that during the visit with Rose at school she was often unable to distinguish between mothers. Gina is sure that the protective service worker could not understand, but Rose "had it straight." The worker used the fact that Lilly had turned down the offer of a Big Sister as an example of "lack of family support." Their failure to return to the mental health center after the first contact was reframed to be lack of commitment [26].

Another mental health worker, other than the one they saw for the one appointment on the recommendation of the protective service worker, stated on the stand that he saw Lilly and Gina on opposite ends of the spectrum: Gina was independent and Lilly was dependent. Gina said he indicated it was almost as if Lilly was under the control of the "horrible" woman, Gina. Lilly feels he stated his opinion as fact and the judge listened.

Lilly and Gina visited the mental health center the October prior to Rose's removal. This meeting occurred at the principal's suggestion be-

cause of a concern about the problems Rose was having in school. Minutes before the meeting, Oscar told Gina he had been locked out of the
house a few days earlier by Gina's son who had been babysitting Oscar
and Rose while Gina and Lilly were working. Oscar said he questioned his
sister and she told him that while Oscar was outside, the son "messed
around" with her. Gina felt it would be best if Oscar were to tell his story
to the doctor, so he accompanied them. They shared with the doctor, in
confidence, their fear of Rose having been sexually molested. At the time,
Gina and Lilly were under the assumption that they were conversing with
a "real psychologist." Gina "did most of the talking, trying to crowd the
years of problems into a half-hour time span so the doctor could make as
clear an analysis as possible." He was also told of an abnormal sexual
problem Rose had that was discovered when she was only four-and-a-half
years old.

When asked by Gina, the doctor "didn't think that it would become
an issue against Gina's son." He then dialed a number for confirmation of
this, hung up the phone, and explained that he had called SRS protective
service and said that "this kind of information can never be held in confidence, if SRS wanted to push the issue," but he didn't think they would.
Gina and Lilly left in shock, never to return to see him.

It was later, when he appeared in court, that Gina and Lilly realized
that the "Doctor" was an intake worker. It was he who testified that
"Gina's son was thought to have possibly molested this child." There was
no mention of any of the problems, sexual or otherwise, that Gina and
Lilly had shared with him when they thought he was a doctor. Rose was
never interviewed or examined during the time the case was in process.
The issue of sexual molestation was never mentioned again in the court
[27].

There were references in the record about a family belief that Rose
was possessed. This they did not deny. There had been one instance when
Rose was about two years old when four or five adults had to hold her
down. Gina and Lilly had discussed this with the Catholic priest in town,
who said that he would pray over the child if they wanted. Gina felt certain that she had more ability to help the child than the priest. They had
talked about this with the protective service worker as an example of how
difficult Rose could be to control. They say that the incident was twisted
in court to make them sound crazy [28].

Lilly said that by the time all this came out in court she was not about
to "go off." She was feeling a great deal of calmness because she had come
to realize that what was occurring with Rose made her like a pawn in a

greater scheme. The court thought that the parental authority of the "couple" was a problem and that demands on Rose were too high. The court thought that Rose had difficulty integrating the family belief system into her development and that she would not develop normally if left in the family. Rose was said to be at risk of physical and emotional abuse, afraid, and without support in the family. Rose never took the stand. Not one professional asked her anything. When the disposition was made, Lilly remembers the district attorney "looking at me as if I had already killed the child." Prior to this hearing and thereafter, Rose's guardian ad litem met with Rose only once. When Gina or Lilly attempted contact later, he was unavailable for their calls [29].

On April 7, 1983, Rose was temporarily placed in SRS custody. She was placed in town, on the demand of Lilly's attorney, in order to allow family visits. At a June hearing she was kept for further evaluation. A review hearing occurred in October. No other court action occurred until a motion to review was filed by Lilly's lawyer in August 1984. A review hearing was held in September and continued until November. At this hearing, the lawyer for the foster care facility in which Rose was placed was present and was allowed to ask questions "like the rest of the attorneys." Lilly and Gina felt he asked nagging questions, but at this hearing, visits were increased. In January 1985, Rose was returned home, but custody remained with SRS. Full custody was finally returned in July 1985, with congratulations from the judge for all the positive changes that had been made.

Lilly says that even today when she sees any of the professionals involved in the case in her role as their waitress at the Holiday Inn, someone always says, "You look so much better." "From July 'til now professionals comment on how different I am and I have not changed since the day they took Rose away. I have no guilt feelings." Gina feels "we made no changes. We remained as we always were. People simply began to see we were not guilty as they first opined we were" [30].

The Foster Care Experience

Lilly remembers the foster care visits as troublesome. She had no transportation, so it took some effort to get to the SRS office to see Rose for just an hour. After a while, visits were allowed at home, but some of these were canceled because of foul weather. She did not meet the foster parents with whom Rose was initially placed. By the June hearing, these foster parents told SRS they wanted Rose removed because she was an uncontrollable child. At the hearing, the SRS foster care worker stated that

SRS had nowhere to place Rose in the city and, therefore, she should be placed out of town. Lilly's lawyer would "have nothing of this," so after the hearing Rose was place at the Emergency Shelter. This is a facility for older children, designed to care for children 90 days or less. Rose was four years younger than the youngest resident and she stayed there for nearly six months [31].

Even though the facility was not really geared to meet Rose's needs, she seemed to adjust well there. The staff made attempts to make both Rose and Lilly comfortable during their weekly visits. Lilly spent time with the staff before taking Rose on walks or home during their time together. Gina never visited Rose at the shelter. She never tried for fear that her attempts would be misinterpreted and cause the family more trouble. During this period workers suggested many out-of-town placements, which Lilly refused. To her knowledge there were no staffings or administrative reviews of Rose's situation [32].

While SRS was attempting to locate an appropriate foster home, the rest of the family began to participate in mental health services as expected by the courts. Both Gina and Lilly were seen separately by the director of the mental health center. After separate intake interviews, she sent a letter asking Gina to consider meeting with her and Lilly's therapist to discuss ways Gina could facilitate therapy for Lilly. She sent a copy of Lilly's letter to Gina and Gina's letter to Lilly. Gina did not participate in any further formal therapy except with Rose's therapist, after Rose returned home [33].

After the first few sessions, Lilly felt that her therapy time was spent helping the therapist with her own child. Lilly would share instructions based on numerology and astrology to give her "a deeper understanding into the behavior patterns of children and adults." Later, after Rose's return home, this same therapist asked Gina to volunteer at the center [34].

Rose was finally placed in a "well-respected" group facility in January 1984. Placement into SRS custody had been on the basis of serious psychological problems, but due to the instability of her earlier placements, therapy did not begin until February 1984, ten months after placement [35].

There were troubles with visits from the beginning of this last placement. Lilly felt that the facility wanted total control. They wanted the visits changed to once a month instead of once a week, as they had been since Rose had come into care. The house parents, who were not therapists, also said that Rose would need two months of adjustment prior to the first visit. Lilly says her lawyer had a "fit" for her and demanded phone calls and visitation rights. The facility agreed, on the condition that Rose comply with the house rules. Lilly feels that the facility never intended to have Rose return to her [36].

There were other difficulties with the placement. When Rose was moved to the facility she had to leave Peacock school and move to a rural school that did not provide the same special help in reading and math that Rose had been receiving since second grade. The children at Peacock sent her letters that Lilly has kept so Rose will have them when she is older. The children in her new school made fun of her [37].

There were problems with phone calls and with how Rose kept her hair. Rose could only speak on the phone with her mother for five minutes if she had obeyed the rules. If her mother was not home from work when she called, Lilly would have to call Rose back long distance or not be able to talk with her. Rose's hair was a constant problem. The staff wanted to cut it. Lilly did not. Finally, they sent her notice that she had three weeks to get it cut or they would do it for her. Shortly afterward, Rose came for a visit and her hair was a mess. She said that she had had no brush for two weeks. Lilly asked the staff person who dropped Rose off for the visit where her hair brush was and how they could let her go around looking as she did. As a result of that confrontation, the facility refused to deliver Rose to her home for visits. From then on the two would meet at the public library and walk home. This change started in cold March weather [38].

In June 1984, Rose told her mother over the phone that she would "rather have fewer visits instead of more visits." She said she "got so excited about seeing her mother that she always got into trouble," so she "thought fewer visits would be better." Lilly felt Rose was coached into saying this. Lilly resented the phone limitation and became even angrier at further suggested limitations. Things "fired up" between the facility and Lilly. Finally, in frustration, the SRS foster care worker asked Lilly what she wanted for Rose. She made a list of her minimal requirements. These included good grooming, good care, and good behavior management. Lilly remembers refusing to play the game of the "wimpy" mother. When SRS asked, she gave them what they wanted. But she has been fascinated that in court she was "put down" for not being "like straightforward Gina and then got into trouble when she made demands like Gina would" [39].

Within the first month of this last placement, the first and only proposed service agreement was mailed to Lilly to sign. Lilly and her lawyer did not like the wording, so the lawyer helped her with a response instead of signing the form. The lawyer saw the statements in the plan as very leading [40].

During the 21 months away from home Rose had three placements. There were seven social workers from SRS, two social workers and three psychologists from the mental health center, three district attorneys, two judges, one guardian ad litem and one lawyer for the parents involved in the case. In the end, Lilly feels that the lawyers took a personal interest in the case. She thinks they felt something was wrong, but didn't know what. During the investigation and placement no one came past the foyer or the front room of the home. When Rose was brought to the house by volunteer drivers or SRS workers, they would just honk and expect Lilly to let Rose run out to the car. Lilly says, "In all sorts of ways people continued to say 'things have to change,' but no one ever said *what* had to be changed" [41].

After Rose's return, there was another protective service contact in October 1985. This time a different protective service worker arrived at the front door to say that they had received a complaint of abuse. Lilly told the woman if she kept pushing, Lilly would take *them* to court. A few days later, Lilly received a form letter saying the concern was unfounded and the case was closed. Until the July 1985, final hearing, Lilly received form letters from SRS asking if she were interested in family services, but the services that were listed were "not of help" [42].

Epilogue

In the fall of 1987, Rose was placed voluntarily by her mother in an emergency shelter pending placement in a more structured treatment environment. Rose's behavior had deteriorated to the point that she was involved in petty crimes and threats of violence to herself and school staff. The "temporary" placement occurred between November and May when Rose was placed in treatment out of the state. The shelter placement was stormy, with particular controversy between Lilly and the facility director about whether or not Lilly deserved to parent Rose. Complaints about the facility led to an investigation by SRS, but no action was taken by the time Rose was placed out of state. Lilly did not pursue the problems with the emergency shelter because she did not want to "rock the boat," since custody had been voluntarily given to SRS. She feared that complaints might result in custody being returned, thereby eliminating this one real chance of helping Rose.

In late May, while in a family meeting, the therapist, in front of Rose, shared a letter from the old mental health center regarding an allegation that Rose had been sexually molested and that this should be a focus of treatment. Lilly was furious, saying that this was one more example of Rose's ability to twist people and reality, and that it certainly should be the focus of treatment, but because it was a lie, not because it was a reality. The session ended "in a shamble" with everyone upset.

Lilly, upon return home, contacted Rose's therapist who confirmed that Rose had really been molested, apparently at the El Rancho motel by a friend of the family who, in 1986, had received the State Foster Parent of the Year award. The therapist had been "trying to figure out the appropriate way to tell" Lilly. It seems that Rose's guardian ad litem notified the mental health center in March when, during his work in defense of another client (the alleged perpetrator), he became aware that Rose had been a molestation victim of this client seven or eight years earlier. The mental health center communicated this information to the court. It is unclear if SRS was ever notified. The mental health center chose not to inform Lilly because they did not "know how she would react."

Sentencing of the perpetrator occurred through plea bargaining around Rose's case, though no one talked to Lilly or Rose. Lilly considered legal action, but her first concern was Rose. From Lilly's perspective, the system set up a situation in which she had insulted her daughter. She feels she now must seek her daughter's forgiveness for not understanding Rose's behavior for more than eight years. Rose continues in placement and Lilly continues to worry that what she does will negatively impact her daughter. Lilly continues to be angry and confused. She cannot understand how the system could withhold such important information from her. Her child was in custody, but her parental rights were not severed. She is still uncertain what else she could have done or whom she could have trusted [43].

Lessons to Be Learned

When I asked why this family was willing to bring all this up again, both Lilly and Gina, in an almost fatalistic way, agreed that Rose has been a pawn in an overall need to change the way SRS and others handle child abuse. They see the laws and the services that were intended to help family as having been hurtful and stressful additions to their lives. Their history with protective services makes no sense to them unless what they experienced helps other children in the future [44].

From the Family

If their story accurately captures the multiple realities of the protective service experience, several important lessons can be learned that may aid in understanding the family perspective in another environment. If the descriptions in this story provided sufficient information about the family's context, then conclusions can be reached about whether transfer into another context is possible. If it is possible, then these lessons or working hypotheses should also have potential for future practice with other families. Table 11–1 offers the family's perspective on some suggested practice principles. They have been derived from their story and are lessons that may be learned from their experience.

TABLE 11–1

Lessons for Professionals Who Protect Children

---

1. When doing an investigation, investigate facts with extreme care. Do not judge or form opinions until you understand the situation. Check all possible sources of information. Do not make assumptions. Remember that your "facts" may be someone else's opinions.

2. Understand the child's situation. Know who the child is; where the child is; what the situation is before judging the behavior of the parents.

3. Determine if parents understand the difference between discipline and punishment and their perception of the child's needs before deciding if what the parents have done is wrong.

4. Care about kids and support families no matter how those families may be constructed. Remember that removing a child from his or her family may be more damaging to the child than allowing the child to remain at home. The system or foster care can be more abusive to the child than what he or she experiences at home.

5. Be honest with parents. Do not do one thing and then tell parents something else. Do not sneak around building a case. Parents have a right to know what professionals think and how that may affect their rights to care for their child at home.

6. Do not respond only to the stubborn, willful, committed families who are determined to get their children back. They will not give

up. Some families care just as much. They just do not have the strength to fight for their children.

7. Be sensitive to different lifestyles and belief systems. Do not judge them as wrong without knowing the emotional state of the children in those homes. If they are developing in a healthy manner, leave them alone.

8. Look for strengths in the family, not weaknesses. You will find what you are looking for. Look for ways to put families together instead of pulling them apart.

9. If it becomes necessary to remove a child from his or her home, remember how scared the child will be. Do not treat the child as if the child is in trouble. Be there to nurture the child, to comfort and assure the child that things will be all right. Do not lie to the child. Be a bridge between the child and the family.

10. While the child is in care, do not set the child up to be torn further from the family. Phone calls and family visits should not be forms of discipline.

11. Give the family help when they request it. Trust them to know what they need. Do not make the family fight for help as a measure of their commitment to their child.

12. Do not talk in public about cases. Talk honestly to all the persons involved, but respect confidentiality and the importance of the issues to the particular family.

13. Guardians ad litem, protect the child you are working for. Do your job based on real facts that come to you. Do not just listen to what the professionals tell you. Be independent. Make an independent judgment about the child's best interest and then be available for the child.

14. Be sensitive to all sources of understanding. Remember that views of the world other than your own, such as those from other cultures, astrology, religions, numerology, and so forth, may be just as valid and useful for raising healthy children.

15. In protecting your children, get the human element back. Do not objectify your work into "cases." Remember that your decisions and your efforts involve persons who have become dependent upon you.

Also important to the family's story were the ways the system may have mistreated Rose. From Gina and Lilly's perspective, the act of removal and placement of a child in one or many different family structures, different from their own, is fraught with risks of mistreatment. For them, Rose did not experience abuse until she came into protective custody [45]. Table 11–2 shows how the system of protection might mistreat the child being protected. These are also lessons derived from the story.

TABLE 11–2

How the System of Protection Might Mistreat the Child Being Protected

1. Removing a child from a family, no matter how dangerous the situation, will remove the child from what is known and loved. The child may feel punished for something he or she does not understand.

2. Explaining to the child the reason for removal can be hurtful to the child if care is not taken with the words used to describe what the parents did and why.

3. Placing a child with a family structure, in a lifestyle or socioeconomic level much different from his or her own requires adjustments to different rules that may be very difficult for the child.

4. Asking the child to adjust to a new set of totally unfamiliar circumstances that are out of the control of the people he or she knows and trusts is asking the child to live in fear.

5. Multiple placements require the child to deal with the same fears, insecurities, and adjustments over and over again.

6. A child's time frame is much different than a system's. A placement that is said to be temporary, but lasts for six months, can seem like a lifetime to a child.

7. Telling a child that he or she must receive therapy in order to grow up to be healthy and then taking months to arrange it, tells the child that no one cares enough to help him or her become healthy.

8. For a child in placement, the family is all-important. A child should not have to choose between a family visit and an exciting activity with the foster family. Nor should family visits or phone calls be used as a means of discipline. Contact with family is a right, not a privilege.

9. Family visits in public places can be a source of embarrassment, instead of a source of security for a child.

10. The material goods provided a child in care, such as new clothes, allowance, shopping trips, may set the child up to prefer those to family love and permanence.

Did anything good happen for Rose while she was in care? This was more difficult. She received new clothes and was able to go places out of town she otherwise wouldn't have. She had an allowance and was able to purchase things she wanted instead of just what she needed. She had lavish birthdays and Christmases. All the family, including Rose, feels this has only deepened the "taste" for satisfying the personal "want" area to the point of Rose's involvement in serious stealing. Was there anything less material? Rose says she received an education for and about different lifestyles. She says she learned to live with extremes. Finally, she learned to eat different foods [46].

From the System of Protection

As a part of the inquiry, the expected behaviors of the district attorney, the SRS worker, and the guardian ad litem were compared with what occurred in this family's case. A first look might suggest professional incompetence, incomplete investigation, and poor casework, and so forth. A closer assessment suggests that, for the most part, the actors did their jobs. But they did their jobs based on a flawed initial decision. Rose was an undetected sexually abused child. Rose was not at risk of child abuse or neglect from her parents. She had already been abused; she was at current risk of poverty; and she lived in a "different" family and home environment. She had some special behavioral needs that the family had identified, did not understand, and had requested help in addressing. The "help" they received was her removal for nearly two years.

The various actors carried out the letter of the state law, but in doing so generally missed the spirit of the federal law that is intended to guard against unnecessary removal. No in-home services were offered or delivered prior to Rose's removal. No family preservation services were offered upon her return. Welfare was provided, but it barely allowed for minimum nutrition, not a lifestyle devoid of economic stress.

The law is attentive to the need for careful placements that recognize the special needs of the child and is supportive of family life. None of Rose's three placements prior to the voluntary removal could be said to be more appropriate for her than if she had remained at home with the therapy Lilly requested in 1981. The law calls for good case planning focused on reunify-

ing the family. In this case, case planning that took well over a year to prepare did not include the family or recognize their strengths. Unfortunately,
when protective service involvement ceased, to get the treatment Rose
needed, which family could not afford, Lilly was forced to give up custody
by saying she was unable to respond to her child's special needs. Even with
this last voluntary placement, it appears that only the family and its lawyer
consistently focused on family reunification. Finally, the law calls for decisive, timely action to secure a permanent home. Nothing in this case was
timely or decisive except Rose's original removal.

Audit Trail Resources
Coding System
For Data Units

(verbal)–(respondent ([interview #]))–(data unit #)

Example: V–L(2)–68

Interpretation: Verbal data, from Lilly, second interview, 68th data unit
(nonverbal)–(respondent ([interview #]))–(data unit #)

Example: NV–L(1)–30

Interpretation: Nonverbal data, from Lilly, first interview, 30th data unit

For Reflexive Journal

(Reflexive journal)–(page number([date]))

Example: R–4(Mar 14)

Interpretation: Reflexive journal, page 4, dated March 14

For Documents

(document)–(number)–(page number)

Example: D–1–2

Interpretation: Document number one, page 2

Raw Data for Audit Trail

1. D–1–18; D–1–4; D–1–21; D–1–2.

2. D–2–121; D–2–114; D–2–122; D–2–124; D–2–129–131; D–2–113.

3. V–DA(2)–25; V–B(1)–14; V–K(2)–5; V–R(1)–52; V–J(2)–78; V–D(1)–14; V–S(1)–7; V–C(1)–29; V–JudgeW(1)–42.

4. R–1(Jan 22); R–1(Jan 24); R–1(Jan 30); R–2(Feb 7); R–3(Feb 21); R–3(Feb 27); R–4(Mar 5); R–4(Mar 14); R–4(Mar 17); R–4(Mar 18); R–5(Mar 19).

5. R–5(Mar 19).

6. R–5(Mar 19).

7. NV–L(1)–1; NV–L(1)–3; NV–L(2)–1; NV–L(1)–4; NV–L(1)–16; NV–L(1)–8.

8. NV–L(1)–7; NV–L(1)–8.

9. NV–L(1)–; NV–L(1)–12.

10. V–L(1)–2; V–L(1)–5; V–L(1)–6; V–L(1)–8; V–L(1)–9.

11. V–L(1)–14; V–L(1)–33.

12. V–L(1)–11.

13. V–L(1)–35; V–L(1)–16; V–L(1)–15.

14. V–L(1)–34; V–L(1)–12.

15. V–L(1)–10; V–L(1)–26.

16. V–L(1)–40; V–L(1)–39; V–L(1)–43; V–L(1)–46.

17. V–L(1)–50; V–L(1)–55.1.

18. V–L(2)–10; V–L(2)–11; V–L(2)–12; V–L(2)–12.1; V–L(4)–5; V–L(1)–56; V–L(1)–53; V–L(1)–45; NV–L(1)–23.

19. V–L(1)–55; V–L(2)–8; V–L(2)–9; V–L(1)–49.

20. V–L(1)–54; V–L(1)61.1.

21. V–L(2)–15; V–L(2)–16; V–L (2)–17; V–L(2)–18; V–L(2)–18.1; V–L(2)–20.

22. V–L(1)–46; V–L(1)–64; V–L(1)–57; V–L(1)–58; V–L(1)–61.1; V–L(1)–63; V–L(1)–42; V–L(1)–66; V–L(1)–65.

23. V–L(20)–19; V–L(2)–22; V–L(2)–23; V–L(2)–24; V–L(2)–25; V–L(2)–26.

24. V–L(1)–27; V–L(2)–32; V–L(2)–39; V–L(1)–28; V–L(2)–83; V–L(2)–33.

25. V–L(2)–7; V–L(1)–7; V–L(1)–29; V–L(1)–30; V–L(2)–7.1; V–L(2)–1.

26. V–L(1)–20; V–L(2)–40; V–L(1)–67; V–L(1)–68; NV–L(1)–30.

27. V–L(1)–19; V–L(2)–41; V–L(2)–42.

28. V–L(2)–36.

29. V–L(2)–31; V–L(2)–2; V–L(2)–3; V–L(2)–4; V–L(2)–5; V–L(2)–6; V–L(2)–37; V–L(2)–38.

30. V–L(2)–37; V–L(2)–47; V–L(2)–57; V–L(2)–78; V–L(2)–79; V–L(2)–81; V–L(2)–84; V–L(2)–94; V–L(1)–38; V–L(2)–35.

31. V–L(2)–49; V–L(2)–48; V–L(2)–50; V–L(2)–51.

32. V–L(2)–52; V–L(2)–36; V–L(2)–53; V–L(2)–55.

33. V–L(2)–45.

34. V–L(2)–88; V–L(2)–89.

35. V–L(2)–54; V–L(2)–57.1.

36. V–L(2)–60; V–L(2)–72; V–L(2)–73; V–L(2)–74; V–L(2)–75.

37. V–L(2)–71; V–L(2)–92.

38. V–L(2)–91; V–L(2)–70; V–L(2)–76.

39. V–L(2)–93; V–L(4)–16; V–L(2)–61; V–L(2)–64; V–L(2)–65; V–L(2)–67.

40. V–L(2)–68; V–L(2)–69.

41. V–L(1)–22; V–L(3)–2; V–L(1)–23; V–L(1)–47; V–L(2)–77.

42. V–L(2)–95; V–L(2)–96; V–L(2)–97; V–L(2)–58.

43. V–L(6)–1; V–L(7)–1.

44. V–L(1)–44; V–L(1)–25; V–L(2)–66; V–L(1)–72; V–L(2)–86; V–L(2)–87.

45. V–L(4)–9; V–L(5)–11; V–L(5)–12; V–L(5)–16; V–L(5)–19; D–7–1.

46. NV–L(2)–33; V–L(2)–183; V–L(2)–184; V–L(2)–185; V–L(2)–186; V–L(2)–187; V–L(2)–188; V–L(2)–191; V–L(2)–192; V–L(2)193; V–L(2)–194; V–L(2)–195; V–L(2)–196.

Discussion Questions

The following questions will require the reader to evaluate the strengths and weaknesses of the research reported in the case study.

1. How is the inquiry question related to the major assumptions of constructivism? What assumptions are clearest? Which might present a problem in this inquiry?

2. As an outside reader, what is your evaluation of the quality of the case study? To what degree do you think transferability is possible? Using either Guba and Lincoln's or Zeller's criteria from Chapter 8, how does this case study measure up? What could have made it more compelling?

3. Given the limited audit trail provided at the end of the case study, is there an indication that the assertions in the case study are grounded in the data? If you were providing a confirmability audit, what would you say?

4. Where is the voice of the inquirer most apparent? Is it clear when the inquirer is speaking and when the voices of the participants are represented. How about in the lessons to be learned? Whose voices are there? Do the lessons go beyond the data? If so, how?

GLOSSARY

audit The process by which the constructivist rigor of trustworthiness and authenticity is attested to by an outside review of the audit trail.

authenticity Dimension of constructivist research rigor focusing on the quality of the research process, rather than on the research product. Composed of fairness, ontological, educative, catalytic, and tactical aspects.

basic science Generally understood to be scientific research that leads to the description of things following positivist assumptions and principles. *See also* natural science.

case report Preferred method of presenting the results of a constructivist study, usually written in a narrative style and providing a thick description of the phenomena under investigation, the context of the investigation, and the results of the co-construction by inquiry participants. *See also* case study.

case study Generally interchangeable with the case report as the primary vehicle for emic inquiry that builds on the reader's tacit knowledge and allows for reader judgment regarding transferability of the information to another known context. *See also* case report.

catalytic authenticity A measure of constructivist research rigor that demonstrates change or reshaping has resulted from the research process. *See also* authenticity.

cause Concept originating with Aristotle who was trying to frame the fundamental nature of things. Usually discussed as efficient cause (any power or agent that effects a result), final cause (the purpose or end for which anything is produced), formal cause (the ideal standard according to which a thing or event is produced), and material cause (the means undertaken to produce a formal cause). In positivistic research, efficient cause is of most interest.

co-construction In relational conversation, the dialogic and dialectical process by which research participants, together with the inquirer, create a reality and share an understanding of it.

cognitive map Conceptual structure that orders bits of information and their relationships.

confirmability A measure of constructivist research rigor that demonstrates that the research results are linked to the data collected during the inquiry. *See also* trustworthiness.

constructed reality What exists is in the minds of individuals; a cognitive process that leads to an infinite number of constructions and, hence, multiple realities; reality is constructed through the use of some common referent terms that could be understood (constructed) differently by different individuals.

constructionism Principally a framework for intervention, based on the assumption that personality and identity are socially constructed and potentially changing from situation to situation. Change comes through linguistic negotiation generated between individuals who judge and correct until agreement is achieved regarding meaning. Linguistic coupling through narrative allows the negotiation of meaning across cognitive, social, and moral structures.

constructivism A philosophical framework and an approach to research and clinical practice that assumes that reality is constructed, based on intersubjectively achieved meaning that cannot generalize beyond the time and context of the encounter; that there are no fundamental causes, but instead networks of relationships that produce multiple and simultaneous shaping to the construction of reality. Focus is on cognitive schemas that construct the subject's experience and action and lead to new interpretive frameworks or structures.

contextual reality A type of constructed reality absolutely imbedded in the particulars of a given situation or environment.

control Methodological and design efforts to guard against bias or the potential influence of intervening variables, in order to assure that findings have no alternative explanation.

credibility A measure of constructivist research rigor that demonstrates the findings are believable. *See also* trustworthiness.

critical paradigm A more radical worldview that assumes knowledge building is only relevant if change results, at both the individual and the societal levels.

critical theory A social theory with Marxist antecedents which looks at ways in which language and linguistic practices shape political and social reality. By emphasizing the individual's reflection on his or her own actions, the belief is that this understanding can influence change.

deduction A reasoning process moving from a more abstract meaning to meanings that are subsumed by it; going from the general to the particular.

dependability A measure of constructivist research rigor which demonstrates that the procedures used to gather, analyze, and interpret data fall within accepted constructivist practices. *See also* trustworthiness.

determinism Refers to limitations placed on events or behaviors and framed in terms of antecedents and consequences. The type of determinism is dependent upon the type of cause that is of interest. With efficient cause, the assumption is that everything is entirely determined by a sequence of causes. *See also* cause.

dialectic Process of meaning making when meaning relations are oppositional, dual, contradictory, or arbitrary; can involve the uniting of opposites into a new totality such as in the synthesis of a thesis and an antithesis.

dichotomous thinking Sometimes called "black and white" or "either/or" thinking wherein meaning can only exist somewhere in a pair of opposites such as good/bad, sweet/sour, and so forth, so that if you are not "good," you must be "bad."

discourse A focused discussion, usually formal and based on reason with the aim of communication and study.

dualism Theory that proposes two realms of explanation to account for the observed facts. Freud's theory of psychic and somatic realms is an example.

educative authenticity A measure of constructivist research rigor that demonstrates there was increased understanding of and respect for the value systems of others as a result of the inquiry process. *See also* authenticity.

effect That which has been produced by or is the result of a cause that has temporally preceded it.

egalitarianism A belief in human equality, especially regarding social, political, and economic affairs.

emergence Describes a research design that allows an orderly development of an inquiry based on what comes forth from the context and process without determining the structure and process beforehand.

emic Providing an insider's view or perspective.

empirical Basing knowledge on what can be observed. Data from these observations can be numbers or words.

empowerment The process by which authority, competence, or power is developed.

epistemology Assumptions related to what can be known and how scientists can be expected to come to know it.

etic Providing an outsider's perspective.

fairness A measure of constructivist rigor that demonstrates there is an evenhanded representation of all viewpoints throughout the research process and in the research product. *See also* authenticity.

functionalism A paradigmatic perspective that assumes the social world is composed of relatively concrete empirical artifacts and relationships that can be identified, studied, and measured through approaches derived from the natural sciences.

gatekeeper A person who, by virtue of position, power, or expertise can provide or prevent access to information or sources of information.

generalizability The ability of a truth to hold across time and circumstance.

grounded theory An explanation or a description of a phenomenon that results as data emerge and are analyzed.

hermeneutic circle In the sense of Gadamer, a circular conversation among and between interested parties (including relevant texts), wherein perspectives and insights are shared, tested, and evaluated. *See also* hermeneutic dialectic.

hermeneutic dialectic The process within the hermeneutic circle where perspectives are compared and placed in contradiction so that, through testing and evaluation, a higher level of sophistication can be achieved, generally filled with at least tension, if not conflict. *See also* hermeneutic circle.

humanism A theory of behavior in which the theorist employs telic or purposeful assumptions that human events always have some intended end, that they are not mechanistic.

ideographic Having the nature of a graphic symbol that represents an object or idea, rather than a word used for the same purpose.

idiographic Descriptions or interpretations that are unique to the individual, that capture what is individually distinctive.

individualism Of or pertaining to the individual, particularly related to his or her best interest.

induction A reasoning process moving from lower to higher levels of abstraction, going from the particular to the general.

inquiry context The physical and psychological backdrop for the research undertaking; the location in which the research is taking place.

interactivity Reciprocal action or effect, mutual shaping.

interpretive paradigm A perspective informed by a concern to understand the world as it is at the level of subjective experience, within the realm of individual consciousness and subjectivity, and from the frame of reference of the participant, as opposed to the observer of action. It sees the social world as an emergent social process that is created by the individuals concerned. Reality is little more than a network of assumptions and intersubjectively shared meanings that hold only as long as meaning is shared.

interventionist research Research that entails altering the context or the intervention being researched for research purposes. Interventionist research, as opposed to naturalistic research, intrudes into the natural rhythm of that which is being investigated.

logical empiricism A philosophical perspective that establishes verifiability as grounds for judging whether or not a question or issue has meaning. Empirical observation is the basis of this approach's measure of good scientific investigation. *See also* logical positivism, positivism.

logical positivism Built on the same assumptions of logical empiricism that all knowledge must be based on observable things and events. *See also* logical empiricism.

meaning construction Based on the assumptions of a socially constructed reality of constructionism and constructivism, it is the communication process through which understanding between individuals and perspectives is achieved by creating relational ties between one item or concept and another with word or symbolic interpretations.

member check Major activity of constructivist rigor of both trustworthiness and authenticity, whereby the inquiry respondents are asked to warrant that what has been understood or produced is an accurate reflection of their reality.

minority report In recognition of multiple realities and the difficulty of gaining consensus through hermeneutic dialectic, the presentation of the claims, concerns, or issues of those for whom consensus was not possible. It is in the form of an addendum to the final constructivist case report.

multiple causality Simultaneous influencing of factors over time in such a way that it is no longer relevant to ask which caused which, sometimes known as mutual causality or mutual simultaneous shaping, because everything influences everything else, in the here and now.

multiple meanings In constructivism, the assumption that each individual will construct his or her own understanding of experience and action, and that even individuals having the same experience will invent different interpretive frameworks or structure to understand, so that the number of interpretations will match the number of individuals having the experience.

multiple perspectives In constructivism, the assumption that our perspective affects what we see, so that any one focus of observation only gives a partial result. In order to hope to achieve a complete picture, many points of view are required. To control biases and develop more than a partial understanding, a plurality of kinds of knowledge must be explored by a multiplicity of methods.

natural science An approach to description of things by reducing all formal and final cause explanations to material and efficient cause explanations, based on the assumption that natural forces work toward a purpose, and the cause can be identified using natural science methods. *See also* cause.

naturalistic research Within the positivist perspective, the systematic study of a phenomenon in its context, without intentional alteration for research purposes. In the interpretive perspective, the original title of what is now known as constructivist research.

negotiated outcomes The required results of a constructivist inquiry. Meanings, interpretations, and the final product must be negotiated with the human sources because it is their construction of reality, and because participants own their own data. The goal of the negotiation is accurate reconstruction of perspectives.

nonrational Not to be confused with irrational, speaks of a logic that is not linear; but instead, tends to be circular and able to consider even the most tangential aspects of a thought process. Nonrational reasoning is reasoning by metaphor and analogy rather than by "if/then" statements.

nomothetic An approach to description of behavior and things based upon what is generally the case. This approach relies on lawlike generalizations that describe everything exactly the same way for all time. Individual differences are minimized and commonalities are emphasized.

objectivity Refers to constructs with meanings that transcend the individual who frames the relationship intended and, therefore, may be understood by all individuals who expend the proper effort. Objective meanings can be understood by anyone who sincerely examines the contents at issue because social reality has concrete existence above and beyond the individual.

ontological authenticity A measure of constructivist research rigor that demonstrates increased awareness of the complexity of the phenomenon under investigation. *See also* authenticity.

ontology Perspective on the nature of reality. Is it above and beyond individual knowledge or is it based on individual consciousness without regard to the outside world?

paradigm How one orders reality; the general organizing principles governing perceptions including beliefs, values, techniques used to describe what exists, where to look, and what scientists expect to discover. It is a worldview with a set of axioms and systems, all related to one another for disciplined inquiry.

paradox Holding seemingly contradictory opinions, interpretations, or two different things as true at the same time.

peer debriefing As a part of peer review, the process whereby the peer reviewer poses searching questions in order to help the researcher understand his or her own perspective and behavior in the research process, and test working hypotheses outside the inquiry context to enhance the emergent design. *See also* peer review.

peer review The process in constructivist research whereby an outside agent or reviewer is engaged to accompany the research process in order to discuss feelings, findings, and conclusions in a process that resembles clinical supervision. *See also* peer debriefing.

persistent observation In constructivism, an activity to increase the probability of credible findings that includes noting, watching, and taking into account the physical and psychosocial dynamics of the time and place of the inquiry. It provides depth in an inquiry because it occurs over time and allows the inquirer to eliminate aspects that are irrelevant, while continuing to address those that are critical to the inquiry.

positivism/positivist paradigm A perspective generally understood to be the same as the logical positivist or logical empiricist, in which theoretical propositions are tested or built according to rules of formal logic to create scientific knowledge. *See also* logical empiricism, logical positivism, post-positivism.

post-positivism Within the tradition of positivism, a perspective that recognizes the value-laden and interactive nature of the research process, so that direct correspondence, or direct, objective knowledge of forms are eliminated. Though generalizability remains the goal, naturalistic and phenomenological approaches and subjective meanings are included so that multiple realities and researcher interpretations become acceptable ways of scientific knowing. *See also* positivism, logical empiricism, logical positivism.

pragmatism A philosophical perspective that tests the validity of all concepts by their practical results.

prediction Inferences that a researcher makes about probable evolution of events or outcomes over time in order to test the validity of research findings.

prolonged engagement In constructivism, an activity that increases the probability of credible findings, including learning about the working, living, and interacting patterns of inquiry participants in their environment by being in the environment over time. "This requires hanging out" to see how participants act, react, and interact to discern and attend to distortions and inaccuracies introduced by the inquirer and the participants. It provides scope in the inquiry by developing trust among the participants.

qualitative methods The preferred means of collecting data in constructivist research because of their adaptability to multiple realities and because they expose more directly the nature of the transaction between investigator and participant. They allow easier access to the biases of the investigator and are more sensitive to mutual shaping influences. The preferred qualitative methods in constructivism are: interviews, participant observations, and focus groups.

quantitative methods The preferred means of collecting data in traditional research in the positivist and post-positivist perspective because of the assumed ability to control intersubjectivity and other biasing effects that could hamper generalizability. Preferred quantitative methods are use of standardized instruments within a controlled research design.

radicalism Favoring fundamental change of the center, foundation, or source as in the social structure. Generally seen to be extreme, mostly used to describe leftist political preferences, as opposed to conservative preferences.

rationalization To explain or interpret on rational grounds. Usually meant to describe a process in which superficially rational or plausible explanations or excuses are devised to support one's acts, beliefs, or desires without one's being aware that these are not the real motives.

reactivity Responding to stimulus, to be affected by some influence, event, experience, and so forth.

realism The philosophical view that the contents of our mind, that which we know, exist independently of our mind. Our understanding of anything is abstracted from an independent reality.

reconstruction The last step in constructivist data analysis after unitizing (a deconstructive process) whereby, through categorizing all data with a constant comparison of one unit to another, the material is brought together in a new and, hopefully, more meaningful way.

reductionism The philosophical assumption that we achieve a better understanding of anything after we have broken down formal and final cause theoretical conceptions to underlying material and efficient cause theoretical conceptions. This is a "building block" conception of reality where little unities constitute bigger totalities and the goal is to reduce everything to the substrata that "make them up." *See also* cause.

reflexive journal During the constructivist inquiry process, a required dimension of trustworthiness that reports on the inquirer's progressive bounding of subjectivity, in which reflections are made regarding inner biases and conflicts, and the strategies devised that are used to cope with or resolve these barriers to understanding. The journal should also chronicle the development of different or deeper insights and understandings of the context and perspectives of the inquiry participants.

reflexivity The ability of the human mind to turn back on itself and, therefore, know that it is knowing.

relativism A perspective on knowledge which maintains that the basis of judgment and/or knowing is relative, differing according to events, persons, and so forth.

rhetoric The use of words effectively in speaking or writing to influence or persuade.

rigor All aspects of the demonstration of quality in constructivist research including trustworthiness, negotiated outcomes, authenticity, and the quality of the hermeneutic circle.

schema In constructivism, the cognitive map or diagram that serves to represent something, principally the result of the data analysis process, but can also refer to the way individuals categorize to make sense out of complexity.

science Knowledge building where validating evidence is employed at some point in coming to understand the object of inquiry.

social science Differing from natural science, the goal is description of things related to human beings, their behavior, and experience. Methods used for explanations or understanding may mirror those of natural science, or they may follow more interpretive perspectives.

stakeholder An individual with a vested interest. In research, stakeholders are all individuals with a perspective or with something to gain or lose, as a result of the process or product of inquiry.

subjectivity Refers to constructs with meanings that are somehow private and, therefore, incapable of being extended beyond the individual who has framed the meaningful relationship intended. Subjective meanings cannot be totally understood, even when we sincerely examine the contents at issue, because social reality exists primarily in the individual's consciousness or mind.

tacit knowledge Intuitions, feelings that have not yet taken propositional (language) form. It cannot be stated, but is somehow known to the subject.

tactical authenticity A measure of constructivist research rigor that demonstrates empowerment or redistribution of power among stakeholders supportive of effective change. *See also* authenticity.

theory A series of two or more schematic labels (words, symbols, concepts, etc.) that have been hypothesized, presumed, or demonstrated to bear a meaningful relationship with one another.

theory building The process by which the relationship between concepts is described.

theory testing The process by which the relationship between concepts is proven or disproved.

transferability A measure of constructivist research rigor that demonstrates sufficient information about the context and the phenomenon under investigation has been provided in the final product, the case report, to allow the reader to make judgments about the similarities of the findings with other contexts. *See also* trustworthiness.

triangulation Using different modes of data collection to cross-check data collected and data analyzed.

trustworthiness The constructivist criteria for testing the rigor of constructivist studies, paralleling the criteria for rigor found in traditional research. It includes credibility (analogous to internal validity), dependability (analogous to reliability), confirmability (analogous to objectivity), and transferability (analogous to external validity).

truth A fact or reality related to actual existence and able to be verified. In traditional science it must also be established to exist across time and context.

values Those things that are desirable or worthy of esteem for their own sakes. That which has intrinsic worth and is regarded in a particularly favorable way.

Verstehen Concept used by Gadamer to describe the results of hermeneutics, which should be agreement or understanding through critical controlled interpretation.

FURTHER READINGS

The following annotated readings should be useful for the constructivist researcher in search of additional technical information. Each reference has been selected because of its compatibility with either interpretive, alternative, or constructivist research perspectives. Care should be taken regarding rigor expectations put forth in some of the texts that are built on traditional positivist assumptions.

Denzin, N. (1989). *Interpretive interactionism.* Newbury Park, CA: Sage.

Coming from a symbolic interactionist and existential perspective, this text considers methods of conducting interpretive research. Highlighted here is hierarchical analysis that includes the used of narrative to compare and contrast different perspectives in a hierarchy of interest. Also emphasized is the use of thick description, a literary style that will allow the reader to experience the world described from the perspectives of the participants. A useful glossary of terms is included.

Denzin, N., & Lincoln, Y. (Eds.). (1994). *Handbook of qualitative research.* Thousand Oaks, CA: Sage.

This text is a compendium on qualitative research created by some of the best minds in qualitative research across disciplines, paradigms, and strategies. It thoughtfully treats the various dimensions of the tensions in qualitative research by going from the general of the history of the qualitative research tradition in various paradigms to the specifics of major research methods of collecting and analyzing qualitative data. The future of qualitative research across disciplines is placed in a new historical moment in research that recognizes complexity and foreshadows a next generation of qualitative research.

Fetterman, D., Kaftarian, S., & Wandersman, A. (Eds.) (1996). *Empowerment evaluation: Knowledge and tools for self-assessment and accountability.* Thousand Oaks, CA: Sage.

Empowerment evaluation uses evaluation methods to foster improvement and self-determination. The text is a training manual with case examples to demonstrate how to implement a four-step model that teaches program participants to evaluate their own programs. Also included is the use of standardized instruments in program evaluation.

Guba, E., & Lincoln, Y. (1989). *Fourth generation evaluation.* Newbury Park, CA: Sage.

This is the second text concerning constructivist methods set within the assumptions of a constructivist perspective. Focus is on implementing the hermeneutic circle and negotiating the co-constructed outcomes of a constructivist inquiry. The text has an adequate treatment of the comparison between the constructivist perspective and a more traditional positivist perspective and also describes and compares more traditional evaluation strategies with those of constructivism.

Hobbs, D., & May, T. (Eds.). (1993). *Interpreting the field: Accounts of ethnography.* NY: Oxford University Press.

This is a collection of examples of ethnographic research experiences complete with the problems that were encountered while undertaking the investigations. Methods addressed are: dealing with diversity, including developing closeness and trust while still maintaining balance, as well as managing confidentiality and risk for both the researcher and the subjects.

Josselson, R., & Lieblich, A. (1995) (Eds.). *Interpreting experience: The narrative study of lives.* Thousand Oaks, CA: Sage.

The research focus is the narrative approach to understanding. The book brings together various researchers interested in interpreting experience. Some techniques are provided, mostly in response to criticism of standard interviewing and analysis styles. Examples of the use of narrative for both research and therapeutic purposes are presented.

Krueger, R. (1994). *Focus groups: A practical guide for applied research.* (2nd ed.). Thousand Oaks, CA: Sage.

This is a "how-to" text for traditional focus group research. The role and skills of the moderator/researcher are detailed. There is a nice discussion of group dynamics and the optimal group size and composition for productive conversation. Though it must be noted that this text is set within a positivist perspective, the strategies for data gathering, including tape recording and note taking, as well as data reduction and writing the final report are useful.

Lambert, L., Walker, D., Zimmermann, D., Cooper, J., Lambert, M., Gardner, M., & Ford Slack, P. (1995). *The constructivist leader.* New York: Teachers College Press.

Though focusing primarily on training and development of constructivist leadership within the educational system, the book is a good, practical application of constructivist theory to a specific context. Also recognized is the importance of language for meaningful dialogue. Details are provided on how to structure a constructivist conversation, the use of narrative to demonstrate changes over time, and the use of metaphor to develop increased understanding in diverse communities.

Lee, R. (1995). *Dangerous fieldwork.* Thousand Oaks, CA: Sage.

This text recognizes the risks involved with outside researchers attempting entrance into a field environment. It addresses the various aspects of danger that may be encountered in the field, with a particular focus on research on drugs and gangs. Attention is given to the special challenges of sexual harassment and assault that may face women researchers. The emphasis here is on techniques to reduce risk regarding personal safety and the findings and policy issues surrounding a research project.

Lincoln, Y., & Guba, E. (1985). *Naturalistic inquiry.* Newbury Park, CA: Sage.

This is the first full text to treat the assumptions and methods of constructivist inquiry (here called naturalistic inquiry). All assumptions of constructivism and the methods that are derived from those assumptions are detailed. A major portion of the book covers standard criticism of "old science" or positivism. From Chapter 8 forward can be found practical advice on how to design, implement, and demonstrate the rigor of a constructivist inquiry.

Lofland, J., & Lofland, L. (1995). *Analyzing social settings: A guide to qualitative observation and analysis.* (3rd ed.). Belmont, CA: Wadsworth.

Participant observation as a research method is the focus of this "how-to" text, which is divided into three sections: gathering, focusing, and analyzing data. Good advice is given about gaining entry into various settings. Of interest is the chapter that helps the researcher to manage the complexity of a context. Also included are how to employ emergent analysis designs, procedures for coding the data, and writing the report.

Martin, R. (1995). *Oral history in social work: Research, assessment, and intervention.* Thousand Oaks, CA: Sage.

The text is a compilation of oral histories of African Americans and Latin Americans with the goal of aiding the social worker and other helping professionals to integrate the material into research and practice. Martin includes 11 steps in conducting an oral history research project.

Miles, M., & Huberman, A. (1994). *Qualitative data analysis: An expanded sourcebook.* (2nd ed.). Thousand Oaks, CA: Sage.

Though set in a traditional research paradigm, the text covers the major technologies of managing word data. Tips for data collection, analysis, display, and report writing are available and useful, as long as the constructivist reader does not stray into the realms of attributing cause and attending to the research rigor needs for generalizability.

Rubin, H., & Rubin, I. (1995). *Qualitative interviewing: The art of hearing data.* Thousand Oaks, CA: Sage.

Built on interpretive social science methods and a feminist model of interviewing, the text outlines a method of rigorous qualitative research. Techniques of data collection including the structured, the unstructured, and the cultural interview are detailed. Also included are means of striking a balance between research ethics and obligations to conversation partners who are research participants, while trying to obtain a certain depth in the material generated. A notable chapter provides guidance in data analysis including hearing themes, coding the material, and identifying major emerging themes. The final chapter provides techniques for writing the final report.

Schwandt, T., & Halpern, E. (1988). *Linking auditing and metaevaluation: Enhancing quality in applied research.* Newbury Park, CA: Sage.

This is the only text solely devoted to auditing techniques for constructivist inquiry and other alternative paradigm research. The authors provide a useful guide to organizing and structuring documentation to create a traceable audit trail. Responsibilities of the auditor and auditee are detailed in order to assure a reliable audit report. Specific steps are included to aid the reader in preparing for the audit, contracting with the auditor, and writing the audit report. Only auditing for trustworthiness is covered.

Van Maanen, J. (Ed.). (1995). *Representation in ethnography.* Thousand Oaks, CA: Sage.

For the constructivist who is interested in sorting out just exactly what ethnography is as a research method, this text is a good start. It contains good treatment of the history and the current issues in ethnographic research. This is an edited work providing a variety of contemporary ethnographic writings that focus on the analysis of text. It is interesting reading, even if it does not provide much specific technology.

Yin, R. (1994). *Case study research: Design and methods.* (2nd ed.). Thousand Oaks, CA: Sage.

Focusing on the case study method of research, the aim is a rigorous process as judged positivistically. Of interest is the use of theory in research and various elements of design and analysis. The reader wishing a primer on preparing the investigator and developing a research protocol will be well served. Also included are issues of triangulation and how to develop the description of the evidence gathered, with various modes of analysis presented.

REFERENCES

Abbott, E. (1918). The social caseworker and the enforcement of industrial legislation. In *Proceedings of the Nations Conference on Social Work, 1918*. Chicago: Rogers and Hall.

Adams, E. (1979). Measurement theory in current research. In P. Asquith & H. E. Kyberg, *Philosophy of Science* (pp. 207–227). East Lansing, MI: Philosophy of Science Association.

Addams, J. (1916). *The long road of woman's memory*. New York: Macmillan.

Addams, J. (1930). *The second twenty years at Hull House, September 1909 to September 1929, with a record of a growing world consciousness*. New York: Macmillan.

Addams, J. (1990). *Twenty years at Hull House: With autobiographical notes by Jane Addams*. Urbana: University of Illinois Press. (Original work published 1910).

Adler, P., & Adler, P. (1993). Observational techniques. In N. Denzin & Y. Lincoln (Eds.), *Handbook of qualitative research* (pp. 377–392). Thousand Oakes, CA: Sage.

Atkinson, P., & Hammersley, M. (1994). Ethnography and participant observation. In N. Denzin & Y. Lincoln (Eds.), *Handbook of qualitative research* (pp. 248–261). Thousand Oakes, CA: Sage.

Austin, D. (1978). Research and social work: Educational paradoxes and possibilities. *Journal of Social Service Research, 2* (2), 159–176.

Bartlett, H. (1958). Toward clarification and improvement of social work practice. *Social Work, 3*, 3–9.

Beckerman, A. (1978). Differentiating between social research and social work research: Implications for teaching. *Journal of Education for Social work, 14*, 9–15.

Benson, J.K. (1983). A dialectical method for the study of organizations. In G. Morgan (Ed.), *Beyond method: Stategies for social research* (pp. 331–346). Beverly Hills, CA: Sage.

Berger, P., & Luckmann, T. (1976). *The social construction of reality*. Harmondsworth, Middlesex, England: Penguin Books.

Berkenkotter, C. (1993). A "Rhetoric for naturalistic inquiry" and the question of genre. *Research in the Teaching of English, 27* (3), 293–304.

Berlin, S. (1990). Dichotomous and complex thinking. *Social Service Review, 64*, 46–59.

Bernstein, R. J. (1985). *Beyond objectivism and relativism: Science, hermeneutics and praxis*. Philadelphia: University of Pennsylvania Press.

Berreth, D. (1986). *Experiences of naturalistic inquirers during inquiry.* Unpublished doctoral dissertation, Indiana University.

Biklin, S., & Bogdan, R. (1986). *On your own with naturalistic evaluation.* New Directions for Program Evaluation, 30. San Francisco: Jossey-Bass.

Birn, R., Hague, P., & Vangelder, P. (1990). *Handbook of market research.* London: Routledge & Kegan Paul.

Blalock, H. M. (1979). Presidential address: Measurement and conceptualization problems. *American Sociological Review, 44,* 881–194.

Bloom, M. (1978). Challenges to the helping profession and the response of scientific practice. *Social Service Review, 25,* 584–595.

Bloom M. (1995). The great philosophy of science war. *Social Work Research, 19* (1), 19–23.

Blumer, H. (1969). *Symbolic interactionism: Perspective and method.* Englewood Cliffs, NJ: Prentice Hall.

Bogdan, R., & Biklen, S. (1982). *Qualitative research for education: An introduction to theory and methods.* Boston: Allyn & Bacon.

Bogdan, R., & Biklen, S. (1992). *Qualitative research in education: An introduction to theory and methods.* (2nd ed.). Boston: Allyn & Bacon.

Bowers, C.A. (1984). *The promise of theory: Education and the politics of cultural change.* New York: Longman.

Brekke, J. (1986, December). Scientific imperatives in social work research: Pluralism is not skepticism. *Social Service Review,* 538–554.

Briar, S. (1964). The family as an organization: An approach to family diagnosis and treatment. *Social Service Review, 38,* 247–255.

Burrell, G., & Morgan, G. (1979). *Sociological paradigms and organisational analysis: Elements of the sociology of corporate life.* London: Heinemann.

Campbell, J. (1995). *Understanding John Dewey.* Chicago: Open Court.

Cancian, F.M., & Armstead, C. (1992). Participatory Research. In E. Borgatta and M. Borgatta (Eds.) *Encyclopedia of sociology* (Vol. 3) (pp. 1427–1432). New York: Macmillan.

Carkhuff, R. (1969). *Helping and human relations: Practice and research.* New York: Holt, Rinehart & Winston.

Carpenter, D. (1996). Constructivism and social work treatment. In F. Turner (Ed.), *Social work treatment: Interlocking theoretical approaches.* (4th ed.) (pp. 146–167). New York: The Free Press.

Chambers, D.,Wedel, K.,& Rodwell, M.K. (1992). *Evaluating social programs.* Boston, MA: Allyn & Bacon.

Chambon, A., & Irving, A. (1994). *Essays on postmoderism and social work.* Toronto: Canadian Scholars' Press.

Charmaz, K. (1983). The grounded theory method: An explication and interpretation. In R. Emerson (Ed.), *Contemporary field research* (pp. 109–126). Boston, MA: Little Brown.

Chelimsky, E. (1985). Comparing and contrasting auditing and evaluation: Some notes on their relationship. *Evaluation Review, 9,* 483–503.

Cook, B. (1992). *Eleanor Roosevelt: 1898–1944.* (Vol. 1) New York: Viking.

Corbin, J., & Strauss, A. (1990). *Basics of qualitative research: Grounded theory procedures and techniques.* Newbury Park, CA: Sage.

Cormier, W., & Cormier, L. (1979). *Interviewing strategies for helpers: A guide to assessment, treatment, and evaluation.* Monterey, CA: Brooks/Cole.

Corsaro, W. (1981). Entering the child's world—research strategies for field entry and data collection in a preschool setting. In J. Green & C. Wallet (Eds.), *Ethnography and language in educational settings* (pp. 117–146). Norwood, NY: Ablex.

Cowger, C. (1984). Statistical significance tests: Scientific ritualism or scientific method? *Social Service Review, 58,* 358–372.

Cronbach, L. (1975). Beyond the two disciplines of scientific psychology. *American Psychologist, 30* (2), 116–127.

Crowley, S. (1995). *Proposal for a constructivist inquiry of implementation of federal housing policy in and between three entitlement jurisdictions.* (Xeroxed). Richmond, VA: Virginia Commonwealth University.

Crowley, S., & Rodwell, M.K. (1994). *A constructivist approach to public policy analysis.* Paper presented at the Ethnographic Research and Urban Policy Problems Conference, Howard University, Washington, DC.

Darkewald, G. (1982). *Adult education: Foundations of practice.* New York: Harper & Row.

Dean, R. (1989). Ways of knowing in clinical practice. *Clinical Social Work Journal 17* (2), 116–127.

Dean, R. (1993). Constructivism: An approach to clinical practice. *Smith College Studies in Social Work, 63,* 127–146.

Dean, R., & Fenby, B. (1989). Exploring epistemologies: Social work action as a reflection of philosophical assumptions. *Journal of Social Work Education 5* (1), 46–54.

Denzin, N. (1970). *The research act.* Chicago: Aldine.

Denzin, N. (1971). The logic of naturalistic inquiry. *Social Forces, 50,* 166–182.

Denzin, N. (1978). The logic of naturalistic inquiry. In N. Denzin (Ed.), *Sociological methods: A sourcebook* (pp. 6–29). New York: McGraw-Hill.

Denzin, N. (1989). *Interpretive interactionism.* Newbury Park, CA: Sage.

Denzin, N. (1993). The art and politics of interpretation. In N. Denzin & Y. Lincoln (Eds.), *Handbook of qualitative research* (pp. 500–515). Thousand Oaks, CA: Sage.

Denzin, N.K., & Lincoln, Y. (Eds.). (1994). *Handbook of qualitative research.* Thousand Oaks, CA: Sage.

Dewey, J. (1933). *How we think.* Boston: D.C. Heath and Co.

Diesing, P. (1991). *How does social science work? Reflections on practice.* Pittsburgh: University of Pittsburgh Press.

Dilthey, W. (1961). *Pattern and meanings in history* (H.P. Rickman, trans.). New York: Harper & Row.

Dilthey, W. (1976). *Selected Writings* (H. P. Rickman, trans.). New York: Cambridge University Press.

Doise, W. (1989). Constructivism in social psychology. *European Journal of Social Psychology, 19,* 389–400.

Dore, R. (1903). A new profession. *Current Literature, 34,* 293–294.

Douglas, H. (1991). Assessing violent couples. *Families in Society, 71* (9), 525–533.

Duffy, T., & Jonassen, D. (1991). Constructivism: New implications for instructional technology. *Educational Technology, 30* (5), 7–12.

Eisner, E. (1979). The use of qualitative forms of evaluation for improving educational practice. *Educational Evaluation and Policy Analysis, 1,* 11–19.

Eisner, E. (1991). *The enlightened eye: Qualitative inquiry and the enhancement of educational practice.* New York: Macmillan.

Fay, B. (1977). How people change themselves: The relationship between critical theory and its audience. In T. Ball (Ed.), *Political theory and praxis* (pp. 200–233). Minneapolis: University of Minnesota Press.

Fetterman, D., Kaftarian, S., Wandersman, A. (Eds.). (1996). *Empowerment evaluation: Knowledge and tools for self-assessment and accountability.* Thousand Oaks, CA: Sage.

Fischer, J. (1978). *Effective casework practice: An eclectic approach.* New York: McGraw-Hill.

Fischer, J. (1981). The social work revolution. *Social Work, 26,* 199–207.

Fischer, J., & Hudson, W. (1983). Measurement of client problems for improved practice. In A. Rosenblatt & D. Waldfogel (Eds.), *Handbook of clinical social work* (pp. 673–693). San Francisco: Jossey-Bass.

Fisher, D. (1991). *An introduction to constructivism for social workers.* New York: Praeger.

Flexner, A. (1915). Is social work a profession? In *Proceedings of the 42nd National Conference of Charities and Corrections* (pp. 576–590). Fort Wayne, IN: Fort Wayne Printing Co.

Fontana, A., & Frey, J. (1994). Interviewing: The art of science. In N. Denzin & Y. Lincoln (Eds.), *Handbook of qualitative research* (pp. 361–376). Thousand Oaks, CA: Sage.

Fostnot, C. (1992). Constructing constructivism. In T. Duffy & D. Jonassen (Eds.), *Constructivism and the technology of instruction: A conversation* (pp. 167–176). Hillsdale, NJ: Erlbaum.

Foucault, Michel. (1980). *Power/knowledge: Selected interviews and other writings, 1972–1977.* (C. Gordon, ed. and trans.). New York: Pantheon Books.

Franklin, C. (1995). Expanding the vision of the social constructionist debates: Creating relevance for practitioners. *Families in Society, 76,* 395–406

Fraser, M., Taylor, M., Jackson, R., & O'Jack, J. (1991). Social work and science: Many ways of knowing? *Social Work Research and Abstracts, 27* (4), 5–15.

Freeman, A., Pretzer, J., Fleming, B., & Simon, K. (1990). *Clinical Applications of cognitive therapy.* New York: Plenum Press.

Freire, P. (1973). *Pedagogy of the oppressed.* New York: Seabury.

Freire, P. (1994). *Pedagogy of the oppressed: New revised 20th anniversary edition.* New York: Continuum.

Gadamer, H. (1989). *Truth and method.* (2nd rev. ed.). (J. Weinsheimer & D. Marshall, Trans.). New York: Crossroads.

Garfinkel, H. (1967). *Studies in ethnomethodology.* New York: Prentice Hall.

Garrett, A. (1949). Historical survey of the evolution of casework. *Social Casework, 30,* 219–229.

Garvin, C. (1986). Assessment and change of group conditions in social group work practice. In P. Glasser & N. Mayadas (Eds.), *Group workers at work: Theory and practice in the 80's* (pp. 103–115). Totowa, NJ: Rowman & Littlefield.

Geertz, C. (1973). Thick description: Toward an interpretive theory of culture. In C. Geertz (Ed.). *The interpretation of cultures* (pp. 3–30). New York: Basic Books.

Gergen, K. (1985). Social constructionist inquiry: Context and implications. In K. Gergen and K. Davis (Eds.), *The social construction of the person* (pp. 3–18.). New York: Springer.

Gergen, K. (1987a). Introduction: Toward metapsychology. In H. Stam, T. Rogers, & K. Gergen, (Eds.), *The analysis of psychological theory* (pp. 1–21). Washington, DC: Hemisphere Publishing Corp.

Gergen, K. (1987b). The language of psychological understanding. In H. Stam, T. Rogers, & K. Gergen, (Eds.), *The analysis of psychological theory* (pp. 115–129). Washington, DC: Hemisphere Publishing Corp.

Gilbert, N. (1977). The search for professional identity. *Social Work, 22* (5), 401–406.

Glaser, B. (1978). *Theoretical sensitivity: Advances in the methodology of grounded theory.* Mill Valley, CA: Sociology Press.

Glaser, B. (1992). *Basics of grounded theory analysis: Emergence vs. forcing.* Mill Valley, CA: Sociology Press.

Glaser, B. (1993). *Examples of grounded theory: A reader.* Mill Valley, CA: Sociology Press.

Glaser, B. (Ed.). (1994). *More grounded theory methodology: A reader.* Mill Valley, CA: Sociology Press.

Glaser, B. (Ed.). (1995). *Grounded theory: 1984–1995.* Mill Valley, CA: Sociology Press.

Glaser, B., & Strauss, A. (1967). *The discovery of grounded theory.* Chicago: Aldine.

Goldstein, H. (1992). If social work hasn't made progress as a science, might it be an art? *Families in Society, 73,* 48–55.

Gordon, W. (1951). *Toward basic research in social work.* Paper delivered at the fiftieth anniversary meeting of the Missouri Association for Social Welfare, October, 1950, St. Louis. Published by the George Warren Brown School of Social Work.

Gordon, W. (1983). Social work revolution or evolution? *Social Work, 28,* 181–185.

Granvold, D. (1994). *Cognitive and behavioral treatment: Methods and applications.* Pacific Grove, CA: Brooks/Cole Publishing.

Gréco, P. (1985). Réduction et construction. *Archives de Psychologie, 53,* 21–35.

Green, J., Doughty, J., Marquart, J., Ray, M., & Roberts, L. (1988). Qualitative evaluation audits in practice. *Evaluation Review, 12* (2), 352–375.

Griffin, R. (1991). Assessing the drug-involved client. *Families in Society, 72* (2), 87–94.

Grinnell, R., Austin, C., Blythe, B., Briar, S., Bronson, D., Coleman, H., Corcoran, K., Epstein, I., Fabricant, M., Festinger, T., Fraser, M., Gibbs, L., Gilcrist, L., Green, R., Harrison, D., Holden, G., Hudson, W., Ismael, J., Ivanoff, A., Jayaratne, S., Jenson, J., Jordon, D., Krysik, J. LeCroy, D., Lie, G., Longres, J., McMurtry, S., Nichols-Casebolt, A., Nurius, P., Proctor, E., Rodway, M., Rogers, G., Royse, D., Sheafor, B., Sieppert, J., Sowers-Hoag, K., Tomlinson, B., Thyer, B., Tripodi, T., Tutty, L., Weinbach, R., & Zastrow, C. (1994, July). Social work researchers' quest for respectability. *Social Work, 39,* 469–470.

Guba, E. (1985). *Perspectives on public policy: What can happen as a result of policy?* Mimeographed. Indiana University, Bloomington, Indiana.

Guba, E. (1987). *Naturalistic evaluation.* New directions for program evaluation, (34). San Francisco: Jossey-Bass.

Guba, E. (Ed.). (1990). *The paradigm dialog.* Newbury Park, CA: Sage.

Guba, E., & Lincoln, Y. (1981). *Effective evaluation.* San Francisco: Jossey-Bass.

Guba, E., & Lincoln, Y. (1982). Epistemological and methodological bases of naturalistic inquiry. *Educational Communications and Technology Journal, 4* (30), 233–252.

Guba, E., & Lincoln, Y. (1986). The countenances of fourth-generation evaluation: Description, judgment, and negotiation. *Evaluation Studies Review Annual, 11,* 70–78.

Guba, E., & Lincoln, Y. (1988). Do inquiry paradigms imply inquiry methodologies? In D. Fetterman (Ed.), *Qualitative approaches to evaluation in education* (pp. 89–115). New York: Praeger.

Guba, E., & Lincoln, Y. (1989). *Fourth generation evaluation.* Newbury Park, CA: Sage.

Halpern, E. (1983). *Auditing naturalistic inquiries: The development and application of a model.* Unpublished doctoral dissertation, Indiana University.

Hammersley, M. (1995). *The politics of social research.* London: Sage.

Harré, R. (1984). Social elements as mind. *British Journal of Medical Psychology, 57,* 127–135.

Harris, J. (1990). *Expressive discourse.* Dallas: Southern Methodist University Press.

Hartman, A. (1990). Many ways of knowing. *Social Work, 35,* 3–4.

Haworth, G. (1984). Social work research, practice, and paradigms. *Social Service Review, 58,* 343–357.

Heineman, M. (1981). The obsolete imperative in social work research. *Social Service Review, 55,* 371–397.

Heineman Pieper, M. (1985). The future of social work research. *Social Work Research and Abstracts, 21,* 3–11.

Heisenberg, W. (1972). *Physics and beyond.* New York: Harper & Row.

Hepworth, D., & Larsen, J. (1993). *Direct social work practice: Theory and skills.* (4th ed.). Pacific Grove, CA: Brooks/Cole.

Hesse, M. (1980). *Revolution and reconstruction in the philosophy of science.* Bloomington: Indiana University Press.

Hodder, I. (1993). The interpretation of documents and material culture. In N. Denzin & Y. Lincoln (Eds.), *Handbook of qualitative research* (pp. 393–402). Thousand Oaks, CA: Sage.

Hollis, E., & Taylor, A. (1951). *Social work education in the United States.* New York: Columbia University Press.

House, E. (1976). Justice in evaluation. In G. Glass (Ed.), *Evaluation Studies Review Annual, 1* (pp. 75–100). Beverly Hills, CA: Sage.

Hudson, J., & McRoberts, H. (1984). Auditing evaluation activities. In L. Rutman (Ed.), *Evaluation research methods: A basic guide.* (2nd ed.) (pp. 219–236). Beverly Hills, CA: Sage.

Hudson, W. (1983). Scientific imperatives in social work research and practice. *Social Service Review, 56,* 246–258.

Hudson, W. (1992). *Walmyr assessment scales.* Tempe, AZ: Walmyr Publishing Co.

Imre, R. (1982). *Knowing and caring: Philosophical issues in social work.* Washington, DC: University Press of America.

Imre, R. (1984). The nature of knowledge in social work. *Social Work, 29,* 41–45.

Imre, R. (1991). What do we need to know for good practice? *Social Work, 36,* 198–200.

Inhelder, B. (1983). On generating procedures and structuring knowledge. In R. Groner, M. Groner, & W. Bischof (Eds.), *Methods of heurisitics* (pp. 131–139). Hillsdale, NJ: Erlbaum.

Inhelder, B., & DeCaprona, D. (1985). Constructisme et création des nouveautés. *Archives de Psychologie, 53,* 7–17.

Jeans, J. (1981). *Physics and philosophy.* New York: Dover Publications.

Joas, H. (1987). Symbolic interactionism. In A. Giddens & J. Turner (Eds.), *Social theory today* (pp. 82–115). Stanford, CA: Stanford University Press.

Josselson, R., & Lieblich, A. (Eds.). (1995). *Interpreting experience: The narrative study of lives.* Thousand Oaks, CA: Sage.

Kadushin, A. (1990). *The social work interview: A guide for human service professionals.* New York: Columbia University Press.

Kahn, R., & Cannell, C. (1957). *The dynamics of interviewing: Theory, technique, and cases.* New York: Wiley.

Kahneman, D., & Tversky, A. (1979). Intuitive prediction. Biases and corrective procedures. *TIMS Studies in Management Science, 12,* 313–327.

Karger, H. (1983). Science, research and social work: Who controls the profession. *Social Work, 28,* 200–205.

Keeney, B. (1983). *Aesthetics of change.* New York: Guilford.

Kirk, J., & Miller, M. (1986). *Reliability and validity in qualitative research.* Beverly Hills, CA: Sage.

Kituse, J., & Spector, M. (1973). Toward a sociology of social problems: Social conditions, value judgments and social problems. *Social Problems, 20,* 407–419.

Knowles, M. (1962). The adult education movement in the US. New York: Holt, Rinehart & Winston.

Knowles, M. (1980). *The modern practice of adult education: From pedagogy to andragogy.* Englewood Cliffs, NJ: Cambridge Adult Education.

Knowles, M. (1984). *Andragogy in action.* San Francisco: Jossey-Bass.

Knowles, M. (1990). *The adult learner: A neglected species.* (4th ed.). Houston: Gulf Publishing.

Kopp, J. (1989). Self-observation: An empowerment strategy in assessment. *Social Casework, 70* (5), 298–299.

Krueger, R. (1994). *Focus groups: A practical guide for applied research.* (2nd ed.). Thousand Oaks, CA: Sage.

Kuhn, T. (1970). *The structure of scientific revolution.* (2nd ed.). Chicago: University of Chicago Press.

Kushner, S., & Norris, N. (1980–81). Interpretation, negotiation and validity in naturalistic research. *Interchange 11* (4), 26–36.

Laird, J. (1994). "Thick description" revisited: Family therapist as anthropologist-constructivist. In E. Sherman & W. Reid (Eds.), *Qualitative research in social work* (pp. 175–189). New York: Columbia University Press.

Laird, J. (1995, March). Family-centered practice in the postmodern era. *Families in Society, 76* (3) 150–162.

Lambert, L., Walker, D., Zimmerman, D., Cooper, J., Lambert, M., Gardner, M., & Ford Slack, P. (1995). *The constructivist leader.* New York: Teachers College Press.

Lather, P. (1986). Research as praxis. *Harvard Educational Review, 56* (3), 257–277.

Lather, P. (1991). *Getting smart: Feminist research and pedagogy with/in the postmodern.* New York: Routledge and Kegan Paul.

Lehne, R. (1978). *The quest for justice: The politics of school finance reform.* New York: Longman.

Levy, C. (1983). Client self-determination. In A. Rosenblatt & D. Waldfogel (Eds.), *Handbook of clinical social work* (pp. 904–919). San Francisco: Jossey-Bass.

Lewin, K. (1946). Action research and minority problems. *Journal of Social Issues, 2,* 34–46.

Lincoln, Y. (1981). *Strategies for insuring the dependability (reliability) of naturalistic studies.* Paper presented at the joint annual meeting of the Evaluation Network and the Evaluation Research Society, Austin, Texas.

Lincoln, Y. (1989). Qualitative research: A response to Atkinson, Delamont, and Hammersley. *Review of Educational Research, 59* (2), 237–329.

Lincoln, Y. (1997). *From theoretical to practical discourses: Contributions of postmodern thinking to educational practice.* Papered presented at the Endowed Spring Lecture, School of Education, Virginia Commonwealth University, Richmond, Virginia.

Lincoln, Y., & Guba, E. (1985). *Naturalistic inquiry.* Beverly Hills, CA: Sage.

Lincoln, Y., & Guba, E. (1986). But is it rigorous? Trustworthiness and authenticity in naturalistic evaluation. In D. Williams (Ed.), *Naturalistic evaluation* (pp. 73–84). San Francisco: Jossey-Bass.

Lincoln, Y., & Guba, E. (1989). Ethics: The failure of positivist science. *Review of Higher Education, 12* (3), 221–140.

Lincoln, Y., & Guba, E. (1990). Judging the quality of case study reports. *International Journal of Qualitative Studies in Education, 3* (1), 53–59.

Lofland, J. (1971a). *Analysing social settings: A guide to qualitative observation and analysis.* Belmont, CA: Wadsworth.

Lofland, J. (1971b). Styles of reporting qualitative field research. *American Sociologist, 9,* 101–111.

Lofland, J., & Lofland, L. (1995). *Analyzing social settings: A guide to qualitative observation and analysis.* (3rd ed.). Belmont, CA: Wadsworth.

Longres, J. (1981). Reactions to working statement on purpose. *Social Work, 26* (1), 85–87.

Maas, H.S., & Varon, E. (1949). The case worker in clinical and socio-psychological research. *Social Service Review,23,* 302–314.

Mahoney, M. (1988a). Constructive metatheory I: Basic features and historical foundations. *International Journal of Personal Construct Psychology, 1* (1), 1–35.

Mahoney, M. (1988b). Constructive metatheory II: Implications for psychotherapy. *International Journal of Personal Construct Psychology, 1*(4), 299–315.

Mahoney, M. (1989). Participatory epistemology and the psychology of science. In B. Gholson, W. Shadish, R. Neimeyer, & A Houts (Eds.), *The psychology of science* (pp. 138–164). Cambridge, England: Cambridge University Press.

Manecas P. (1981). *A history and philosophy of the social sciences.* San Francisco: Jossey-Bass.

Manning, K. (1997). Authenticity in constructivist inquiry: Methodological consider-ations without prescription. *Qualitative inquiry, 3* (1), 93–115.

Marshall, C., & Rossman, G. (1995). *Designing qualitative research.* (2nd ed.). Thousand Oaks, CA: Sage.

Marx, K. (1988). *The economic and philosophic manuscripts of 1844 and the Commu-nist manifesto.* Buffalo: Prometheus.

Maturana, H. (1988). Reality: The search for objectivity or the quest for a compelling argument. *Irish Journal of Psychology, 9,* 25–82.

Maxwell, J. (1992, December). *A synthesis of similarity/continuity distinctions.* Poster session presented at the annual meeting of the American Anthropological Association, San Franciso.

McMillan, J., & Schumacher, S. (1993). *Research in education: A conceptual introduction.* (3rd ed.). New York: HarperCollins.

Meltzer, B., Petras, J., & Reynolds, L. (1975). *Symbolic interactionism: Genesis, varieties and criticism.* London: Routledge & Kegan Paul.

Merleau-Ponty, M. (1994). *Phenomenology of perception* (C. Smith, trans.). New York: Routledge and Kegan Paul.

Miles, M., & Huberman, A. (1994). *Qualitative data analysis: An expanded sourcebook.* (2nd ed.). Thousand Oaks, CA: Sage.

Minnich, E. (1990). *Transforming knowledge.* Philadelphia: Temple University Press.

Morgan, D. (1988). *Focus groups as qualitative research.* Newbury Park, CA: Sage.

Morine-Dershimer, G. (1991, April). *Tracing conceptual change in pre-service teachers.* Paper presented at the Annual Meeting of the American Educational Research Association, Chicago.

National Association of Case Workers (1929/1974). *Social case work: Generic and specific: A report on the Milford Conference.* Washington, DC.: Author.

Neil, J. (1996). *The lived experience of having a chronic wound: A constructivist inquiry.* (Xeroxed). Richmond, VA: Virginia Commonwealth University.

Neimeyer, R. (1985). *The development of personal construct psychology.* Lincoln: University of Nebraska Press.

Neimeyer, R. (1992). Constructivist approaches to the measurement of meaning. In G. Neimeyer (Ed.), *Casebook of constructivist assessment* (pp. 58–103). Newbury Park, CA: Sage.

Neimeyer, R. (1993). An appraisal of constructivist psychotherapies. *Journal of Consulting and Clinical Psychology, 61* (2), 221–234.

Neimeyer, R., & Harter, S. (1988). Facilitating individual change in personal construct therapy. In G. Dunnett (Ed.), *Working with people* (pp. 175–185). London: Routledge and Kegan Paul.

Newman, D., & Brown, R. (1996). *Applied ethics for program evaluation.* Thousand Oaks, CA: Sage.

Nurius. P., & Hudson, W. (1988). Computer-based practice: Future dream or current technology. *Social Work, 33,* 357–362.

Nurius, P., & Hudson, W. (1993). *Computer assisted practice: Theory, methods, and software.* Belmont, CA: Wadsworth.

Owen, I. (1992). Applying social constructionism to psychotherapy. *Counselling Psychology Quarterly, 5* (4), 385–402.

Patton, M. (1980) *Qualitative evaluation methods.* Beverly Hills, CA: Sage.

Patton, M. (1987). *Creative evaluation.* (2nd ed.). Beverly Hills, CA: Sage.

Patton, M. (1990). *Qualitative research and evaluation methods.* (2nd ed.). Newbury Park, CA: Sage.

Pecora, P., Whittaker, J., & Maluccio, A. (1992). *The child welfare challenge policy, practice, and research.* New York: Aldine de Gruyter.

Peile, C. (1988, March). Research paradigms in social work: From stalemate to creative synthesis. *Social Service Review,* 1–19.

Piaget, J. (1932). *The moral judgment of the child.* London: Routledge and Kegan Paul.

Piaget, J. (1954). *The construction of reality in the child.* New York: Basic Books. (Original work published 1937.)

Plummer, K. (Ed.). (1987). *Symbolic interactionism: Vol. 1. Foundations and history.* Brookfield, VT: Edward Elgar.

Plummer, K. (Ed.). (1991). *Symbolic interactionism: Vol. 2. Classic and contemporary issues.* Hauts, England: Edward Elgar.

Polanyi, M. (1958). *Personal knowledge: Toward a post-critical philosophy.* London: Routledge and Kegan Paul.

Polanyi, M. (1966). *The tacit dimension.* Garden City, NY: Doubleday.

Popper, K. (1968). *The logic of scientific discovery.* New York: Harper & Row.

Popple, P. (1985, December). The social work profession: A reconceptualization. *Social Service Review,* 560–575.

Prager, E. (1980). Evaluation in mental health: Enter the consumer. *Social Work Research and Abstracts, 16,* 5–10.

Punch, M. (1986). *The politics and ethics of fieldwork.* Beverly Hills, CA: Sage

Rawls, J. (1971). *A theory of justice.* Cambridge, MA: Harvard University Press.

Reason, P. (1993). Three approaches to participative inquiry. In N. Denzin & Y. Lincoln (Eds.), *Handbook of qualitative research* (pp. 324–339). Thousand Oaks, CA: Sage.

Reason, P. (Ed.).(1994). *Participation in human inquiry.* London: Sage.

Reid, W. (1994). Reframing the epistemological debate. In E. Sherman & W. Reid (Eds.), *Qualitative research in social work* (pp. 464–481). New York: Columbia University Press.

Reinharz, S. (1979). *On becoming a social scientist.* San Francisco: Jossey-Bass.

Richmond, M. (1917). *Social diagnosis.* New York: Russell Sage Foundation.

Richmond, M. (1922). *What is social casework? An introductory description.* New York: Russell Sage.

Robinson, V. (1930). *A changing psychology in social case work.* Chapel Hill: University of North Carolina Press.

Robinson, V. (1934). *A changing psychology in social case work.* Chapel Hill: University of North Carolina Press. (Original work published 1930).

Robinson, V. (1962). *Jessey Taft: Therapist and social work educator, a professional biography.* Philadelphia: University of Pennsylvania Press.

Rodwell, M.K. (1987). Naturalistic inquiry: An alternative model for social work assessment. *Social Service Review, 61,* 231–246.

Rodwell, M.K. (1990). Person/environment construct: Positivist versus naturalist, dilemma or opportunity for health social work research and practice? *Social Science and Medicine, 31* (1), 27–34.

Rodwell, M.K. (1994). Constructivist research: A qualitative approach. In P. Pecora et al., *Evaluating family preservation services* (pp. 191–214). New York: Aldine de Gruyter.

Rodwell, M.K. (1995). Using research for social justice: An example of constructivist research with street children in Brasil. Paper presented at the *Southern Sociological Society Annual Meeting,* Atlanta, Georgia.

Rodwell, M. K., & Blankenbaker, A. (1992). Strategies for the development of cross-cultural sensitivity: Wounding as metaphor. *Journal of Education in Social Work, 28* (2), 153–165.

Rodwell, M.K., & Byers, K. (1997). Auditing constructivist inquiry: Perspectives of two stakeholders. *Qualitative Inquiry, 3* (1), 116–134.

Rodwell, M.K., & Wood, L. (1996). *"Hugs and Kisses" play evaluation: Final evaluation report.* Richmond, VA: Virginia Commonwealth University.

Rodwell, M.K., & Woody, D. (1994). Constructivist evaluation: The policy/practice context. In E. Sherman & W. Reid, (Eds.), *Qualitative research in social work* (pp. 325–327). New York: Columbia University Press.

Rosen, A. (1978). Issues in educating for the knowledge-building research doctorate. *Social Service Review, 52,* 437–448.

Rosenberg, A. (1988). *Philosophy of social science.* Boulder, CO: Westview Press.

Rosengren, K. (Ed.).(1981). *Advances in content analysis.* Beverly Hills, CA: Sage.

Rubin, H., & Rubin, I. (1995). *Qualitative interviewing: The art of hearing data.* Thousand Oaks, CA: Sage.

Ryle, G. (1968). *The thinking of thoughts.* (University Lectures, No. 18). Saskatoon: University of Saskatchewan.

Saleebey, D. (1990). Philosophical disputes in social work: Social justice denied. *Journal of Sociology and Social Welfare, 17,* 29–40.

Sampson. E. (1987). A critical constructionist view of psychology and personhood. In H. Stam, T. Rogers, & K. Gergen, (Eds.), *The analysis of psychological theory* (pp. 41–59). Washington, DC: Hemisphere Publishing Corporation.

Saxton, S. (1993). Sociologist as citizen-scholar: A symbolic interactionist alternative to normal sociology. In T. Vaughan, G. Sjoberg, & L. Reynolds (Eds.), *A critique of contemporary American sociology* (pp. 232–252). Dix Hills, NY: General Hall.

Schatzman, L., & Strauss, A. (1973). *Field research.* Englewood Cliffs, NJ: Prentice-Hall.

Schön, D. (1983). *The reflective practitioner: How professionals think in action.* New York: Basic Books.

Schwandt, T. (1994). Constructivist, interpretivist approaches to human inquiry. In N. Denzin & Y. Lincoln (Eds.), *Handbook of qualitative research* (pp. 118–137). Thousand Oaks, CA: Sage.

Schwandt, T., & Halpern, E. (1988). *Linking auditing and metaevaluation: Enhancing quality in applied research.* Newbury Park, CA: Sage.

Scott, D. (1989). Meaning construction and social work practice. *Social Service Review, 63,* 39–52.

Shulman, L. (1984). *The skills of helping individuals and groups.* (2nd ed.). Itasca, IL: F.E. Peacock.

Silverman, D. (1985). *Qualitative methodology and sociology.* Aldershot, UK: Gower.

Simon, B. (1994). *The empowerment tradition in American social work.* New York: Columbia University Press.

Skrtic, T. (1985a). Doing naturalistic research into educational organizations. In Y. Lincoln (Ed.), *Organizational theory and inquiry: The paradigm revolution* (pp. 185–220). Beverly Hills, CA: Sage.

Skrtic, T. (1985b*). Naturalistic policy research and the organizational context of special education.* Paper presented at the Second Annual Pittsburgh Symposium on Research with the Handicapped, Pittsburgh, Pennsylvania.

Smith, J. (1984). The problem of criteria for judging interpretive inquiry. *Educational Evaluation and Policy Analysis, 6* (4), 379–391.

Smith, M., & Lincoln, Y. (1984, November/December). Another kind of evaluation. *Journal of Extension*, 5–10.

Spector, M., & Kituse, J. (1977). *Constructing social problems*. Hawthorne, New York: Aldine de Gruyter.

Speed, B. (1991). Reality exists O.K.? An argument against constructivism and social constructionism. *Family Therapy, 13*, 395–409.

Spradley, J. (1979). *The ethnographic interviews*. New York: Holt, Rinehart & Winston.

Spradley, J. (1980). *Participant observation*. New York: Holt, Rinehart & Winston.

Stone, D. (1988). *Policy paradox and political reason*. New York:HarperCollins

Strauss, A., & Corbin, J. (1990). *Basics of qualitative research. Grounded theory procedures and techniques*. Newbury Park, CA: Sage.

Strike, K. (1982). *Educational policy and the just society*. Champaign: University of Illinois Press.

Taft, J. (1937). The relation of function to process in social case work. *Journal of Social Work Process, 1*, 1–18.

Thayer, B. (1986). On pseudoscience and pseudoreasoning. *Social Work Research and Abstracts 22* (2), 371–372.

Thyer, B. (1989). In response to Dean, R., & Fenby, B. (1989). Exploring epistemologies. *Journal of Social Work Education, 25* (1), 174–176.

Towle, C. (1936). Factors in treatment. In *Proceedings of the National Conference on Social Work 63rd Annual Session, Atlantic City* (pp. 179–191). Chicago: University of Chicago Press.

Tripodi, T., & Epstein, I. (1978). Incorporating knowledge of research methodology into social work practice. *Journal of Social Service Research, 2*, 65–78.

Tyson, K. (1992). A new approach to relevant and scientific research for practitioners: The heuristic paradigm. *Social Work, 37*, 541–556.

Tyson, K. (1993, May 27–29). *Advancing clinical social work: Prior approaches and a view toward the future based on intrapsychic humanism*. Keynote address presented at the Conference on Clinical Social Work, Scuola per Assistenti Sociali, Scuola Diretta a Fini Speciali per Assistenti Sociali, Universita Cattolica del Sacro Cour, and School of Social Work, Loyola University of Chicago, Rome.

Tyson, K. (1995). *New foundations for scientific social and behavioral research: The heuristic paradigm*. Boston: Allyn & Bacon.

Varela, F. (1989). Reflections on the circulation of concepts between the biology of cognition and systemic family therapy. *Family Process, 28*, 15–24.

Viney, L. (1993). Listening to what my clients and I say: Content analysis categories and scales. In Neimeyer, G. (Ed.), *Constructivist assessment: A casebook* (pp. 104–142). Newbury Park, CA: Sage.

von Glasersfeld, E. (1984). An introduction to radical constructivism. In P. Watzlawick (Ed.). *The invented reality* (pp. 17–40). New York: Norton.

Vygotsky, L. (1962). *Thought and language*. Cambridge, MA: MIT Press.

Wakefield, J. (1988, June). Psychotherapy, distributive justice, and social work: Part 1: Distributive justice as a conceptual framework for social work. *Social Service Review*, 187–211.

Watzlawick, P. (1984). *The invented reality*. New York: W.W. Norton.

Weber, M. (1949). *The methodology of social sciences*. Glencoe, IL: Free Press.

Weick, A. (1987). Reconceptualizing the philosophical perspective of social work. *Social Service Review, 61,* 218–230.

Weick, A. (1993). Reconstructing social work education. *Journal of Teaching in Social Work, 8* (1/2), 11–30.

Weick, A., & Pope, L. (1988). Knowing what's best: A new look at self-determination. *Social Casework, 69,* 10–16.

Weick, K. (1995). *Sensemaking in organizations.* Thousand Oaks, CA: Sage.

Williams, D. (1986). *When is naturalistic evaluation appropriate?* (New Directions for Program Evaluation, 30). San Francisco: Jossey-Bass.

Witkin, S. (1989). Towards a scientific social work. *Journal of Social Service Research, 12,* 83–89.

Woolgar, S. (1989). Representation, cognition and self. In S. Fuller, M. DeMey, T. Shinn, & S. Woolgar (Eds.), *The cognitive turn* (pp. 201–223). Dordrecht, the Netherlands: Kluwer.

Zeller, N. (1987). *A rhetoric for naturalistic inquiry.* Unpublished doctoral dissertation, Indiana University, Bloomington.

Zeller, N. (1991). *A new use for new journalism: Humanizing the case report.* Paper presented at the Annual Meeting of the American Educational Research Association, Chicago, April.

Zimmerman, D. (1995). The Linquistics of Leadership. In L. Lambert, D. Walker, D. Zimmerman, J. Cooper, M. Lambert, M. Gardner, & P. Slack, *The constructivist leader* (pp. 104–120). New York: Teachers College Press.

INDEX